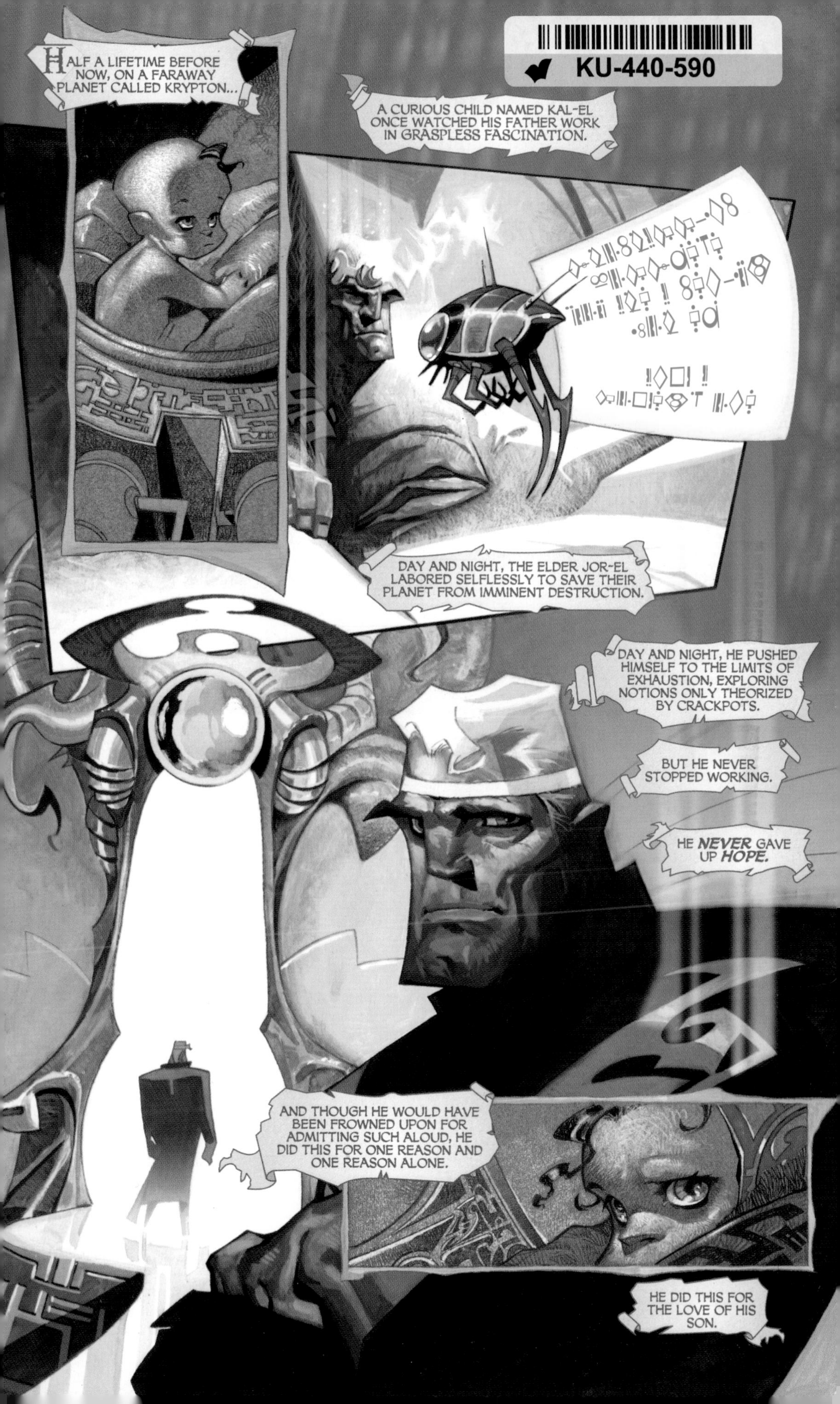
HALF A LIFETIME BEFORE NOW, ON A FARAWAY PLANET CALLED KRYPTON...
A CURIOUS CHILD NAMED KAL-EL ONCE WATCHED HIS FATHER WORK IN GRASPLESS FASCINATION.
DAY AND NIGHT, THE ELDER JOR-EL LABORED SELFLESSLY TO SAVE THEIR PLANET FROM IMMINENT DESTRUCTION.
DAY AND NIGHT, HE PUSHED HIMSELF TO THE LIMITS OF EXHAUSTION, EXPLORING NOTIONS ONLY THEORIZED BY CRACKPOTS.
BUT HE NEVER STOPPED WORKING.
HE NEVER GAVE UP HOPE.
AND THOUGH HE WOULD HAVE BEEN FROWNED UPON FOR ADMITTING SUCH ALOUD, HE DID THIS FOR ONE REASON AND ONE REASON ALONE.
HE DID THIS FOR THE LOVE OF HIS SON.

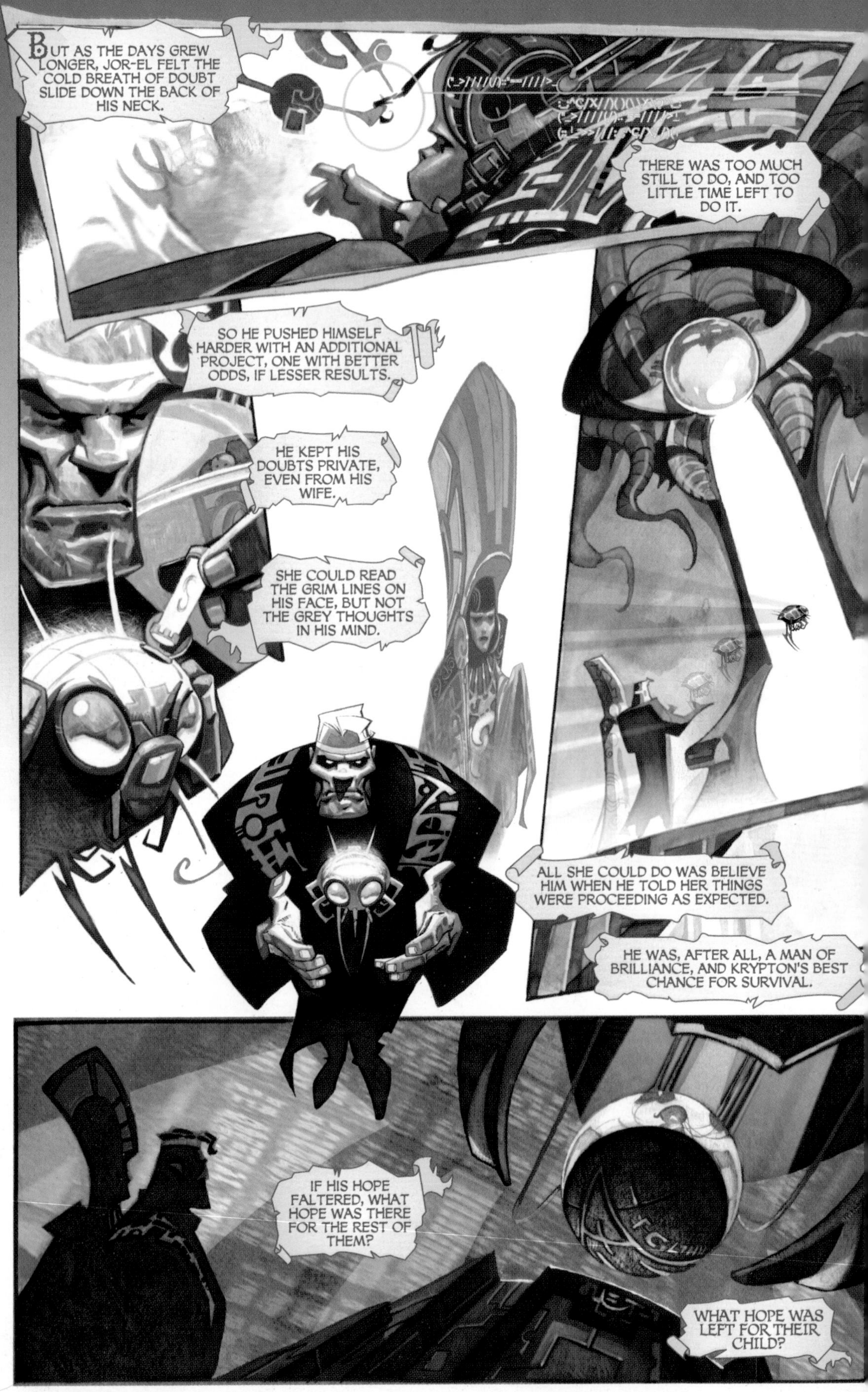
BUT AS THE DAYS GREW LONGER, JOR-EL FELT THE COLD BREATH OF DOUBT SLIDE DOWN THE BACK OF HIS NECK.
THERE WAS TOO MUCH STILL TO DO, AND TOO LITTLE TIME LEFT TO DO IT.
SO HE PUSHED HIMSELF HARDER WITH AN ADDITIONAL PROJECT, ONE WITH BETTER ODDS, IF LESSER RESULTS.
HE KEPT HIS DOUBTS PRIVATE, EVEN FROM HIS WIFE.
SHE COULD READ THE GRIM LINES ON HIS FACE, BUT NOT THE GREY THOUGHTS IN HIS MIND.
ALL SHE COULD DO WAS BELIEVE HIM WHEN HE TOLD HER THINGS WERE PROCEEDING AS EXPECTED.
HE WAS, AFTER ALL, A MAN OF BRILLIANCE, AND KRYPTON'S BEST CHANCE FOR SURVIVAL.
IF HIS HOPE FALTERED, WHAT HOPE WAS THERE FOR THE REST OF THEM?
WHAT HOPE WAS LEFT FOR THEIR CHILD?

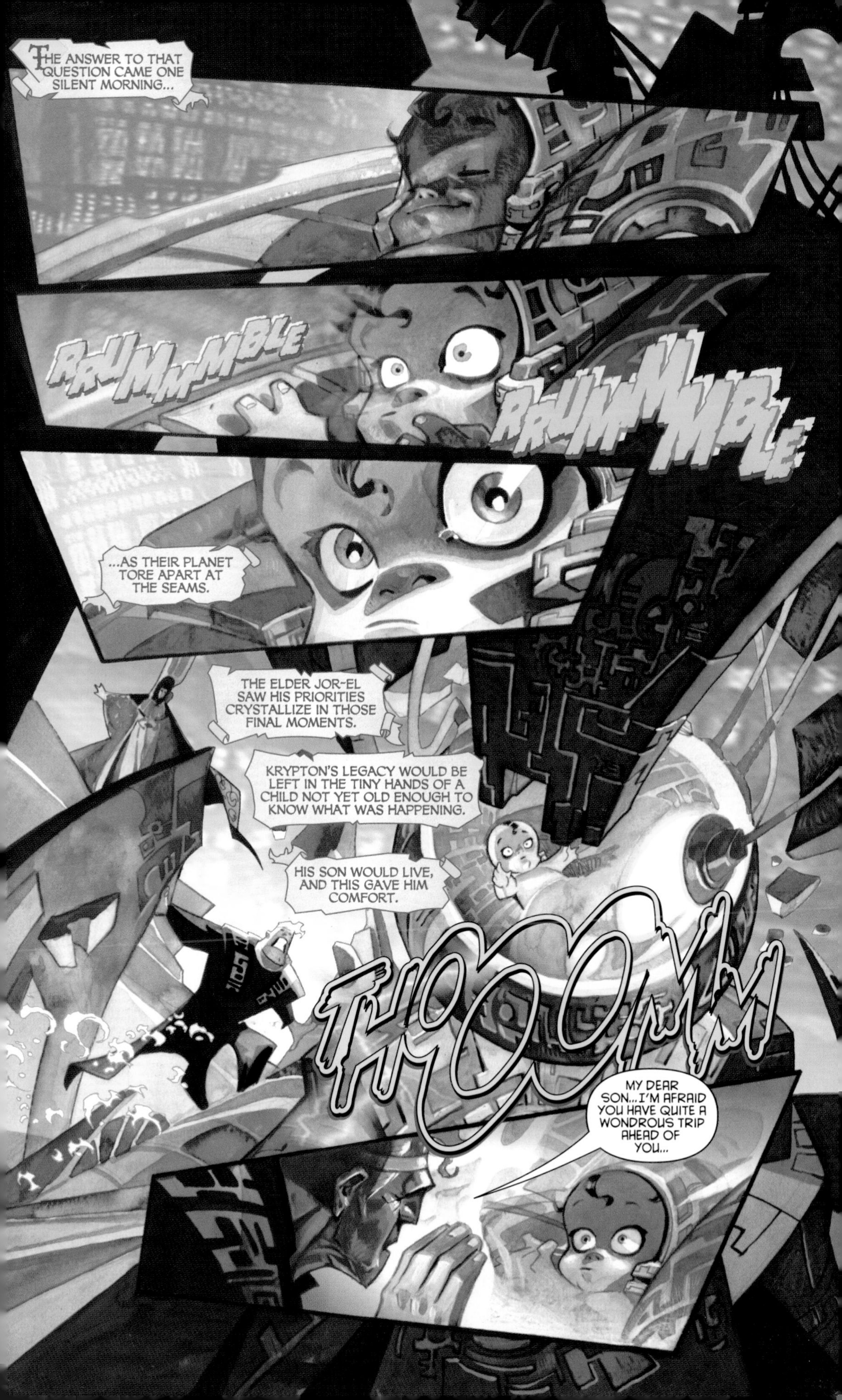
THE ANSWER TO THAT QUESTION CAME ONE SILENT MORNING...
RRUMMMBLE
RRUMMMMBLE
...AS THEIR PLANET TORE APART AT THE SEAMS.
THE ELDER JOR-EL SAW HIS PRIORITIES CRYSTALLIZE IN THOSE FINAL MOMENTS.
KRYPTON'S LEGACY WOULD BE LEFT IN THE TINY HANDS OF A CHILD NOT YET OLD ENOUGH TO KNOW WHAT WAS HAPPENING.
HIS SON WOULD LIVE, AND THIS GAVE HIM COMFORT.
THOOMM
MY DEAR SON...I'M AFRAID YOU HAVE QUITE A WONDROUS TRIP AHEAD OF YOU...

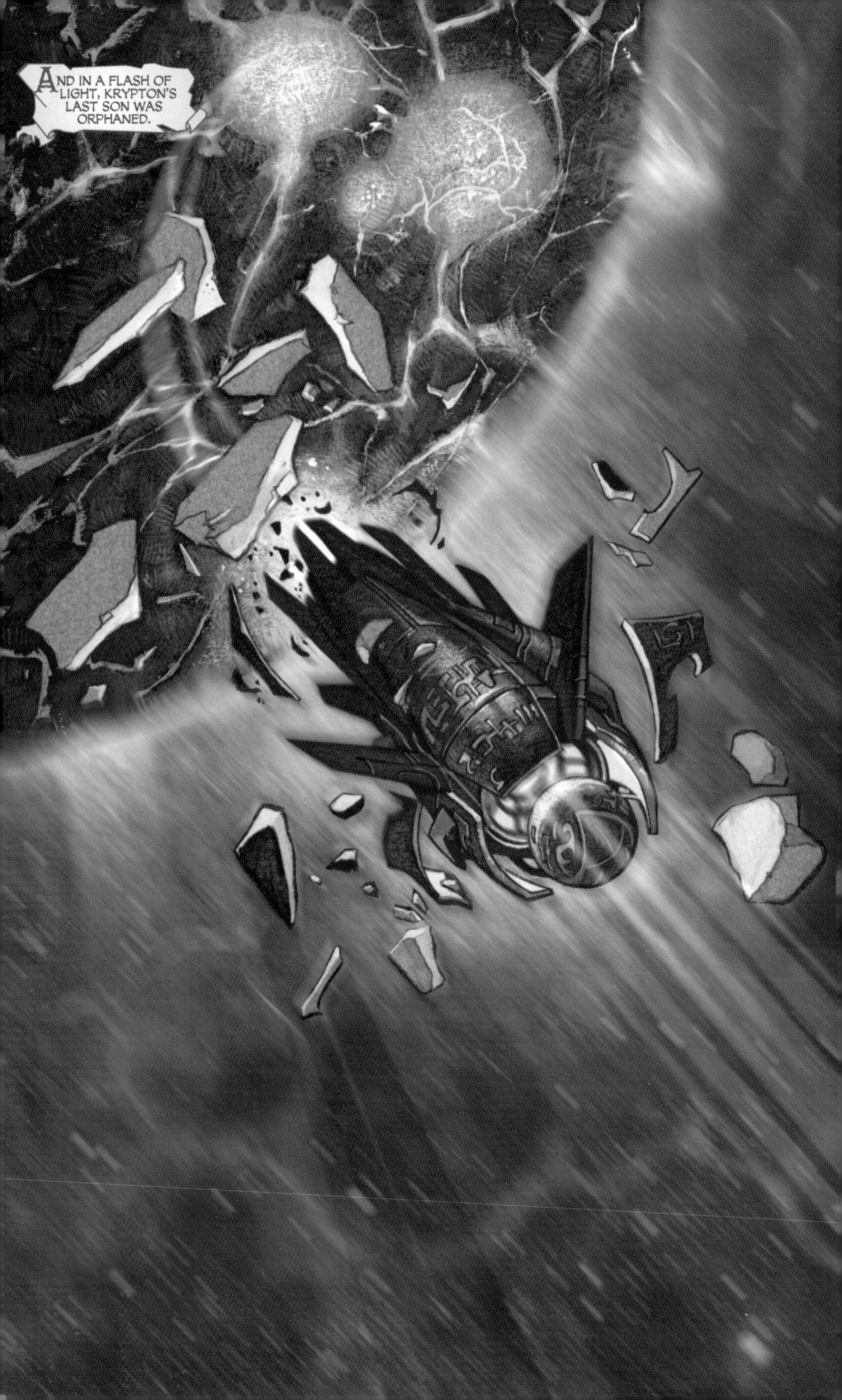
AND IN A FLASH OF LIGHT, KRYPTON'S LAST SON WAS ORPHANED.

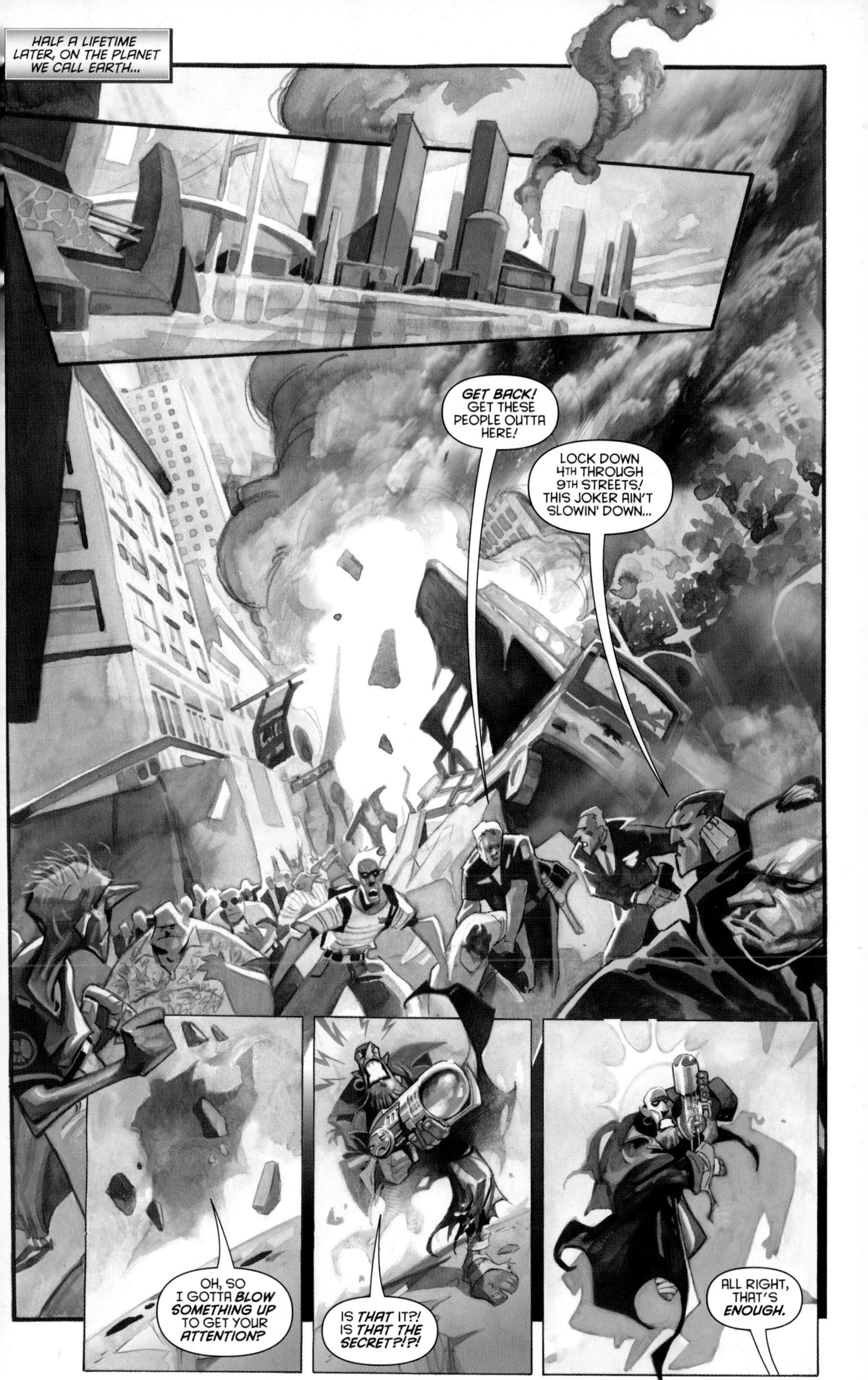
HALF A LIFETIME LATER, ON THE PLANET WE CALL EARTH...
GET BACK! GET THESE PEOPLE OUTTA HERE!
LOCK DOWN 4TH THROUGH 9TH STREETS! THIS JOKER AIN'T SLOWIN' DOWN...
OH, SO I GOTTA BLOW SOMETHING UP TO GET YOUR ATTENTION?
IS THAT IT?! IS THAT THE SECRET?!?!
ALL RIGHT, THAT'S ENOUGH.

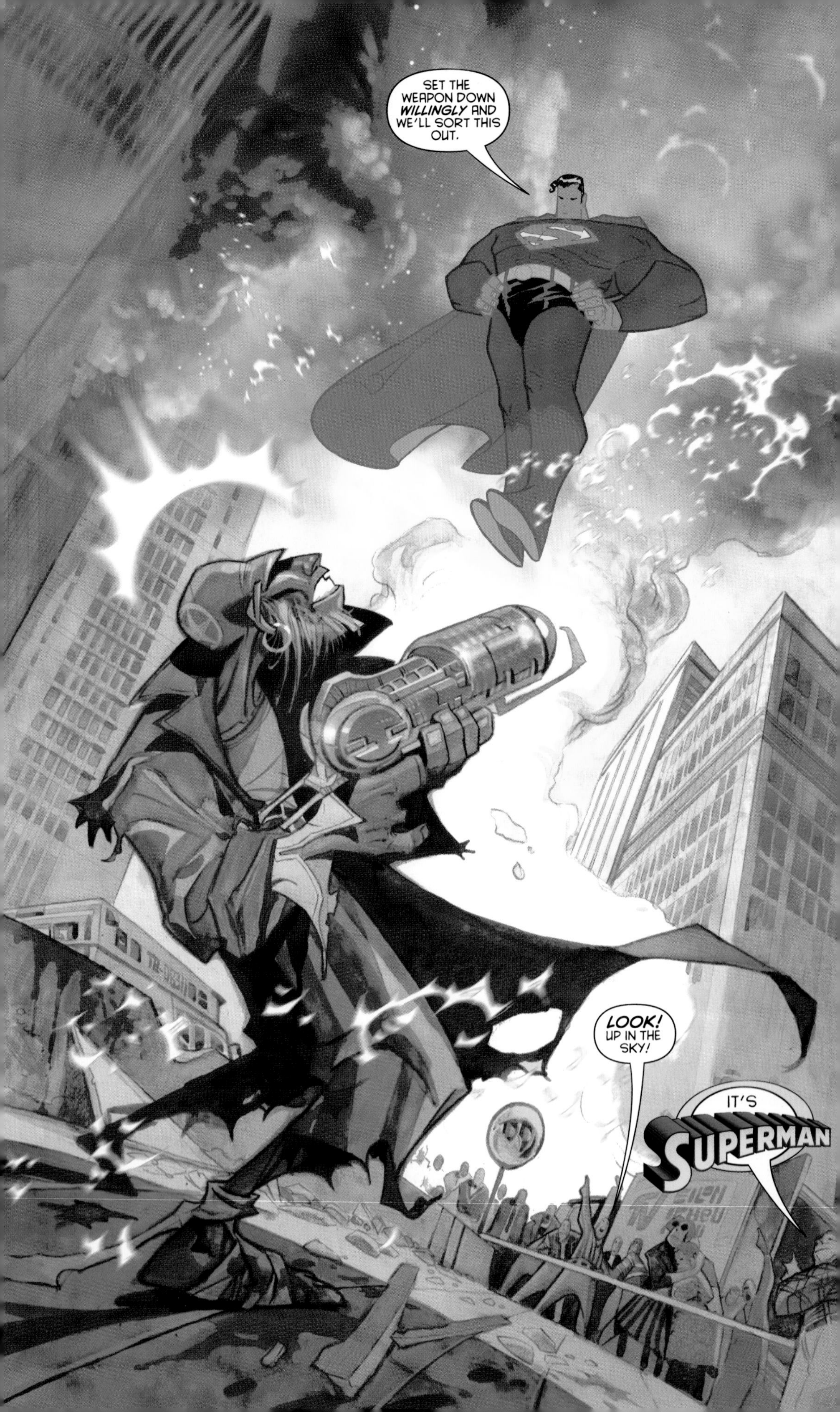
SET THE WEAPON DOWN *WILLINGLY* AND WE'LL SORT THIS OUT.
*LOOK!* UP IN THE SKY!
IT'S
SUPERMAN

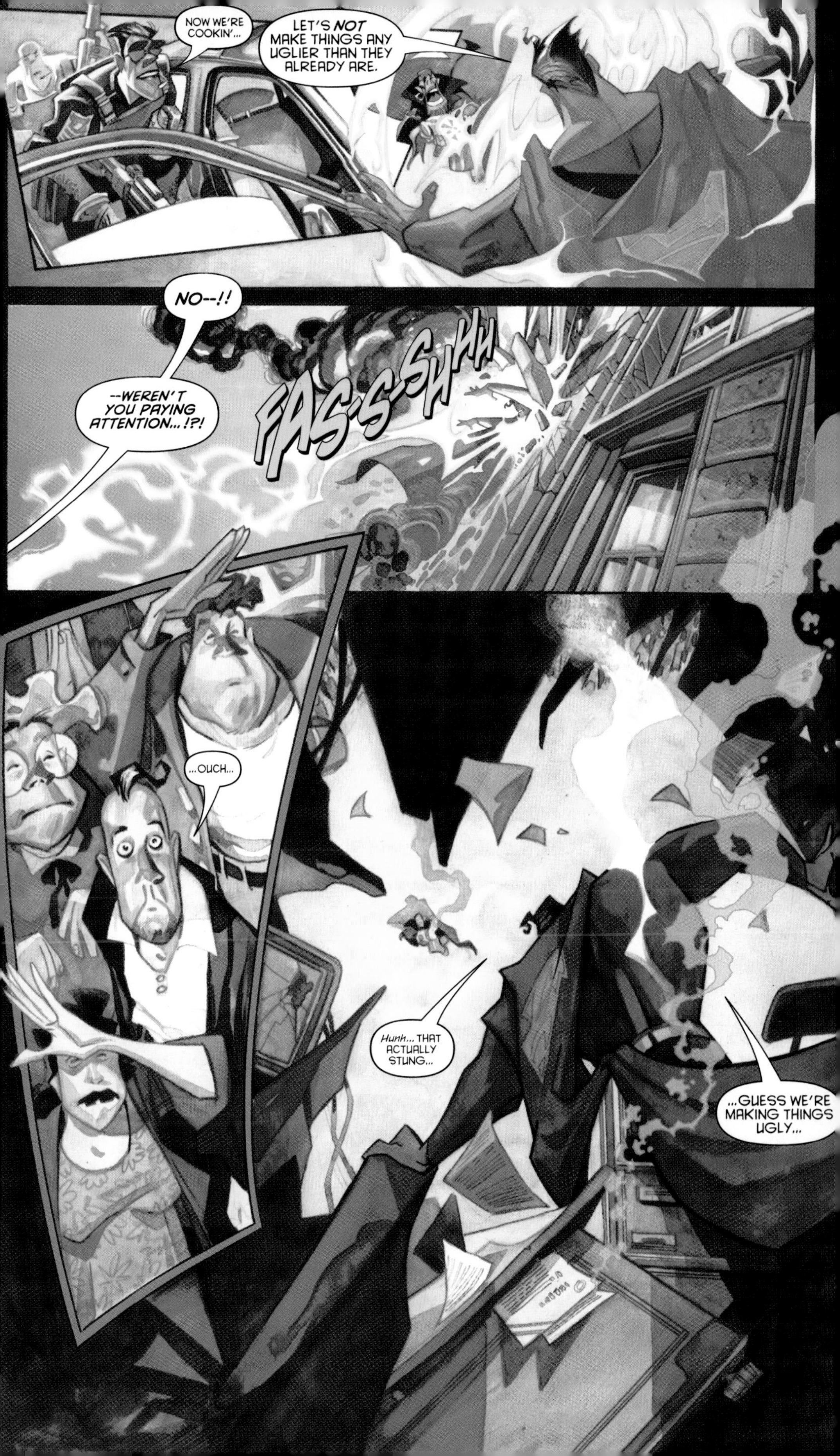
NOW WE'RE COOKIN'...
LET'S *NOT* MAKE THINGS ANY UGLIER THAN THEY ALREADY ARE.
NO--!!
--WEREN'T YOU PAYING ATTENTION...!?!
FAS-S-SHHH
...OUCH...
*Hunh...* THAT ACTUALLY STUNG...
...GUESS WE'RE MAKING THINGS UGLY...

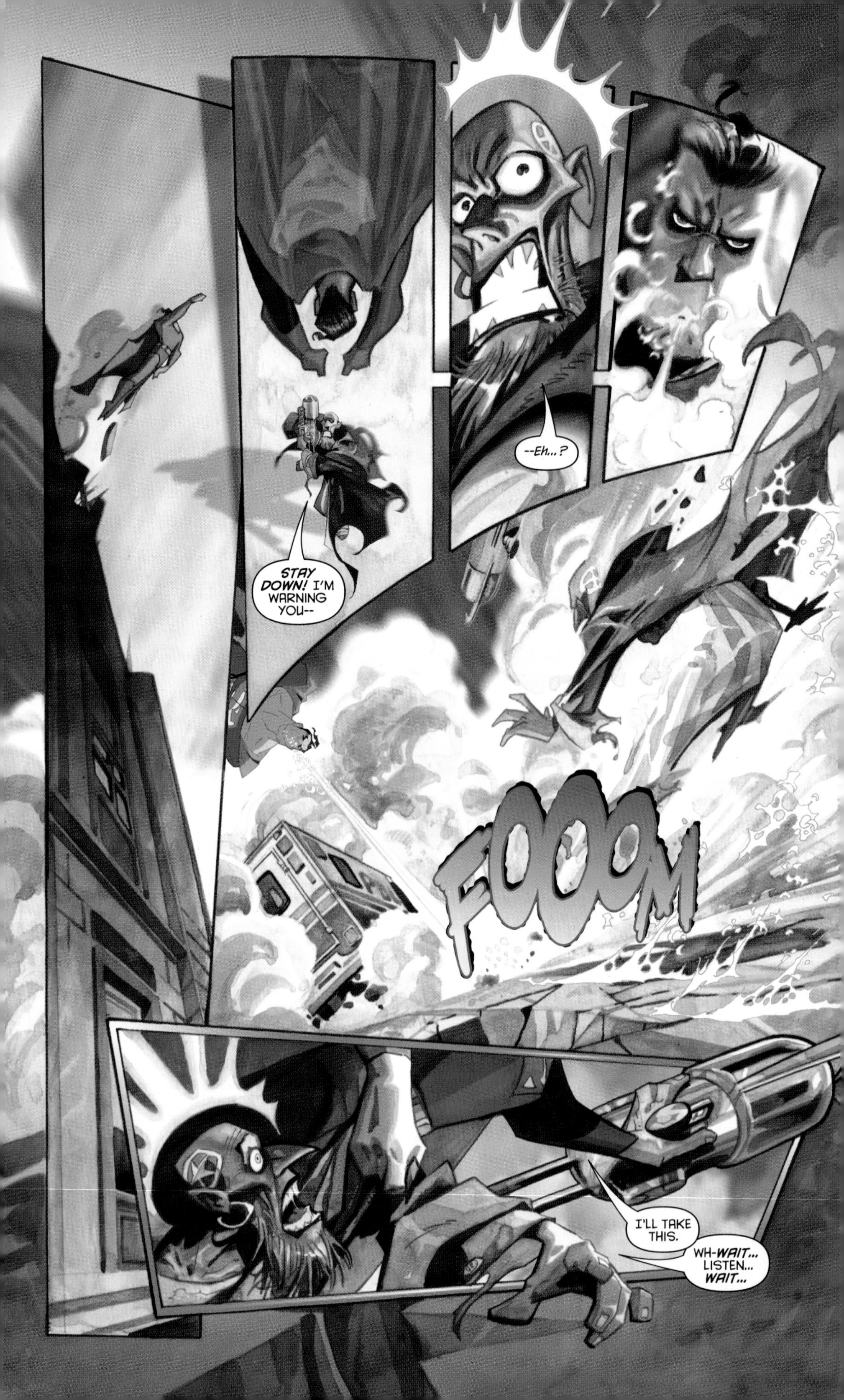
STAY DOWN! I'M WARNING YOU--
--Eh...?
FOOOM
I'LL TAKE THIS.
WH-WAIT... LISTEN... WAIT...

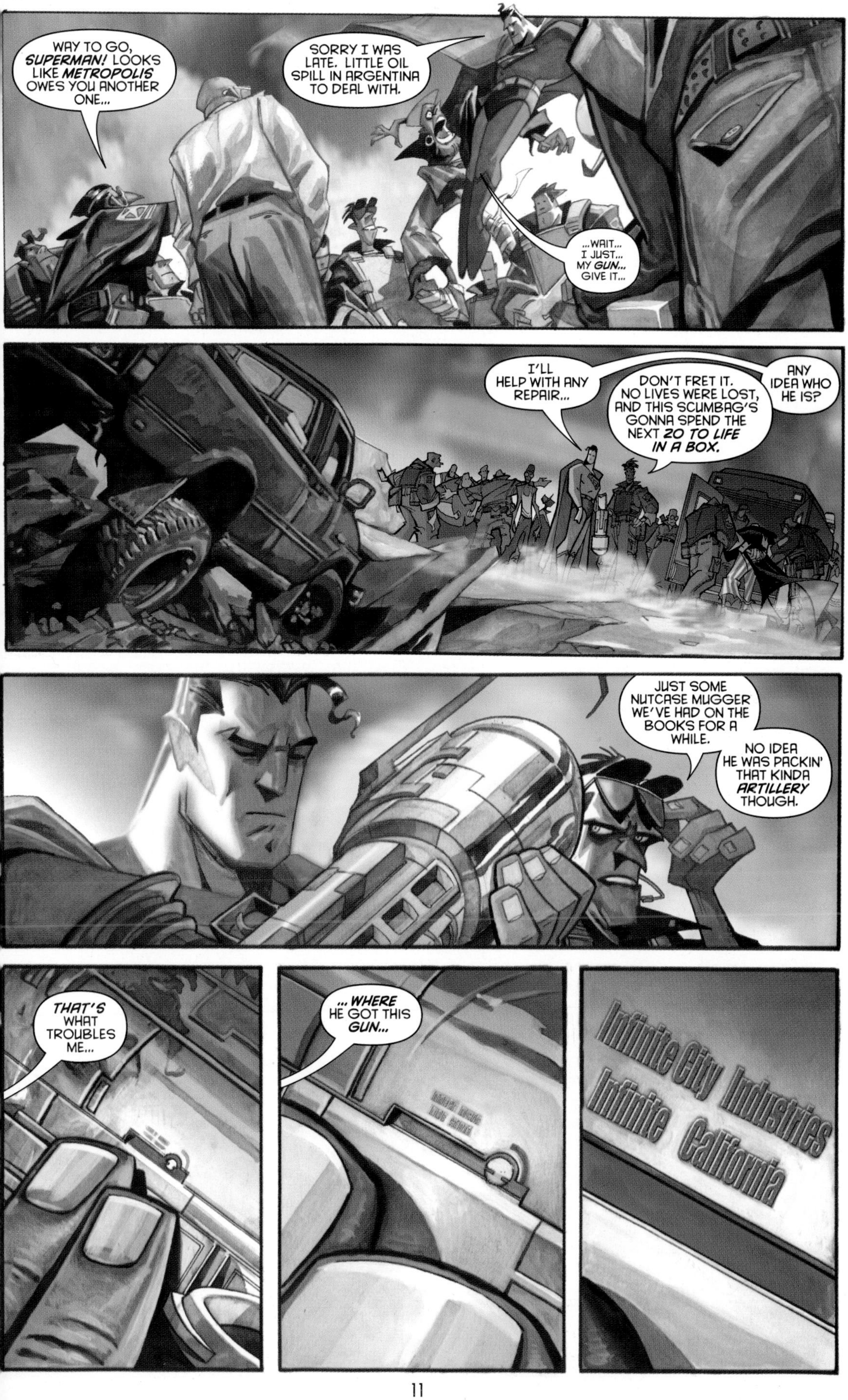
WAY TO GO, SUPERMAN! LOOKS LIKE METROPOLIS OWES YOU ANOTHER ONE...
SORRY I WAS LATE. LITTLE OIL SPILL IN ARGENTINA TO DEAL WITH.
...WAIT... I JUST... MY GUN... GIVE IT...
I'LL HELP WITH ANY REPAIR...
DON'T FRET IT. NO LIVES WERE LOST, AND THIS SCUMBAG'S GONNA SPEND THE NEXT 20 TO LIFE IN A BOX.
ANY IDEA WHO HE IS?
JUST SOME NUTCASE MUGGER WE'VE HAD ON THE BOOKS FOR A WHILE.
NO IDEA HE WAS PACKIN' THAT KINDA ARTILLERY THOUGH.
THAT'S WHAT TROUBLES ME...
...WHERE HE GOT THIS GUN...
Infinite City Industries
Infinite California

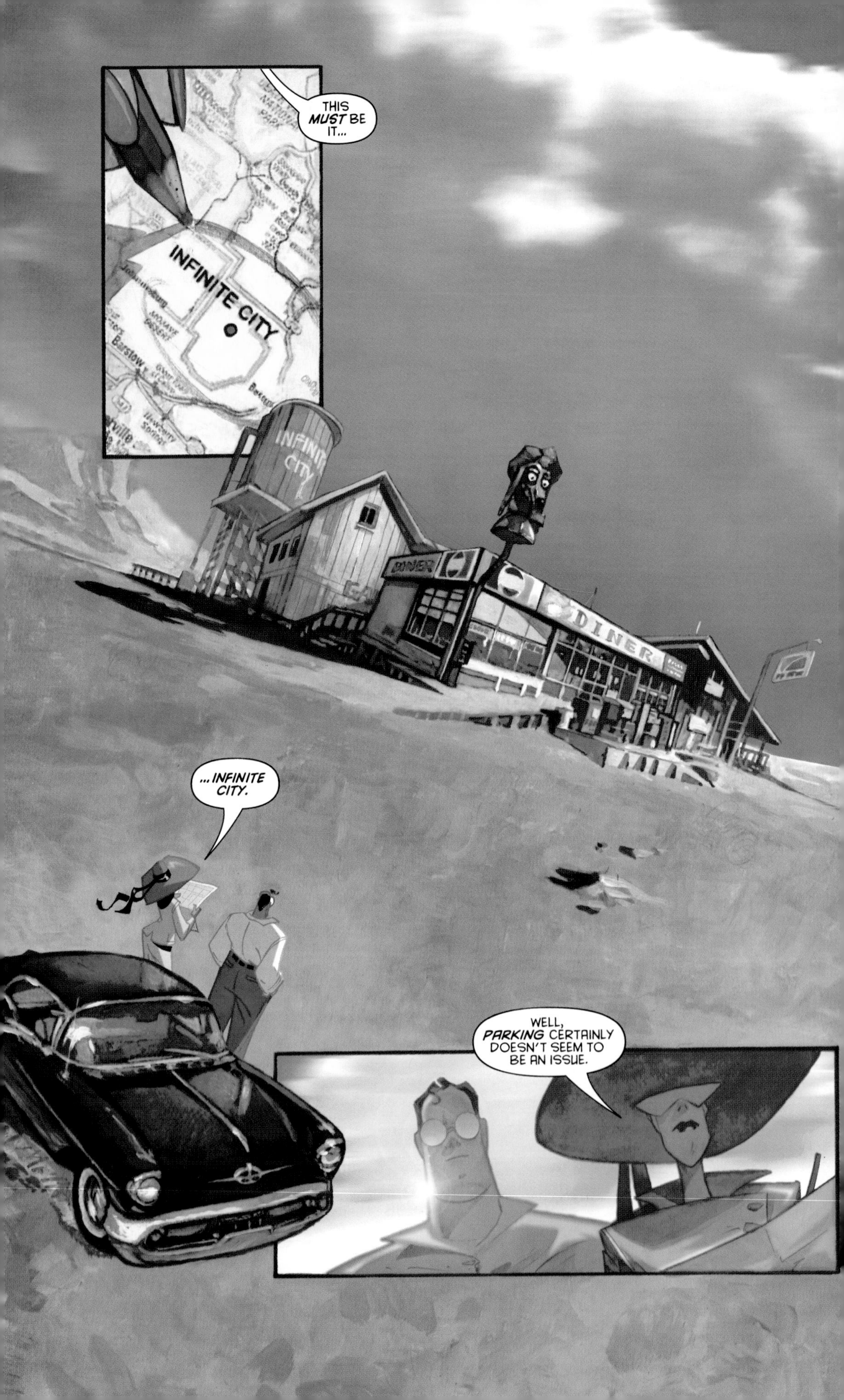
THIS MUST BE IT...
INFINITE CITY
Barstow
INFINITE CITY
DINER
DINER
...INFINITE CITY.
WELL, PARKING CERTAINLY DOESN'T SEEM TO BE AN ISSUE.

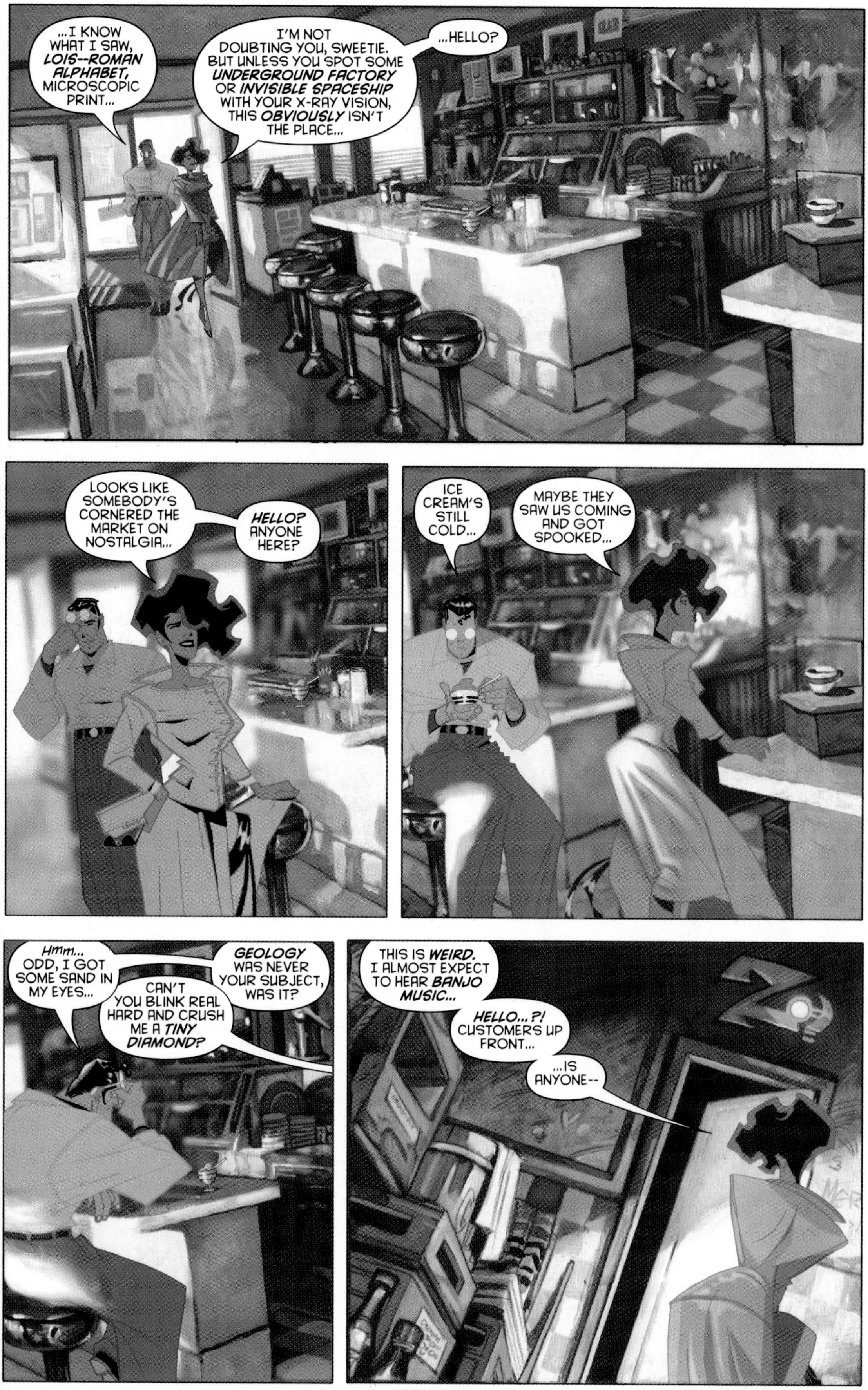
...I KNOW WHAT I SAW, LOIS--ROMAN ALPHABET, MICROSCOPIC PRINT...
I'M NOT DOUBTING YOU, SWEETIE. BUT UNLESS YOU SPOT SOME UNDERGROUND FACTORY OR INVISIBLE SPACESHIP WITH YOUR X-RAY VISION, THIS OBVIOUSLY ISN'T THE PLACE...
...HELLO?
LOOKS LIKE SOMEBODY'S CORNERED THE MARKET ON NOSTALGIA...
HELLO? ANYONE HERE?
ICE CREAM'S STILL COLD...
MAYBE THEY SAW US COMING AND GOT SPOOKED...
Hmm... ODD, I GOT SOME SAND IN MY EYES...
GEOLOGY WAS NEVER YOUR SUBJECT, WAS IT?
CAN'T YOU BLINK REAL HARD AND CRUSH ME A TINY DIAMOND?
THIS IS WEIRD. I ALMOST EXPECT TO HEAR BANJO MUSIC...
HELLO...?! CUSTOMERS UP FRONT...
...IS ANYONE--

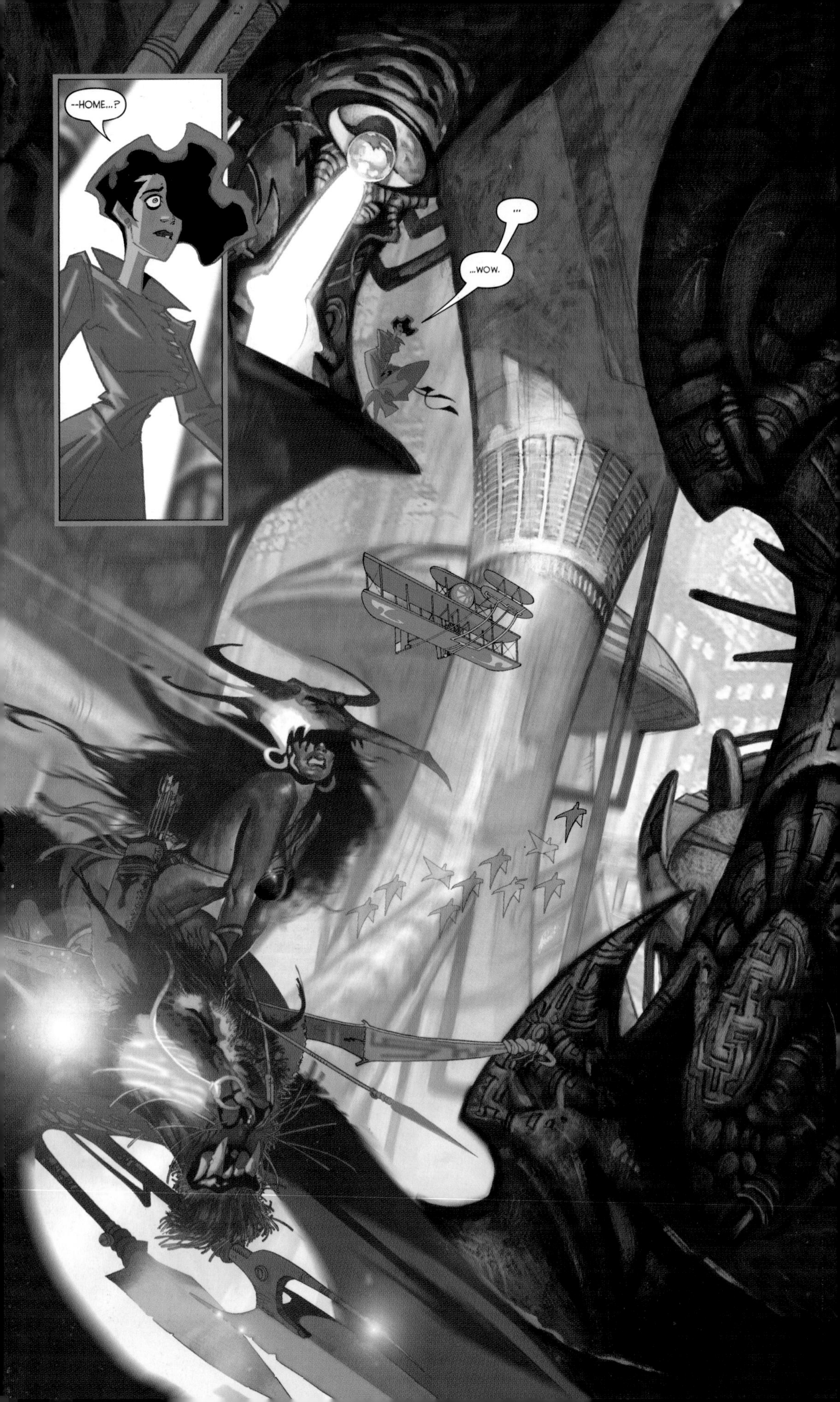
--HOME...?
...
...WOW.

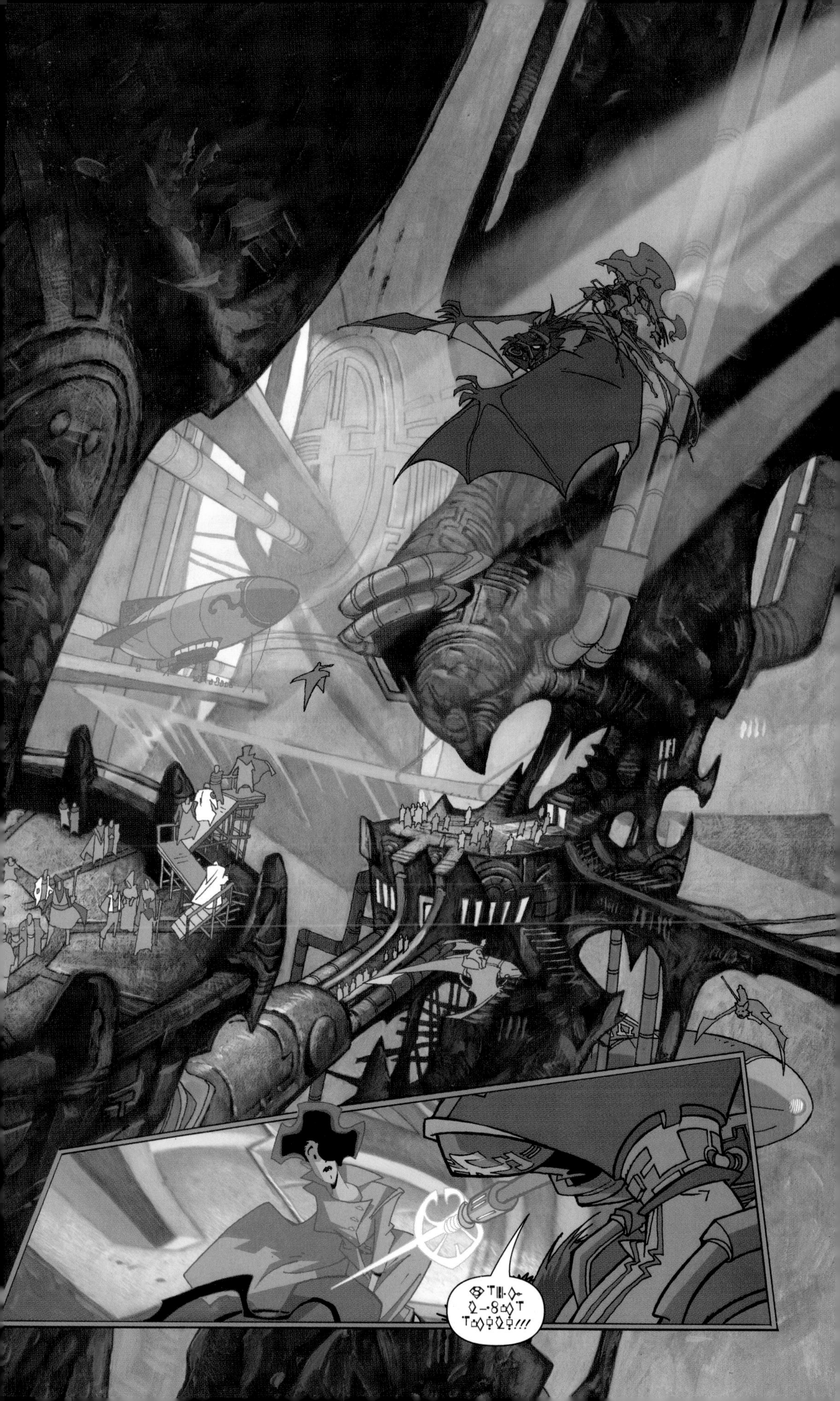

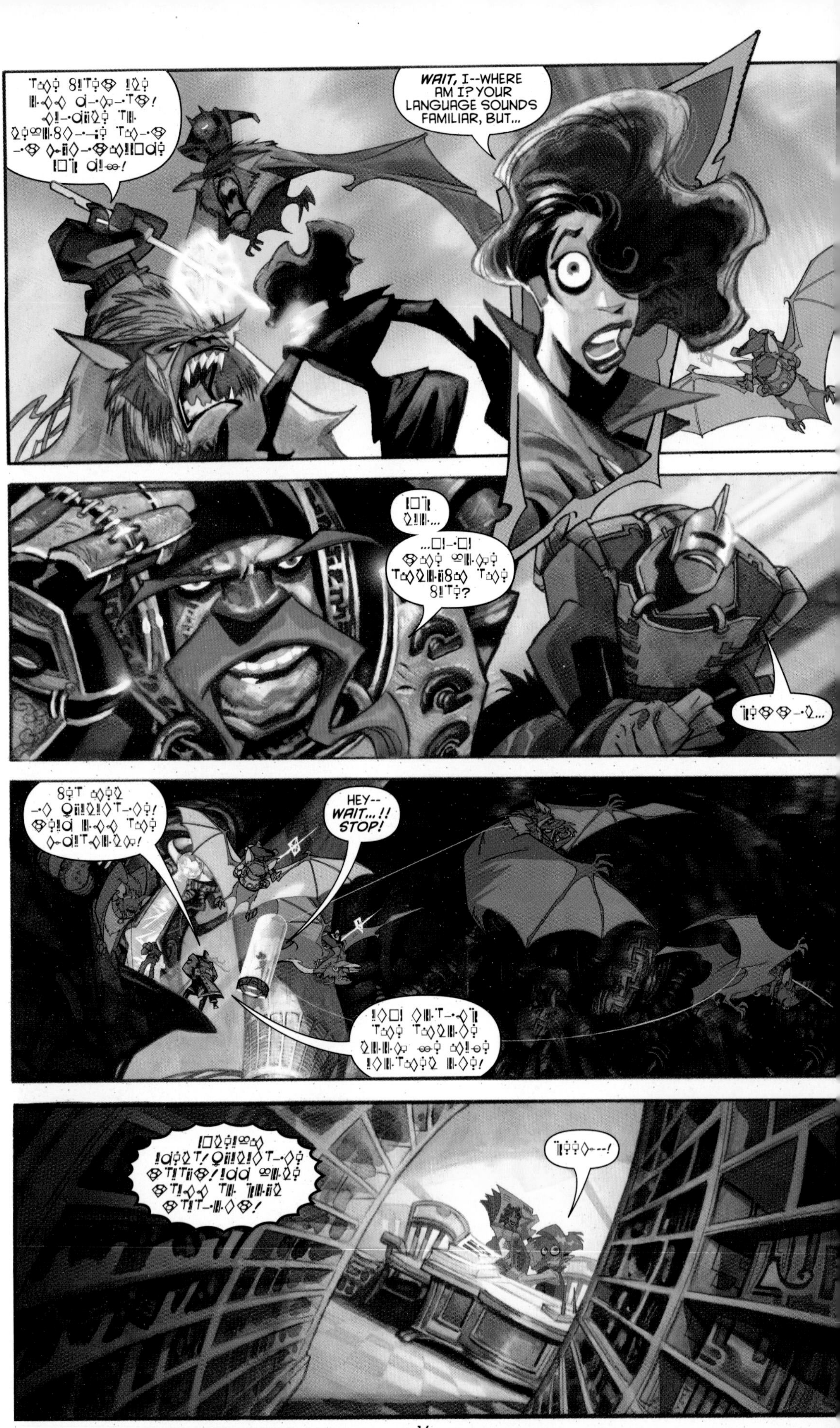
WAIT, I--WHERE AM I? YOUR LANGUAGE SOUNDS FAMILIAR, BUT...
HEY-- WAIT...!! STOP!

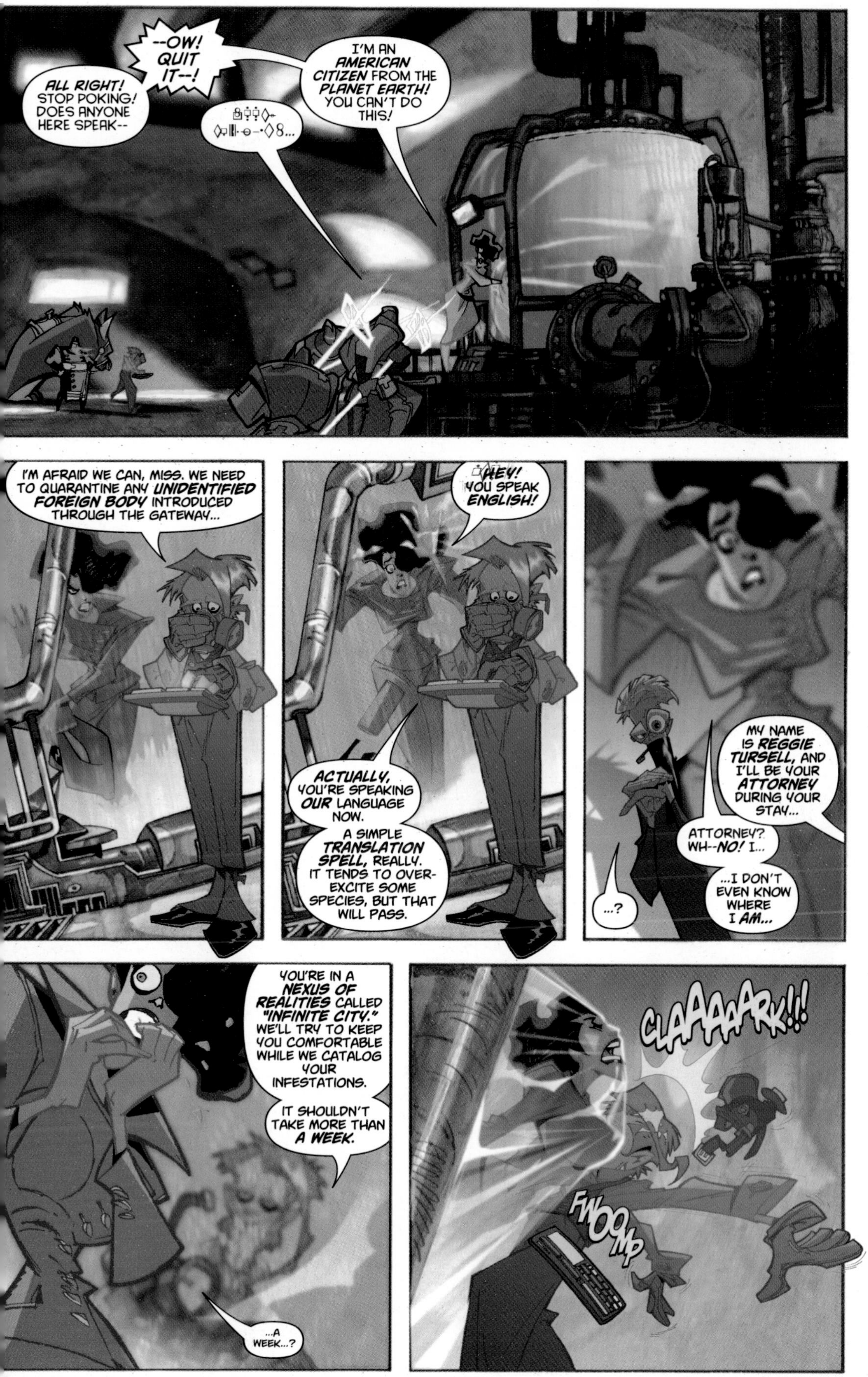

ALL RIGHT! STOP POKING! DOES ANYONE HERE SPEAK--
--OW! QUIT IT--!
I'M AN AMERICAN CITIZEN FROM THE PLANET EARTH! YOU CAN'T DO THIS!
I'M AFRAID WE CAN, MISS. WE NEED TO QUARANTINE ANY UNIDENTIFIED FOREIGN BODY INTRODUCED THROUGH THE GATEWAY...
HEY! YOU SPEAK ENGLISH!
ACTUALLY, YOU'RE SPEAKING OUR LANGUAGE NOW.
A SIMPLE TRANSLATION SPELL, REALLY. IT TENDS TO OVER-EXCITE SOME SPECIES, BUT THAT WILL PASS.
MY NAME IS REGGIE TURSELL, AND I'LL BE YOUR ATTORNEY DURING YOUR STAY...
...?
ATTORNEY? WH--NO! I...
...I DON'T EVEN KNOW WHERE I AM...
YOU'RE IN A NEXUS OF REALITIES CALLED "INFINITE CITY." WE'LL TRY TO KEEP YOU COMFORTABLE WHILE WE CATALOG YOUR INFESTATIONS.
IT SHOULDN'T TAKE MORE THAN A WEEK.
...A WEEK...?
CLAAAAARK!!!
FWOOOMP

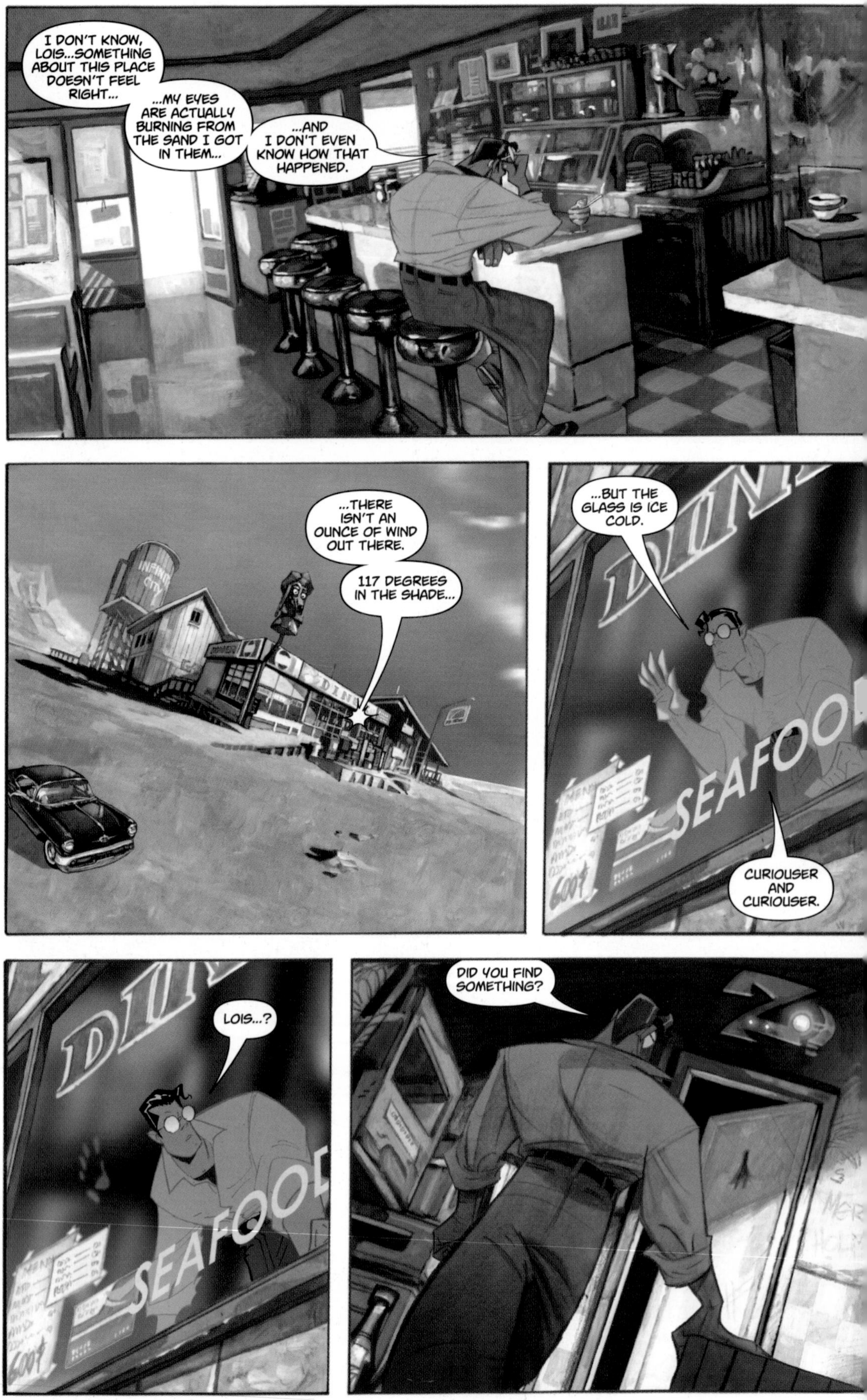
I DON'T KNOW, LOIS...SOMETHING ABOUT THIS PLACE DOESN'T FEEL RIGHT...
...MY EYES ARE ACTUALLY BURNING FROM THE SAND I GOT IN THEM...
...AND I DON'T EVEN KNOW HOW THAT HAPPENED.
...THERE ISN'T AN OUNCE OF WIND OUT THERE.
117 DEGREES IN THE SHADE...
...BUT THE GLASS IS ICE COLD.
CURIOUSER AND CURIOUSER.
SEAFOOD
LOIS...?
DID YOU FIND SOMETHING?

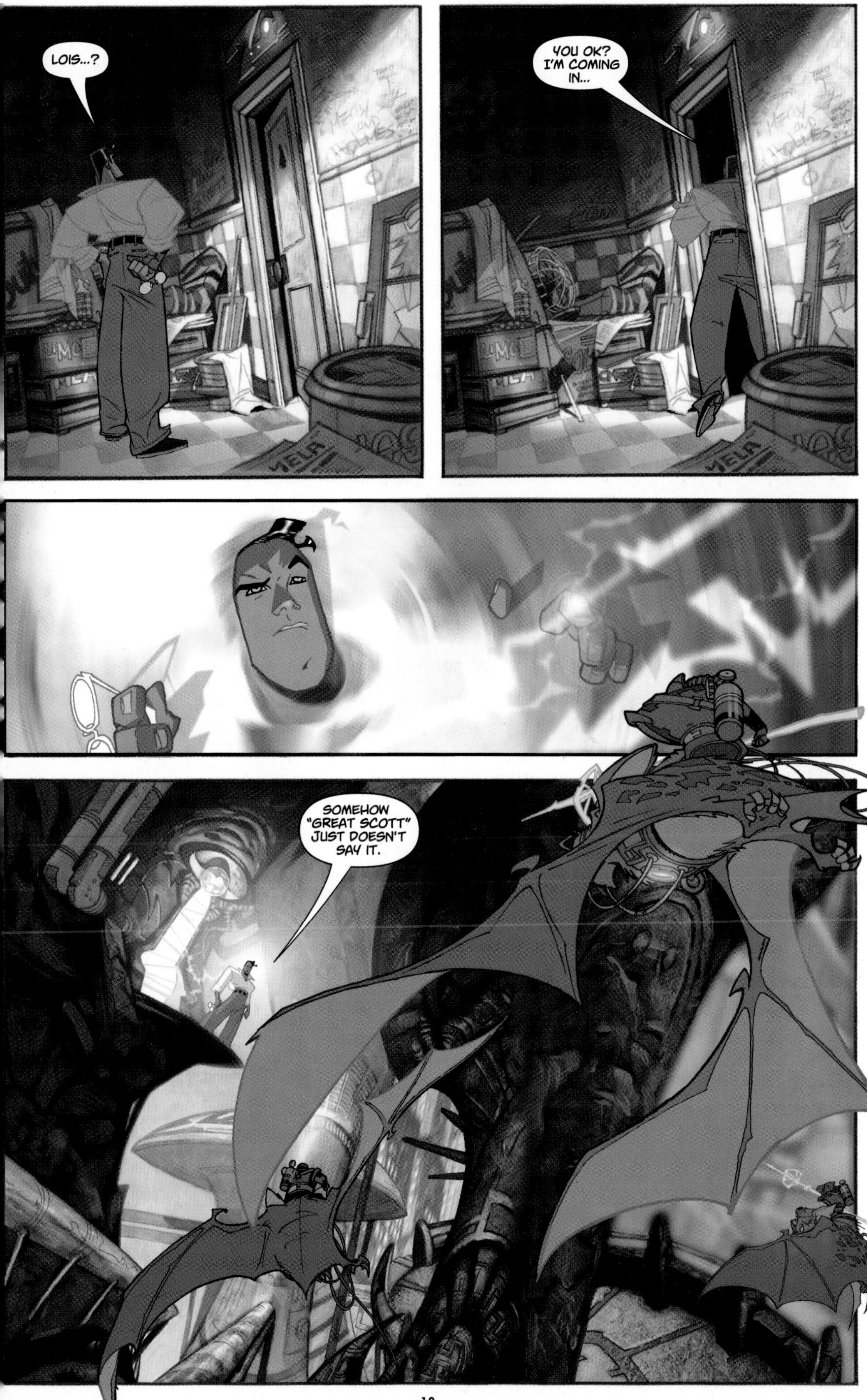
LOIS...?
YOU OK? I'M COMING IN...
SOMEHOW "GREAT SCOTT" JUST DOESN'T SAY IT.

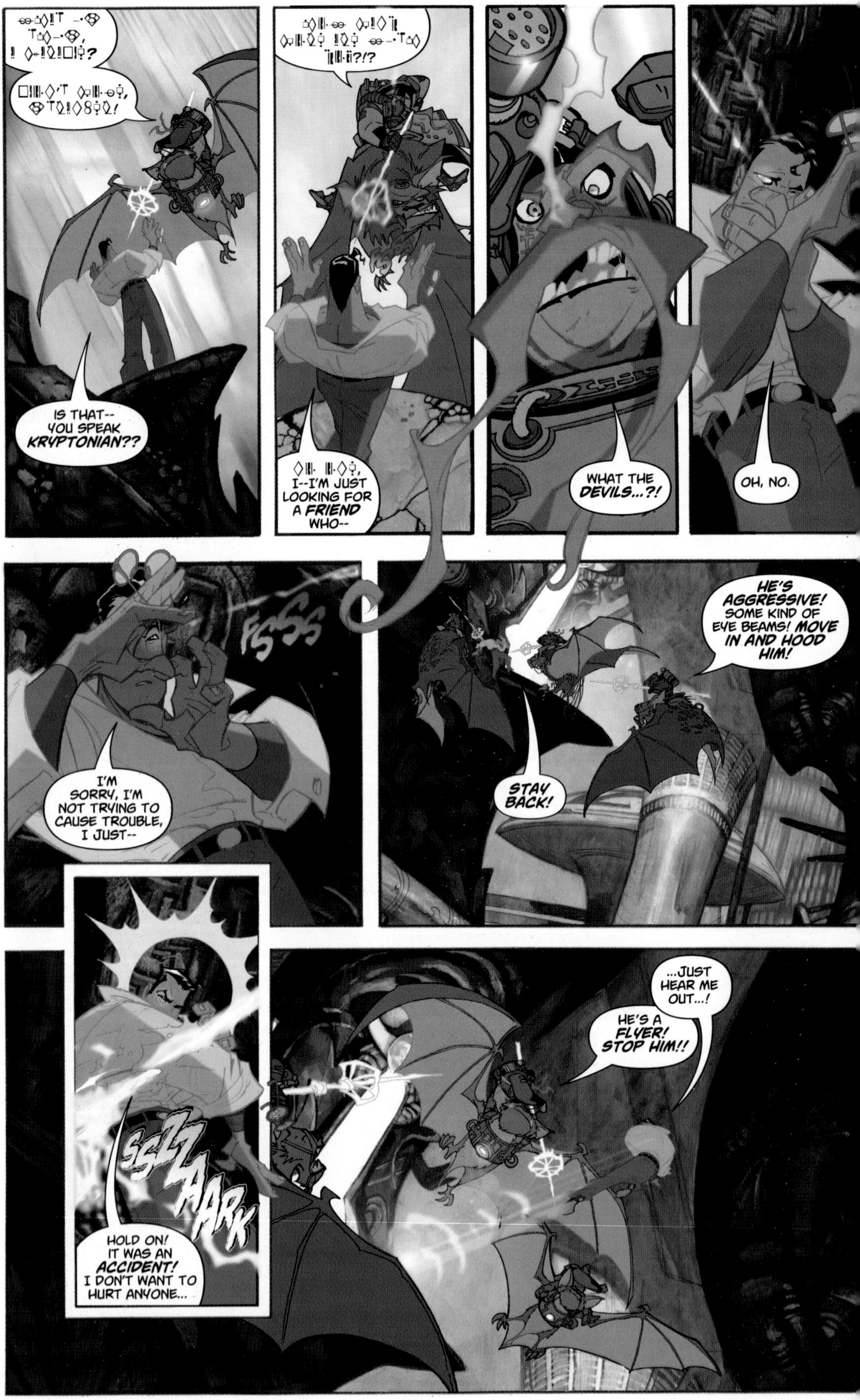
IS THAT-- YOU SPEAK KRYPTONIAN??
I--I'M JUST LOOKING FOR A FRIEND WHO--
WHAT THE DEVILS...?!
OH, NO.
FSSS
I'M SORRY, I'M NOT TRYING TO CAUSE TROUBLE, I JUST--
HE'S AGGRESSIVE! SOME KIND OF EYE BEAMS! MOVE IN AND HOOD HIM!
STAY BACK!
SSZZAARK
HOLD ON! IT WAS AN ACCIDENT! I DON'T WANT TO HURT ANYONE...
...JUST HEAR ME OUT...!
HE'S A FLYER! STOP HIM!!

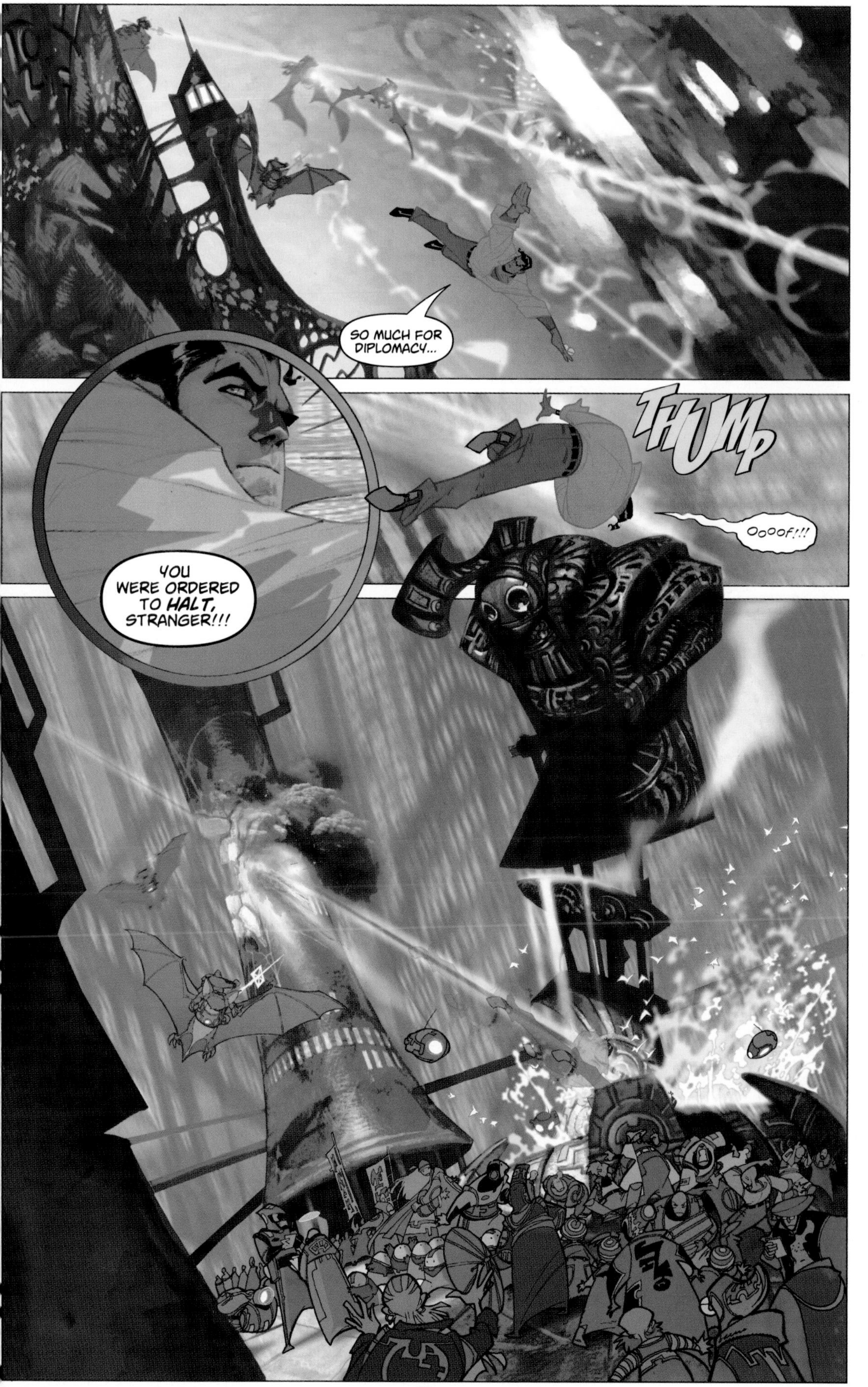
SO MUCH FOR DIPLOMACY...
THUMP
OOOOF!!!
YOU WERE ORDERED TO HALT, STRANGER!!!

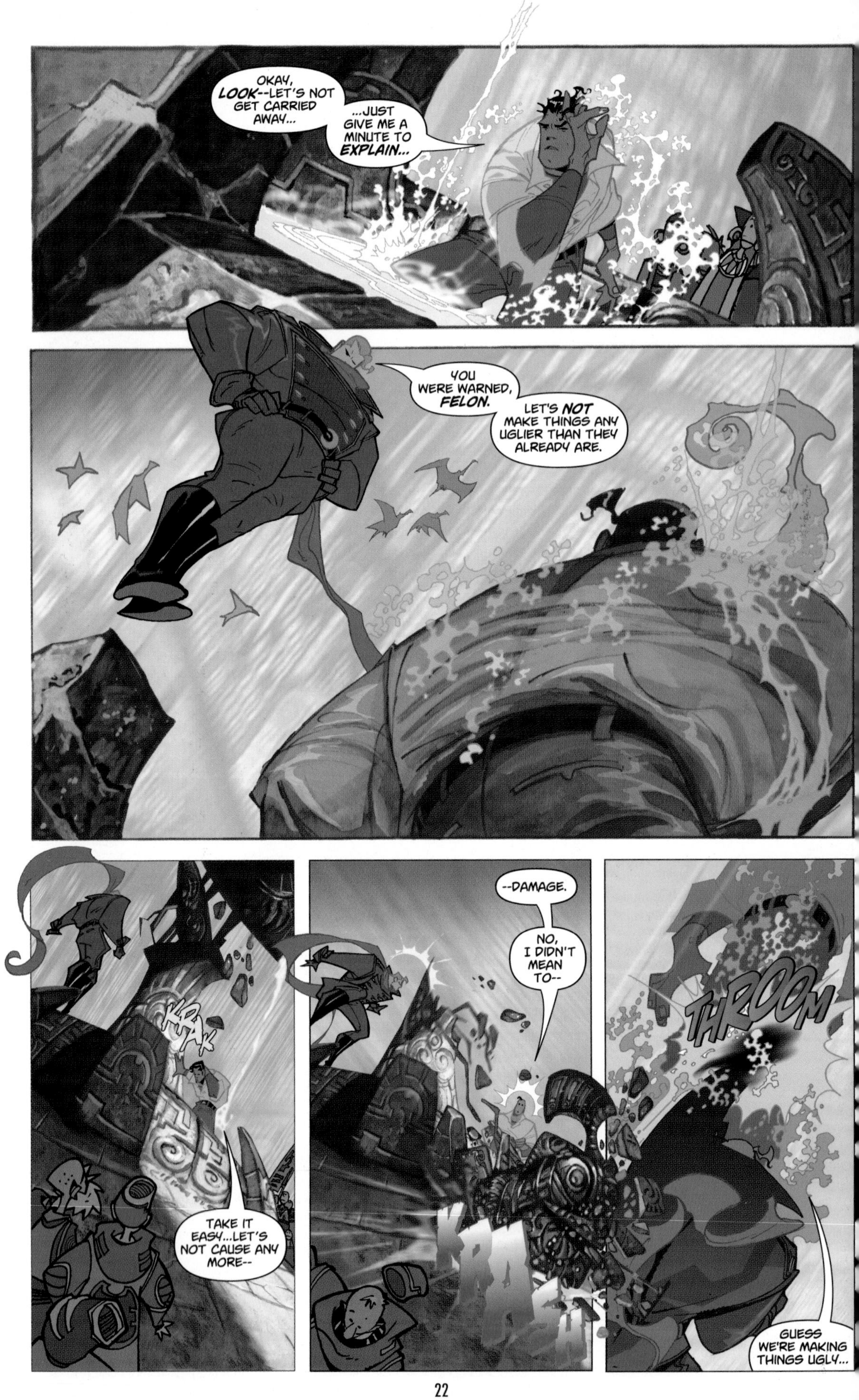
OKAY, LOOK--LET'S NOT GET CARRIED AWAY...
...JUST GIVE ME A MINUTE TO EXPLAIN...
YOU WERE WARNED, FELON.
LET'S NOT MAKE THINGS ANY UGLIER THAN THEY ALREADY ARE.
KRAK
TAKE IT EASY...LET'S NOT CAUSE ANY MORE--
--DAMAGE.
NO, I DIDN'T MEAN TO--
KRASH
THROOM
GUESS WE'RE MAKING THINGS UGLY...

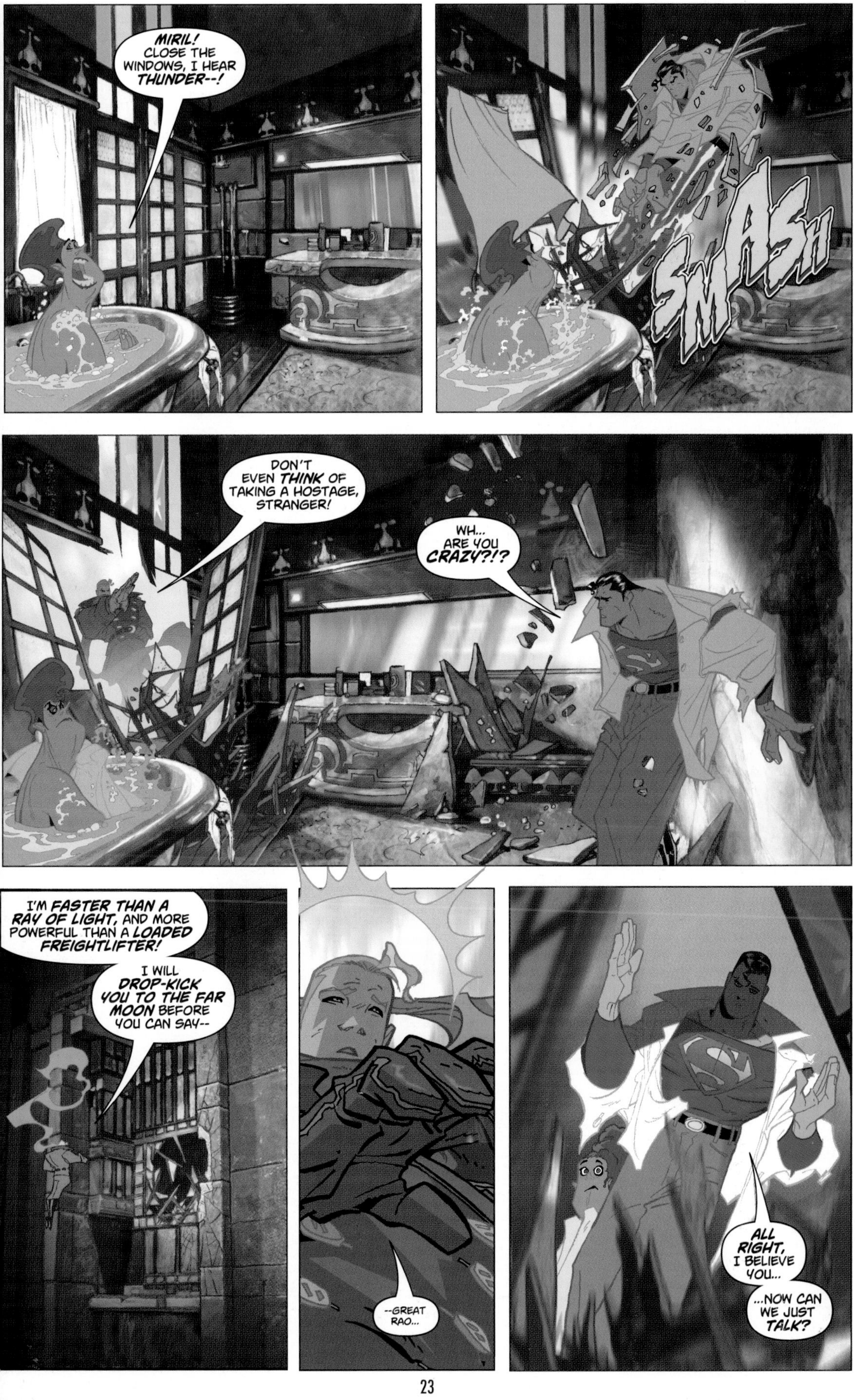

MIRIL! CLOSE THE WINDOWS, I HEAR THUNDER--!
SMASH
DON'T EVEN THINK OF TAKING A HOSTAGE, STRANGER!
WH... ARE YOU CRAZY?!?
I'M FASTER THAN A RAY OF LIGHT, AND MORE POWERFUL THAN A LOADED FREIGHTLIFTER!
I WILL DROP-KICK YOU TO THE FAR MOON BEFORE YOU CAN SAY--
--GREAT RAO...
ALL RIGHT, I BELIEVE YOU...
...NOW CAN WE JUST TALK?

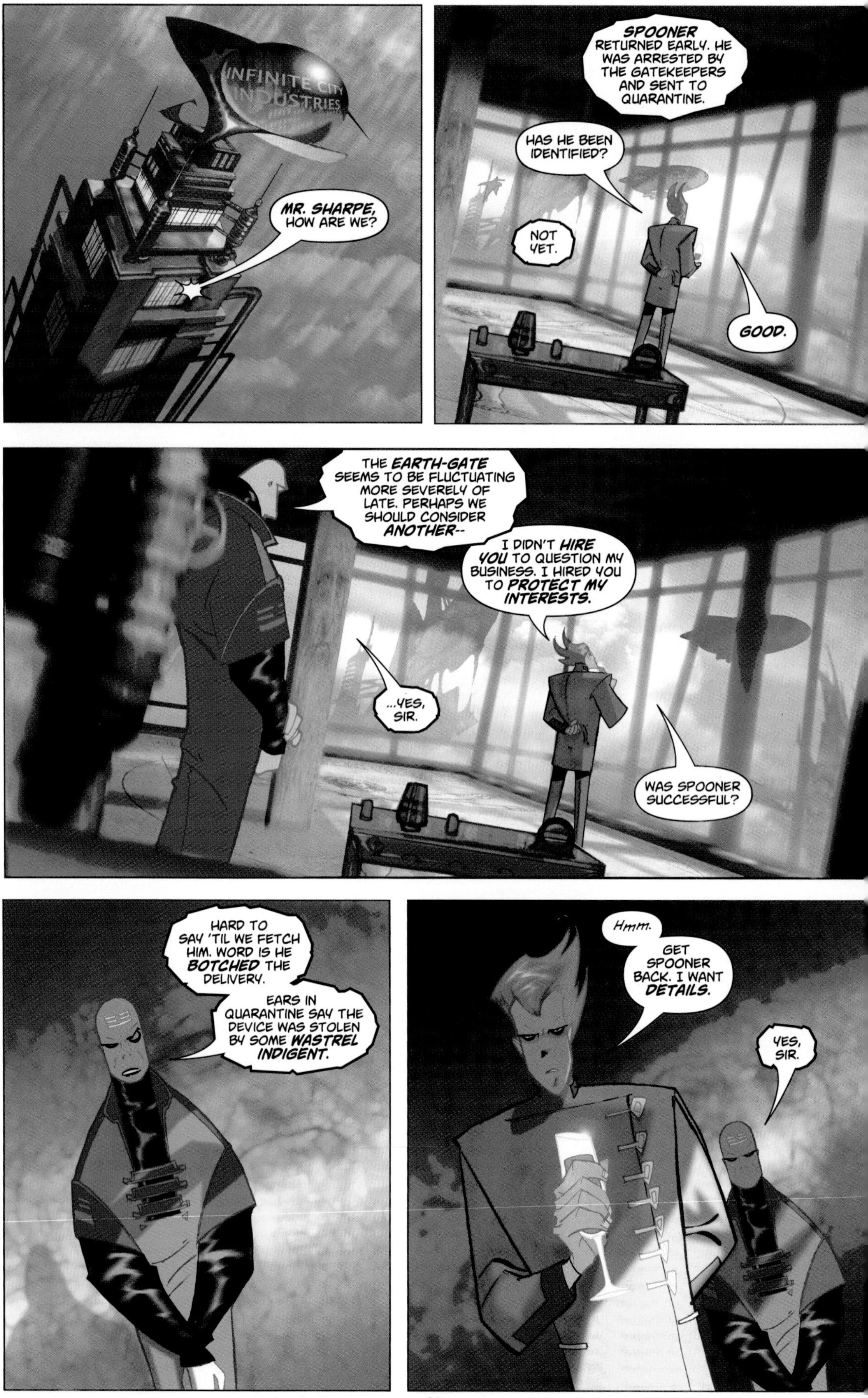
INFINITE CITY INDUSTRIES
MR. SHARPE, HOW ARE WE?
SPOONER RETURNED EARLY. HE WAS ARRESTED BY THE GATEKEEPERS AND SENT TO QUARANTINE.
HAS HE BEEN IDENTIFIED?
NOT YET.
GOOD.
THE EARTH-GATE SEEMS TO BE FLUCTUATING MORE SEVERELY OF LATE. PERHAPS WE SHOULD CONSIDER ANOTHER--
I DIDN'T HIRE YOU TO QUESTION MY BUSINESS. I HIRED YOU TO PROTECT MY INTERESTS.
...YES, SIR.
WAS SPOONER SUCCESSFUL?
HARD TO SAY 'TIL WE FETCH HIM. WORD IS HE BOTCHED THE DELIVERY.
EARS IN QUARANTINE SAY THE DEVICE WAS STOLEN BY SOME WASTREL INDIGENT.
Hmm.
GET SPOONER BACK. I WANT DETAILS.
YES, SIR.

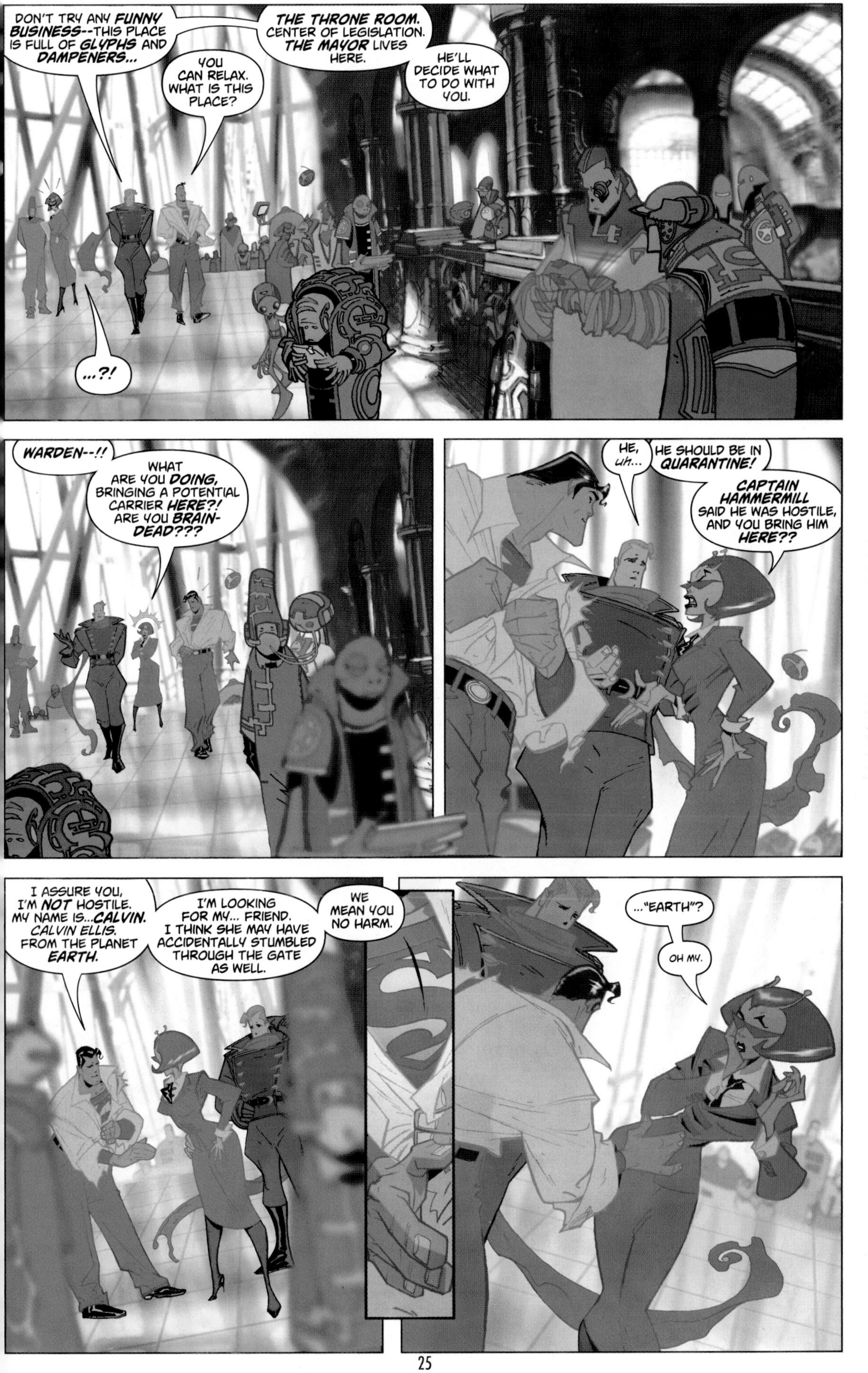

DON'T TRY ANY FUNNY BUSINESS--THIS PLACE IS FULL OF GLYPHS AND DAMPENERS...
YOU CAN RELAX. WHAT IS THIS PLACE?
THE THRONE ROOM. CENTER OF LEGISLATION. THE MAYOR LIVES HERE.
HE'LL DECIDE WHAT TO DO WITH YOU.
...?!
WARDEN--!!
WHAT ARE YOU DOING, BRINGING A POTENTIAL CARRIER HERE?! ARE YOU BRAIN-DEAD???
HE, uh...
HE SHOULD BE IN QUARANTINE!
CAPTAIN HAMMERMILL SAID HE WAS HOSTILE, AND YOU BRING HIM HERE??
I ASSURE YOU, I'M NOT HOSTILE. MY NAME IS...CALVIN. CALVIN ELLIS. FROM THE PLANET EARTH.
I'M LOOKING FOR MY... FRIEND. I THINK SHE MAY HAVE ACCIDENTALLY STUMBLED THROUGH THE GATE AS WELL.
WE MEAN YOU NO HARM.
..."EARTH"?
OH MY.

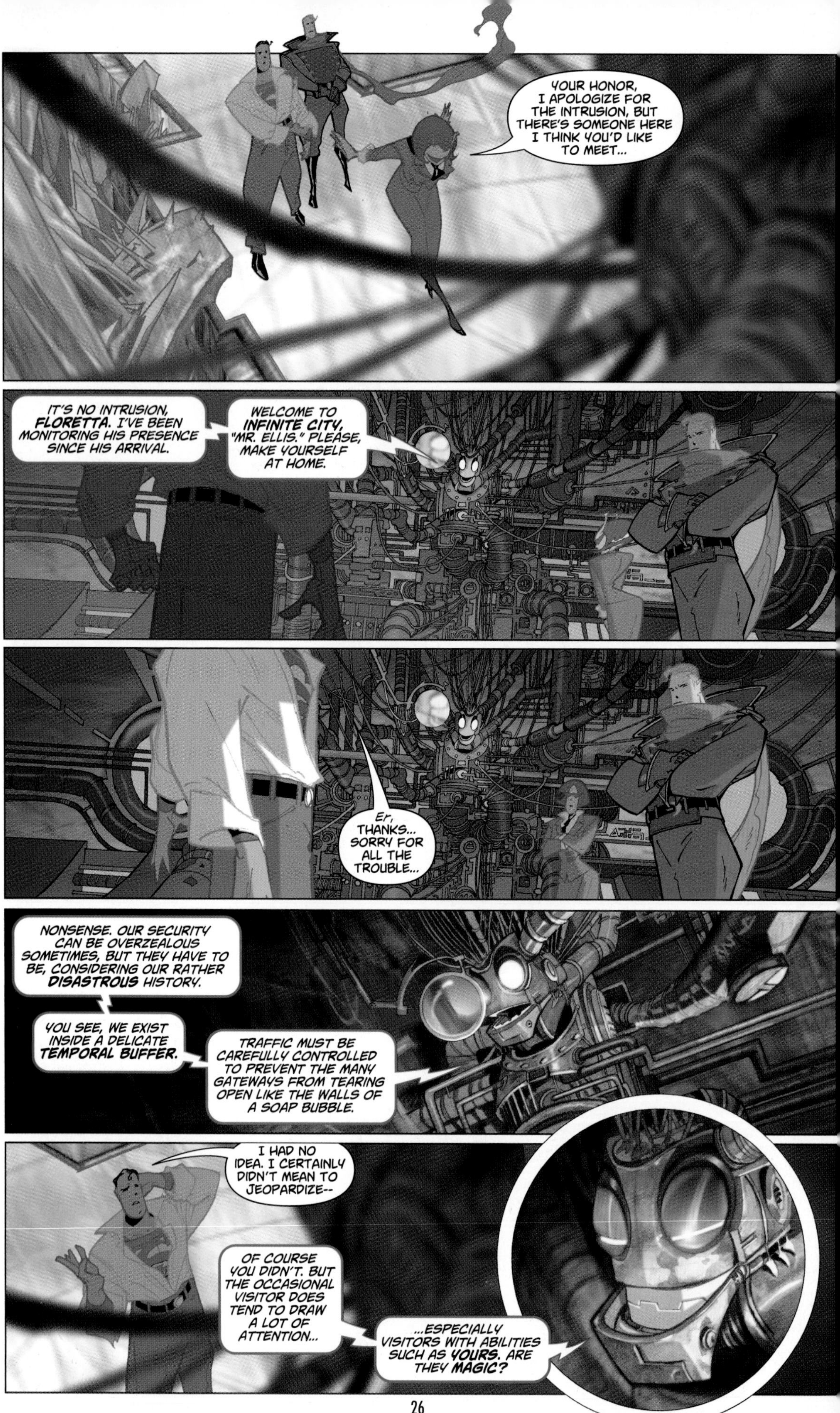
YOUR HONOR, I APOLOGIZE FOR THE INTRUSION, BUT THERE'S SOMEONE HERE I THINK YOU'D LIKE TO MEET...
IT'S NO INTRUSION, FLORETTA. I'VE BEEN MONITORING HIS PRESENCE SINCE HIS ARRIVAL.
WELCOME TO INFINITE CITY, "MR. ELLIS." PLEASE, MAKE YOURSELF AT HOME.
Er, THANKS... SORRY FOR ALL THE TROUBLE...
NONSENSE. OUR SECURITY CAN BE OVERZEALOUS SOMETIMES, BUT THEY HAVE TO BE, CONSIDERING OUR RATHER DISASTROUS HISTORY.
YOU SEE, WE EXIST INSIDE A DELICATE TEMPORAL BUFFER.
TRAFFIC MUST BE CAREFULLY CONTROLLED TO PREVENT THE MANY GATEWAYS FROM TEARING OPEN LIKE THE WALLS OF A SOAP BUBBLE.
I HAD NO IDEA. I CERTAINLY DIDN'T MEAN TO JEOPARDIZE--
OF COURSE YOU DIDN'T. BUT THE OCCASIONAL VISITOR DOES TEND TO DRAW A LOT OF ATTENTION...
...ESPECIALLY VISITORS WITH ABILITIES SUCH AS YOURS. ARE THEY MAGIC?

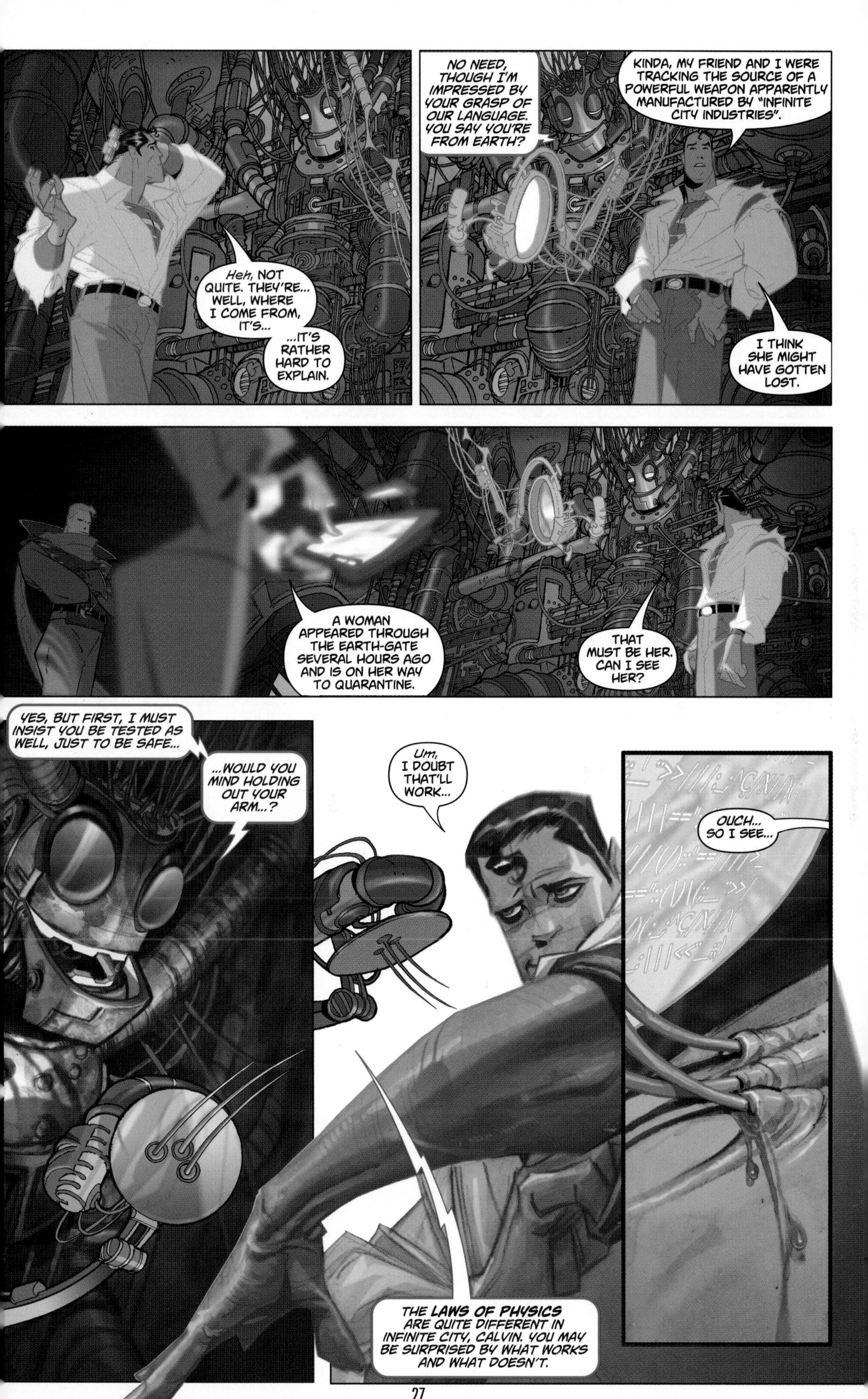
Heh, NOT QUITE. THEY'RE... WELL, WHERE I COME FROM, IT'S...
...IT'S RATHER HARD TO EXPLAIN.
NO NEED, THOUGH I'M IMPRESSED BY YOUR GRASP OF OUR LANGUAGE. YOU SAY YOU'RE FROM EARTH?
KINDA, MY FRIEND AND I WERE TRACKING THE SOURCE OF A POWERFUL WEAPON APPARENTLY MANUFACTURED BY "INFINITE CITY INDUSTRIES".
I THINK SHE MIGHT HAVE GOTTEN LOST.
A WOMAN APPEARED THROUGH THE EARTH-GATE SEVERAL HOURS AGO AND IS ON HER WAY TO QUARANTINE.
THAT MUST BE HER. CAN I SEE HER?
YES, BUT FIRST, I MUST INSIST YOU BE TESTED AS WELL, JUST TO BE SAFE...
...WOULD YOU MIND HOLDING OUT YOUR ARM...?
Um, I DOUBT THAT'LL WORK...
OUCH... SO I SEE...
THE LAWS OF PHYSICS ARE QUITE DIFFERENT IN INFINITE CITY, CALVIN. YOU MAY BE SURPRISED BY WHAT WORKS AND WHAT DOESN'T.

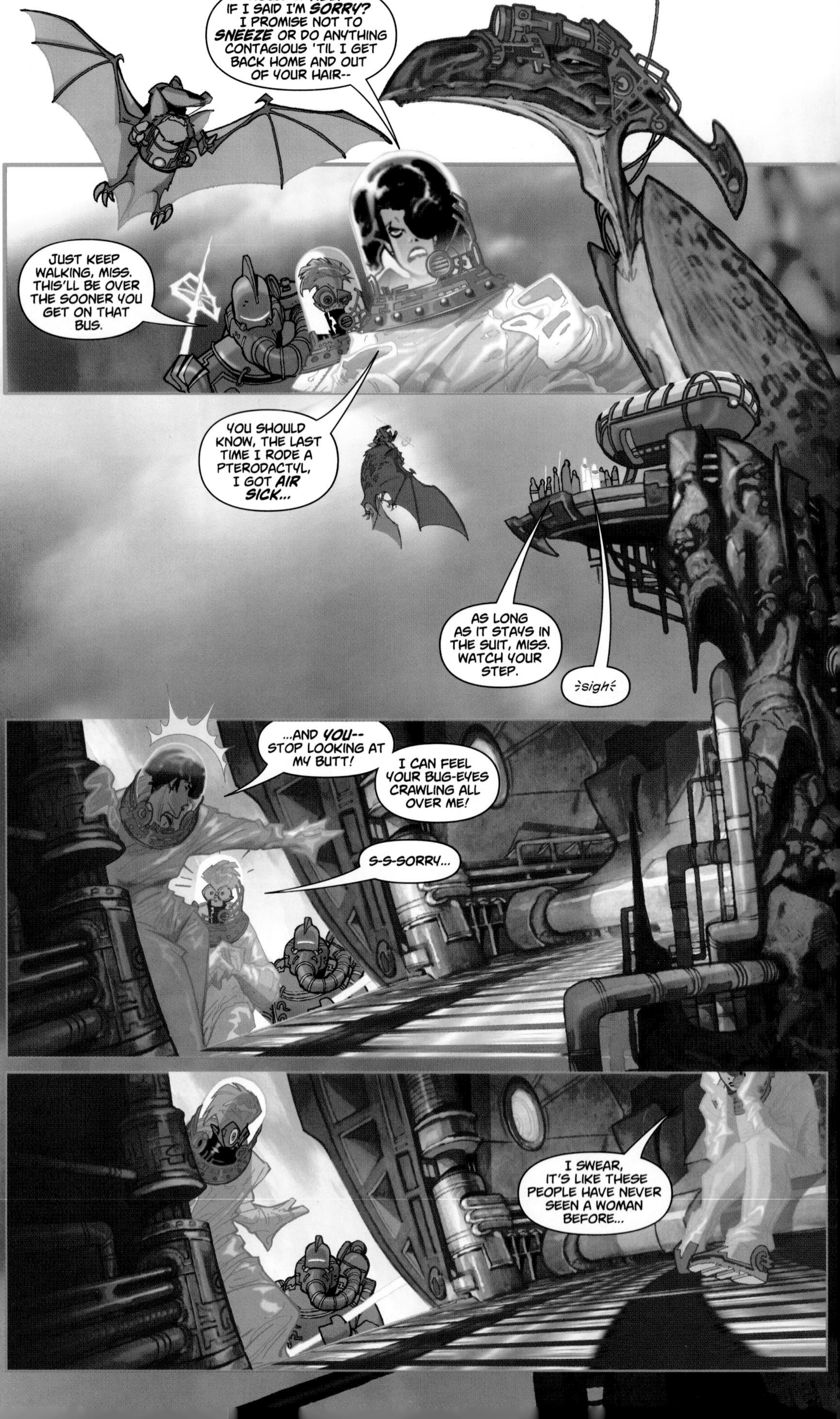
WOULD IT HELP IF I SAID I'M SORRY? I PROMISE NOT TO SNEEZE OR DO ANYTHING CONTAGIOUS 'TIL I GET BACK HOME AND OUT OF YOUR HAIR--
JUST KEEP WALKING, MISS. THIS'LL BE OVER THE SOONER YOU GET ON THAT BUS.
YOU SHOULD KNOW, THE LAST TIME I RODE A PTERODACTYL, I GOT AIR SICK...
AS LONG AS IT STAYS IN THE SUIT, MISS. WATCH YOUR STEP.
sigh
...AND YOU-- STOP LOOKING AT MY BUTT!
I CAN FEEL YOUR BUG-EYES CRAWLING ALL OVER ME!
S-S-SORRY...
I SWEAR, IT'S LIKE THESE PEOPLE HAVE NEVER SEEN A WOMAN BEFORE...

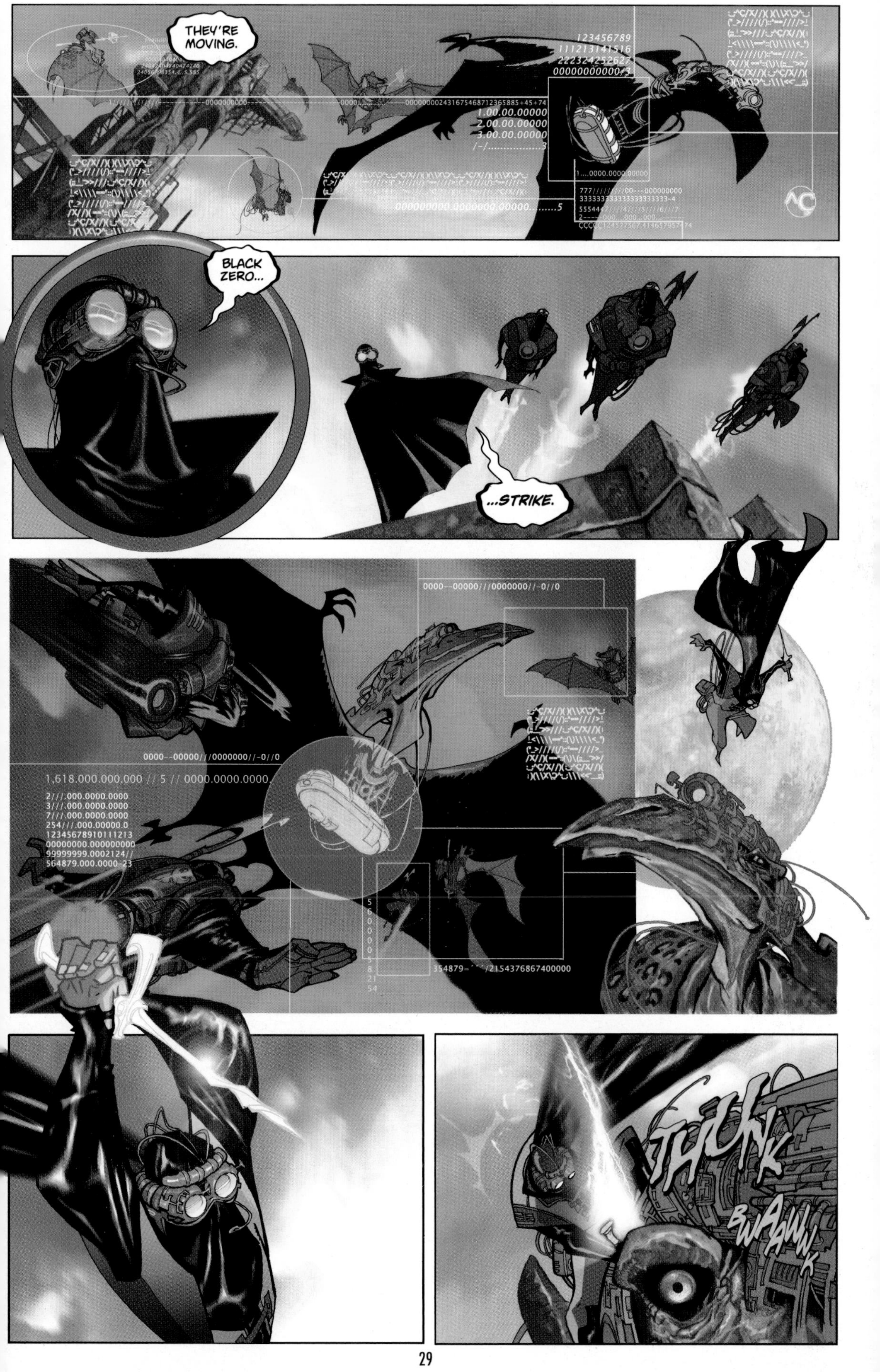
THEY'RE MOVING.
BLACK ZERO...
...STRIKE.
THUNK
BWAAWK

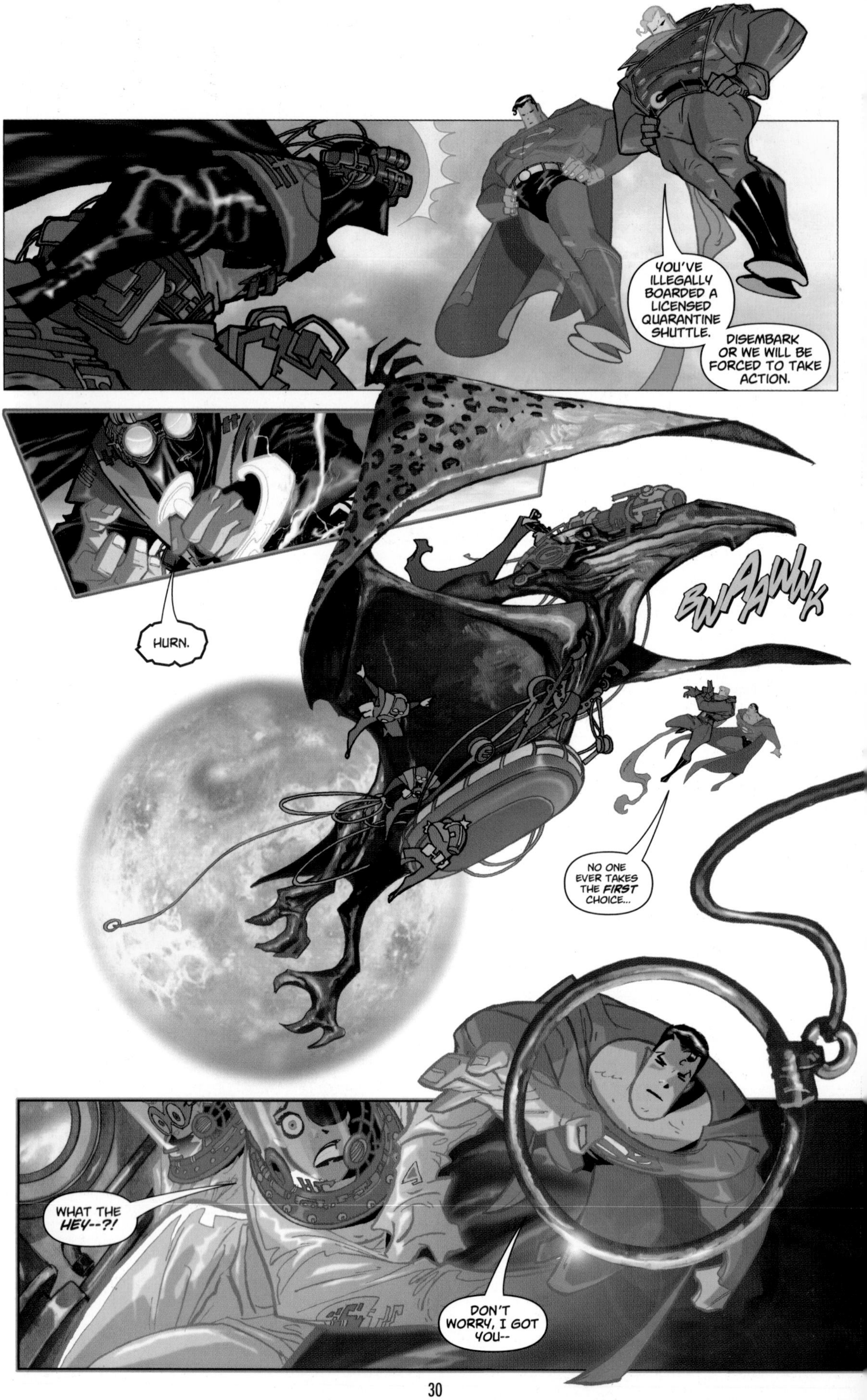
YOU'VE ILLEGALLY BOARDED A LICENSED QUARANTINE SHUTTLE.
DISEMBARK OR WE WILL BE FORCED TO TAKE ACTION.
HURN.
BWAAWWK
NO ONE EVER TAKES THE *FIRST* CHOICE...
WHAT THE *HEY--?!*
DON'T WORRY, I GOT YOU--

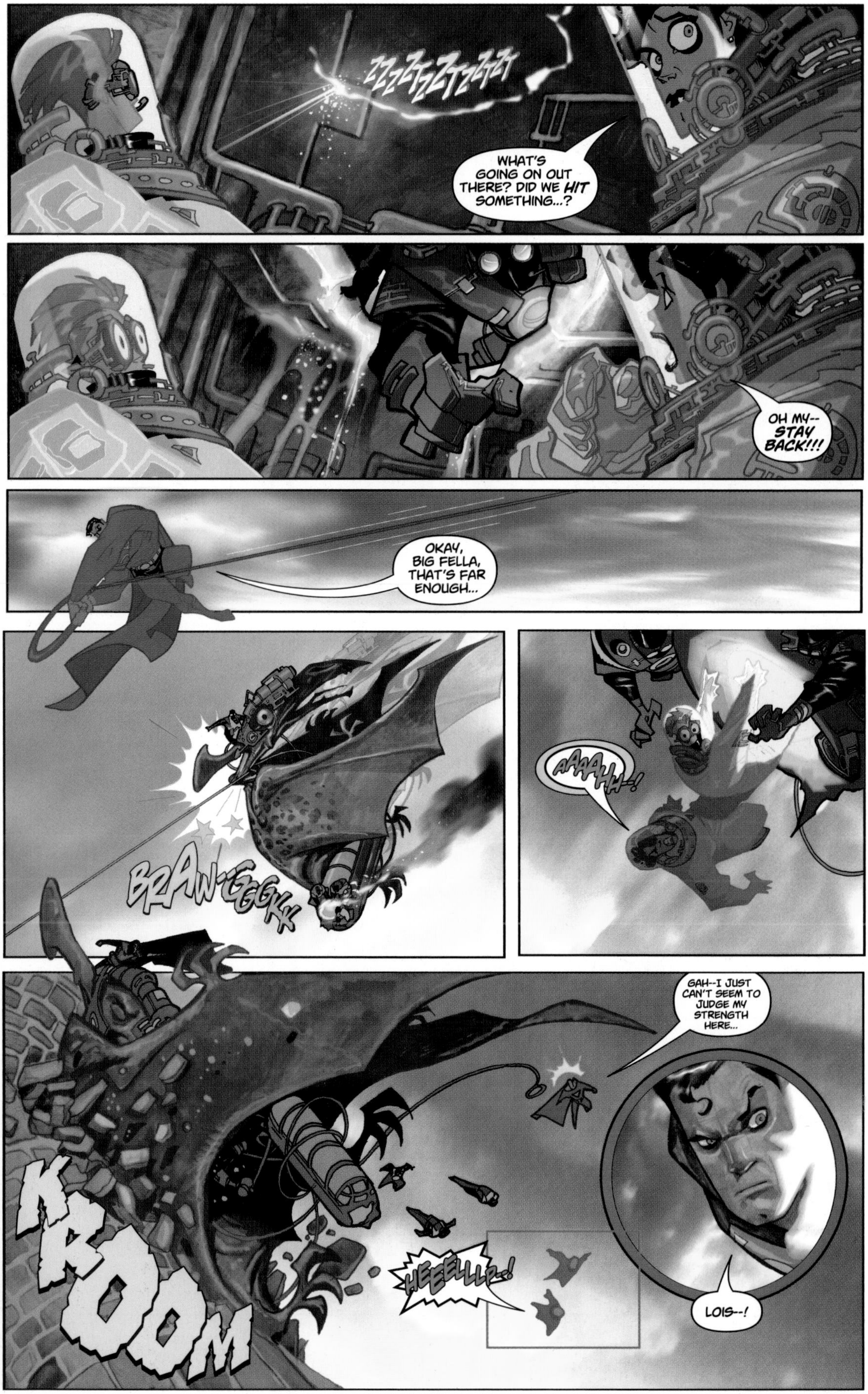
ZZZZTZZTZZTZT
WHAT'S GOING ON OUT THERE? DID WE HIT SOMETHING...?
OH MY-- STAY BACK!!!
OKAY, BIG FELLA, THAT'S FAR ENOUGH...
BRAW-GGGKK
AAAAHH--!
GAH--I JUST CAN'T SEEM TO JUDGE MY STRENGTH HERE...
KROOM
HEEELLLP--!
LOIS--!

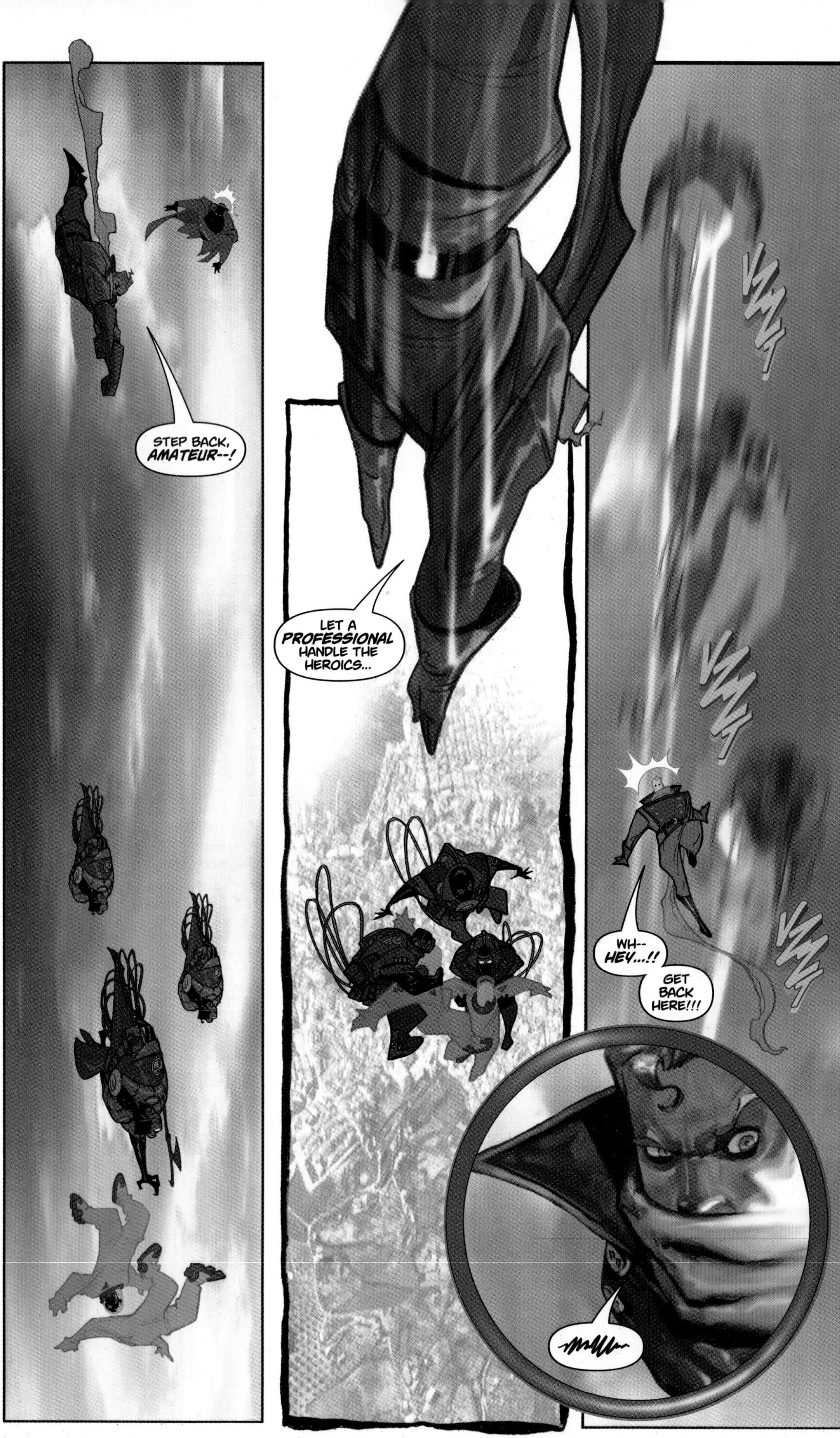
STEP BACK, AMATEUR--!
LET A PROFESSIONAL HANDLE THE HEROICS...
WH-- HEY...!!
GET BACK HERE!!!

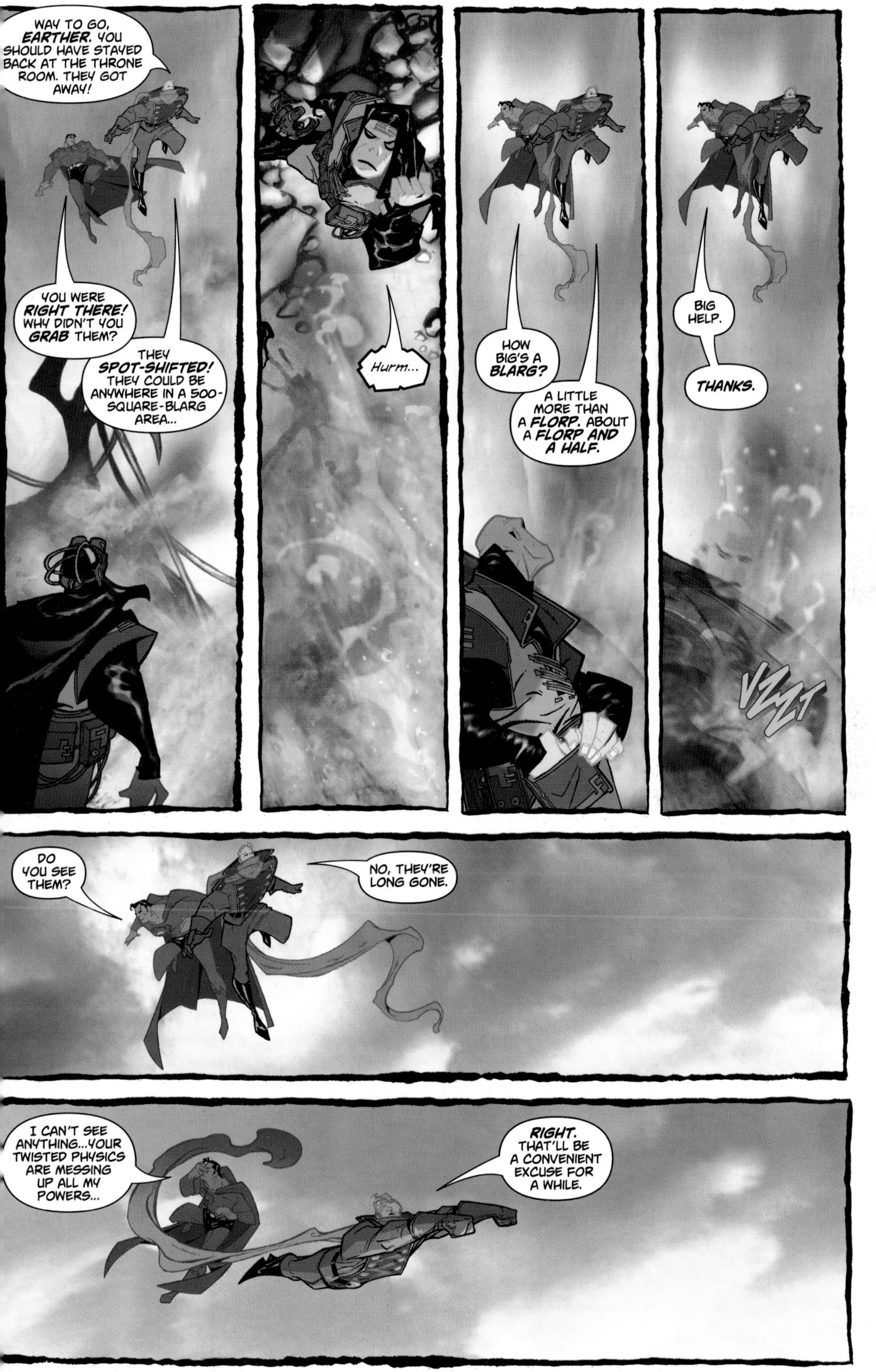
WAY TO GO, EARTHER. YOU SHOULD HAVE STAYED BACK AT THE THRONE ROOM. THEY GOT AWAY!
YOU WERE RIGHT THERE! WHY DIDN'T YOU GRAB THEM?
THEY SPOT-SHIFTED! THEY COULD BE ANYWHERE IN A 500-SQUARE-BLARG AREA...
Hurm...
HOW BIG'S A BLARG?
A LITTLE MORE THAN A FLORP. ABOUT A FLORP AND A HALF.
BIG HELP.
THANKS.
VZZT
DO YOU SEE THEM?
NO, THEY'RE LONG GONE.
I CAN'T SEE ANYTHING...YOUR TWISTED PHYSICS ARE MESSING UP ALL MY POWERS...
RIGHT. THAT'LL BE A CONVENIENT EXCUSE FOR A WHILE.

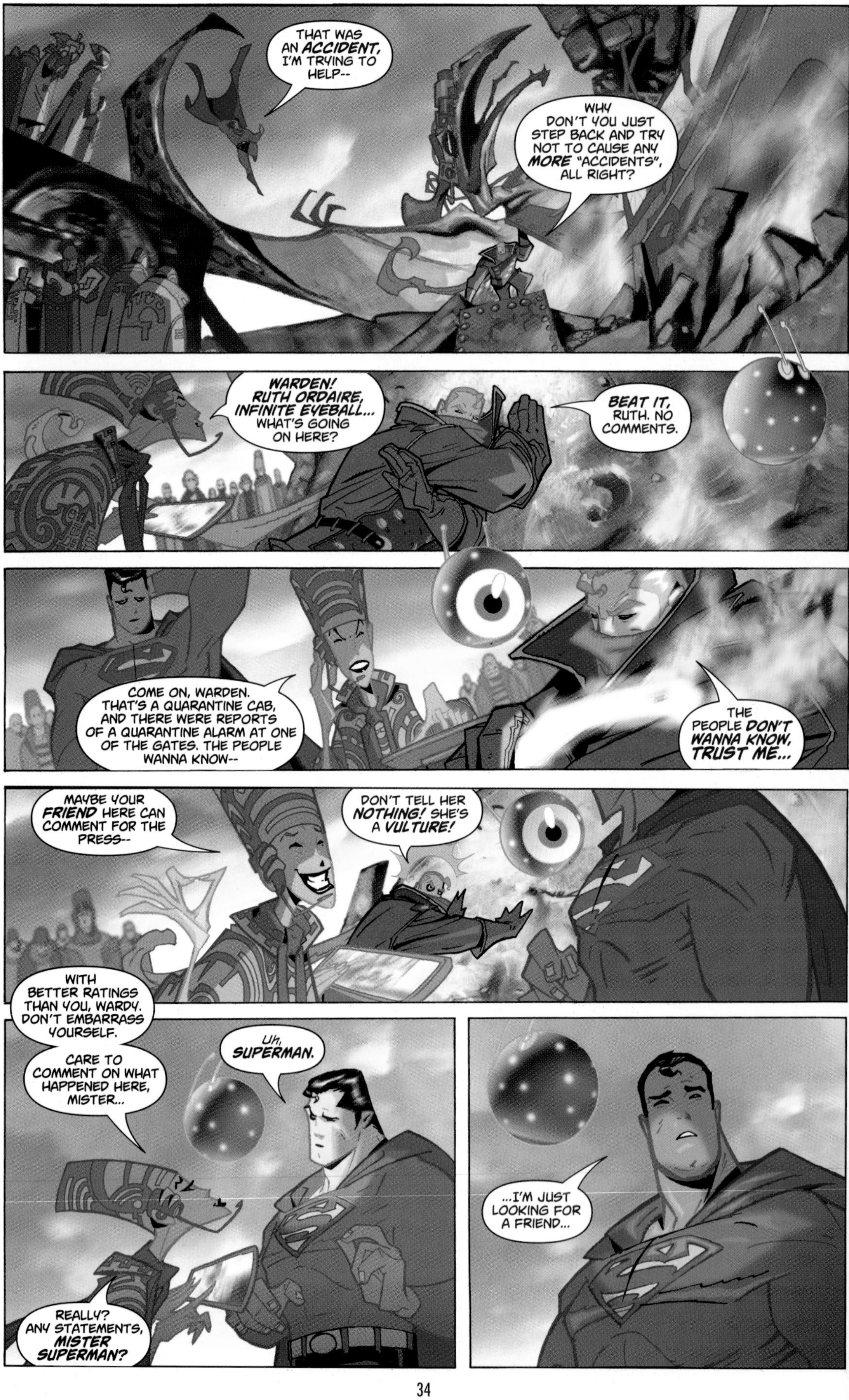
THAT WAS AN ACCIDENT, I'M TRYING TO HELP--
WHY DON'T YOU JUST STEP BACK AND TRY NOT TO CAUSE ANY MORE "ACCIDENTS", ALL RIGHT?
WARDEN! RUTH ORDAIRE, INFINITE EYEBALL... WHAT'S GOING ON HERE?
BEAT IT, RUTH. NO COMMENTS.
COME ON, WARDEN. THAT'S A QUARANTINE CAB, AND THERE WERE REPORTS OF A QUARANTINE ALARM AT ONE OF THE GATES. THE PEOPLE WANNA KNOW--
THE PEOPLE DON'T WANNA KNOW, TRUST ME...
MAYBE YOUR FRIEND HERE CAN COMMENT FOR THE PRESS--
DON'T TELL HER NOTHING! SHE'S A VULTURE!
WITH BETTER RATINGS THAN YOU, WARDY. DON'T EMBARRASS YOURSELF.
CARE TO COMMENT ON WHAT HAPPENED HERE, MISTER...
Uh, SUPERMAN.
REALLY? ANY STATEMENTS, MISTER SUPERMAN?
...I'M JUST LOOKING FOR A FRIEND...

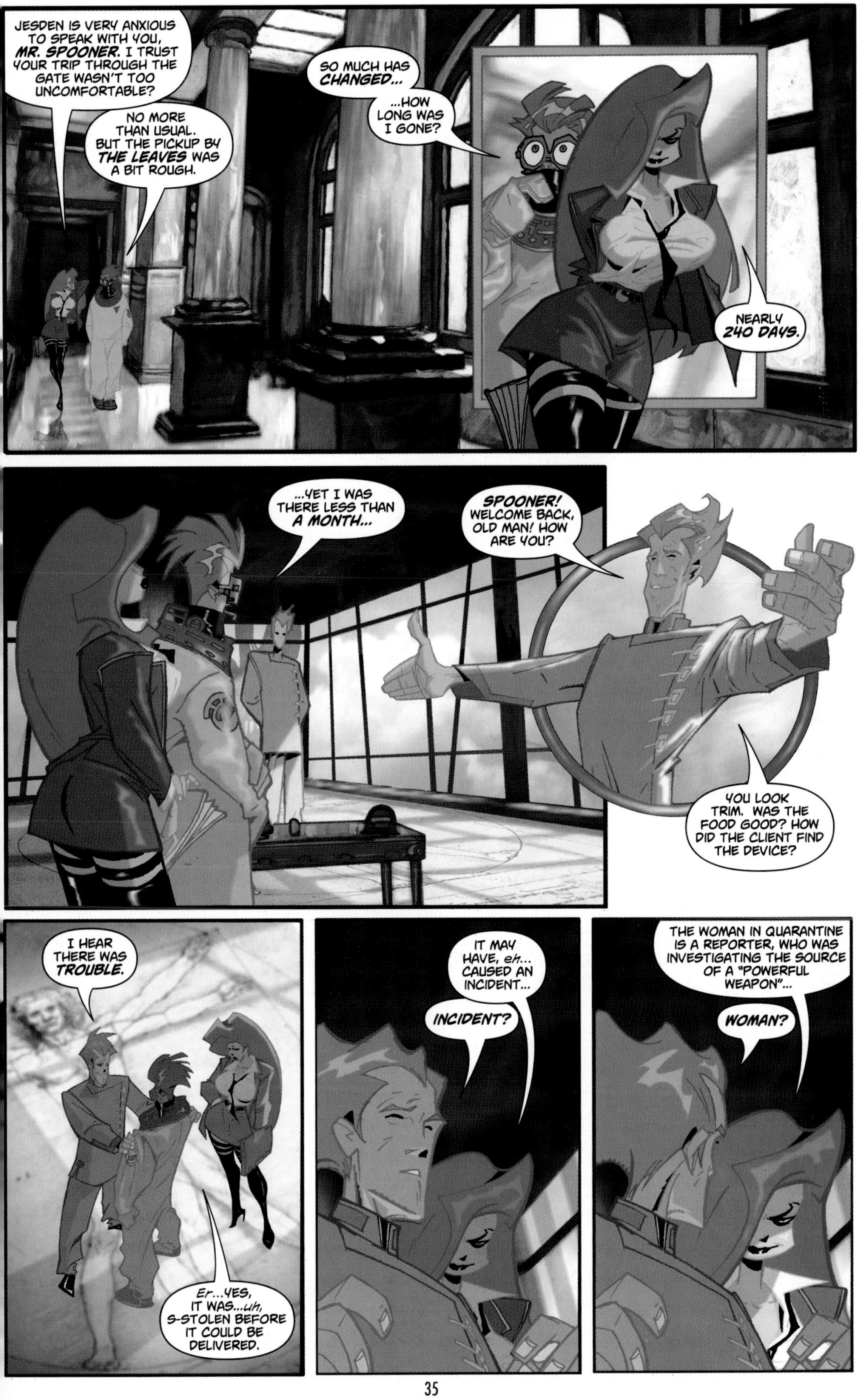
JESDEN IS VERY ANXIOUS TO SPEAK WITH YOU, MR. SPOONER. I TRUST YOUR TRIP THROUGH THE GATE WASN'T TOO UNCOMFORTABLE?
NO MORE THAN USUAL. BUT THE PICKUP BY THE LEAVES WAS A BIT ROUGH.
SO MUCH HAS CHANGED...
...HOW LONG WAS I GONE?
NEARLY 240 DAYS.
...YET I WAS THERE LESS THAN A MONTH...
SPOONER! WELCOME BACK, OLD MAN! HOW ARE YOU?
YOU LOOK TRIM. WAS THE FOOD GOOD? HOW DID THE CLIENT FIND THE DEVICE?
I HEAR THERE WAS TROUBLE.
Er...YES, IT WAS...uh, S-STOLEN BEFORE IT COULD BE DELIVERED.
IT MAY HAVE, eh... CAUSED AN INCIDENT...
INCIDENT?
THE WOMAN IN QUARANTINE IS A REPORTER, WHO WAS INVESTIGATING THE SOURCE OF A "POWERFUL WEAPON"...
WOMAN?

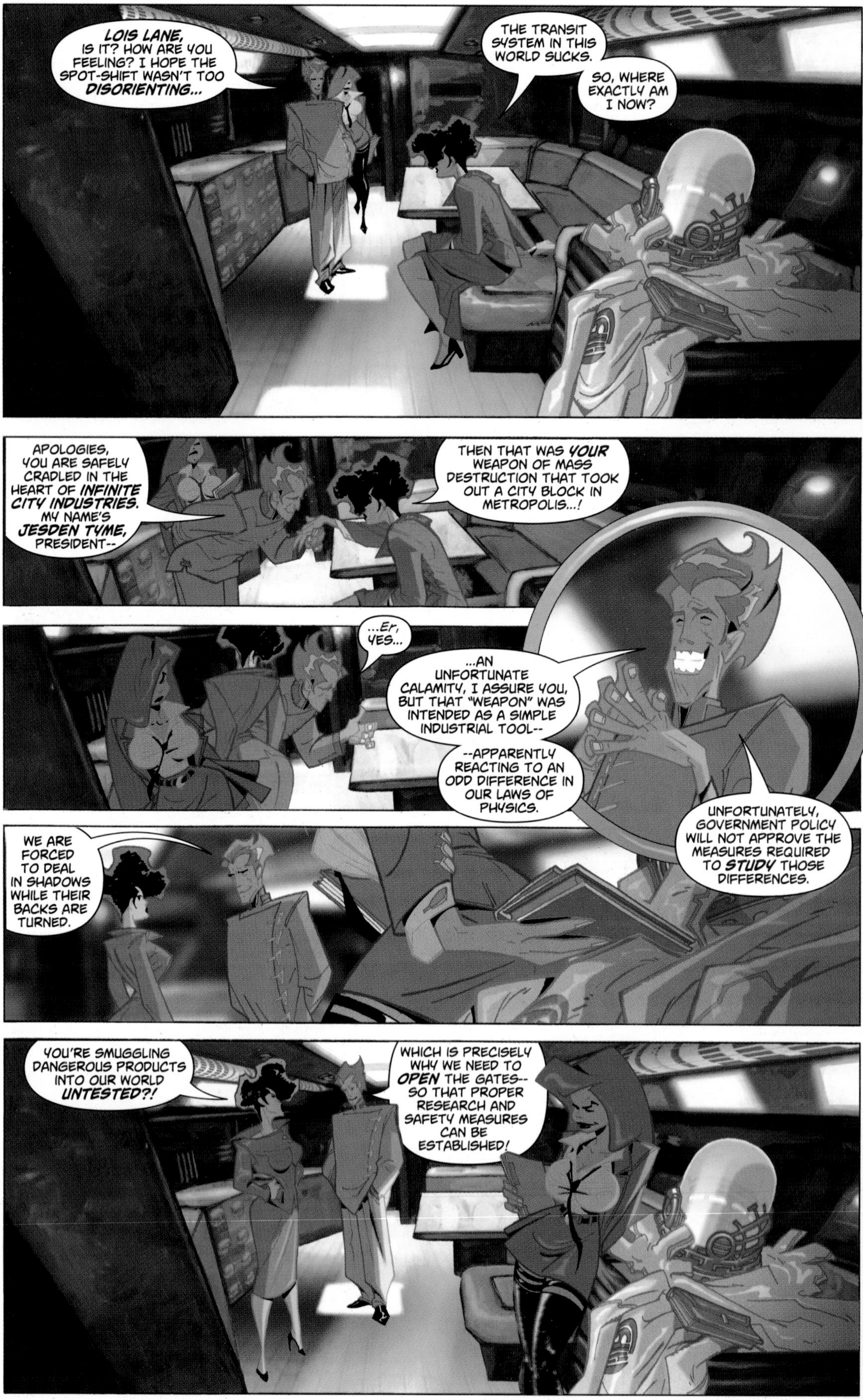
LOIS LANE, IS IT? HOW ARE YOU FEELING? I HOPE THE SPOT-SHIFT WASN'T TOO DISORIENTING...
THE TRANSIT SYSTEM IN THIS WORLD SUCKS.
SO, WHERE EXACTLY AM I NOW?
APOLOGIES, YOU ARE SAFELY CRADLED IN THE HEART OF INFINITE CITY INDUSTRIES. MY NAME'S JESDEN TYME, PRESIDENT--
THEN THAT WAS YOUR WEAPON OF MASS DESTRUCTION THAT TOOK OUT A CITY BLOCK IN METROPOLIS...!
...Er, YES...
...AN UNFORTUNATE CALAMITY, I ASSURE YOU, BUT THAT "WEAPON" WAS INTENDED AS A SIMPLE INDUSTRIAL TOOL--
--APPARENTLY REACTING TO AN ODD DIFFERENCE IN OUR LAWS OF PHYSICS.
UNFORTUNATELY, GOVERNMENT POLICY WILL NOT APPROVE THE MEASURES REQUIRED TO STUDY THOSE DIFFERENCES.
WE ARE FORCED TO DEAL IN SHADOWS WHILE THEIR BACKS ARE TURNED.
YOU'RE SMUGGLING DANGEROUS PRODUCTS INTO OUR WORLD UNTESTED?!
WHICH IS PRECISELY WHY WE NEED TO OPEN THE GATES-- SO THAT PROPER RESEARCH AND SAFETY MEASURES CAN BE ESTABLISHED!

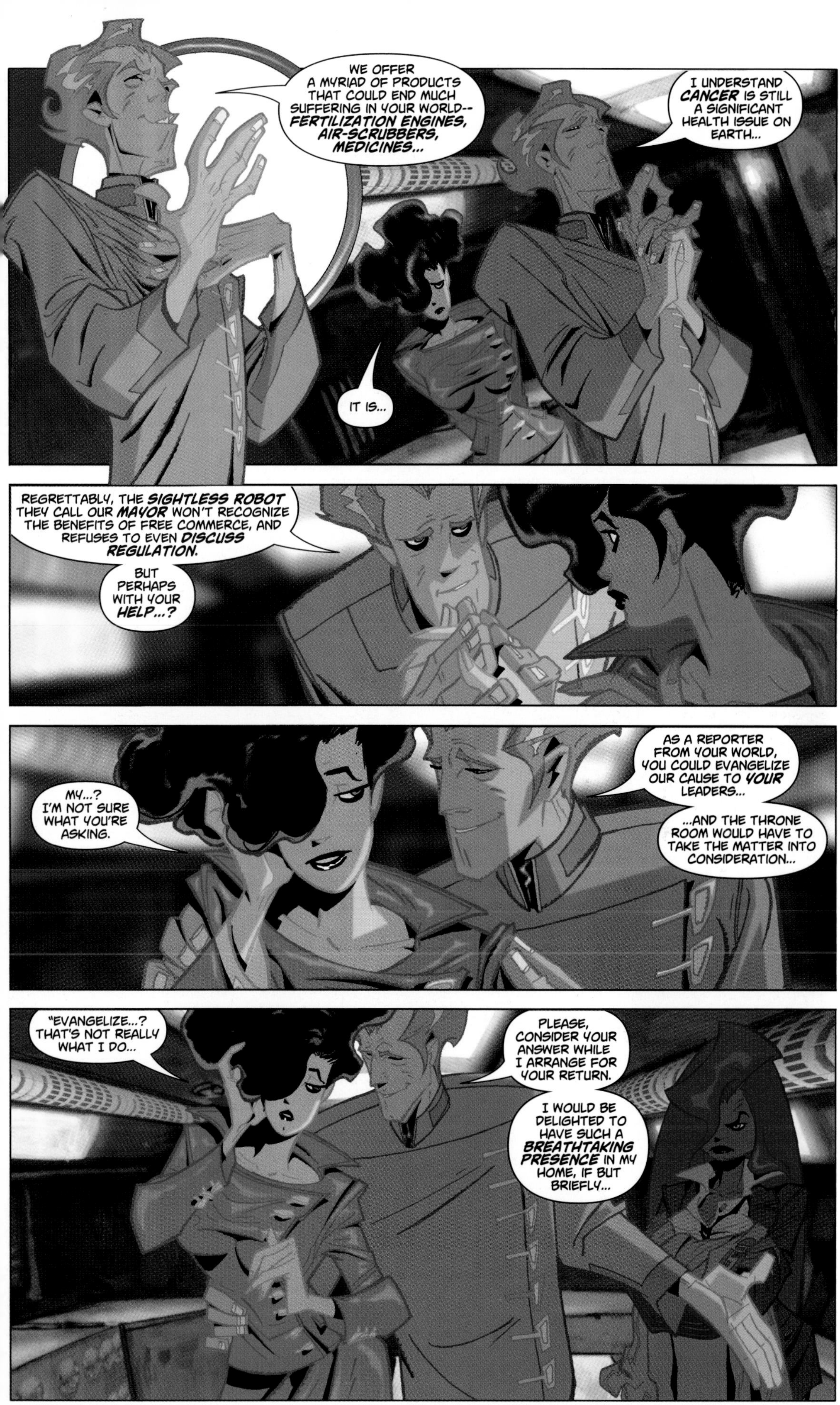
WE OFFER A MYRIAD OF PRODUCTS THAT COULD END MUCH SUFFERING IN YOUR WORLD-- FERTILIZATION ENGINES, AIR-SCRUBBERS, MEDICINES...
I UNDERSTAND CANCER IS STILL A SIGNIFICANT HEALTH ISSUE ON EARTH...
IT IS...
REGRETTABLY, THE SIGHTLESS ROBOT THEY CALL OUR MAYOR WON'T RECOGNIZE THE BENEFITS OF FREE COMMERCE, AND REFUSES TO EVEN DISCUSS REGULATION.
BUT PERHAPS WITH YOUR HELP...?
MY...? I'M NOT SURE WHAT YOU'RE ASKING.
AS A REPORTER FROM YOUR WORLD, YOU COULD EVANGELIZE OUR CAUSE TO YOUR LEADERS...
...AND THE THRONE ROOM WOULD HAVE TO TAKE THE MATTER INTO CONSIDERATION...
"EVANGELIZE...? THAT'S NOT REALLY WHAT I DO...
PLEASE, CONSIDER YOUR ANSWER WHILE I ARRANGE FOR YOUR RETURN.
I WOULD BE DELIGHTED TO HAVE SUCH A BREATHTAKING PRESENCE IN MY HOME, IF BUT BRIEFLY...

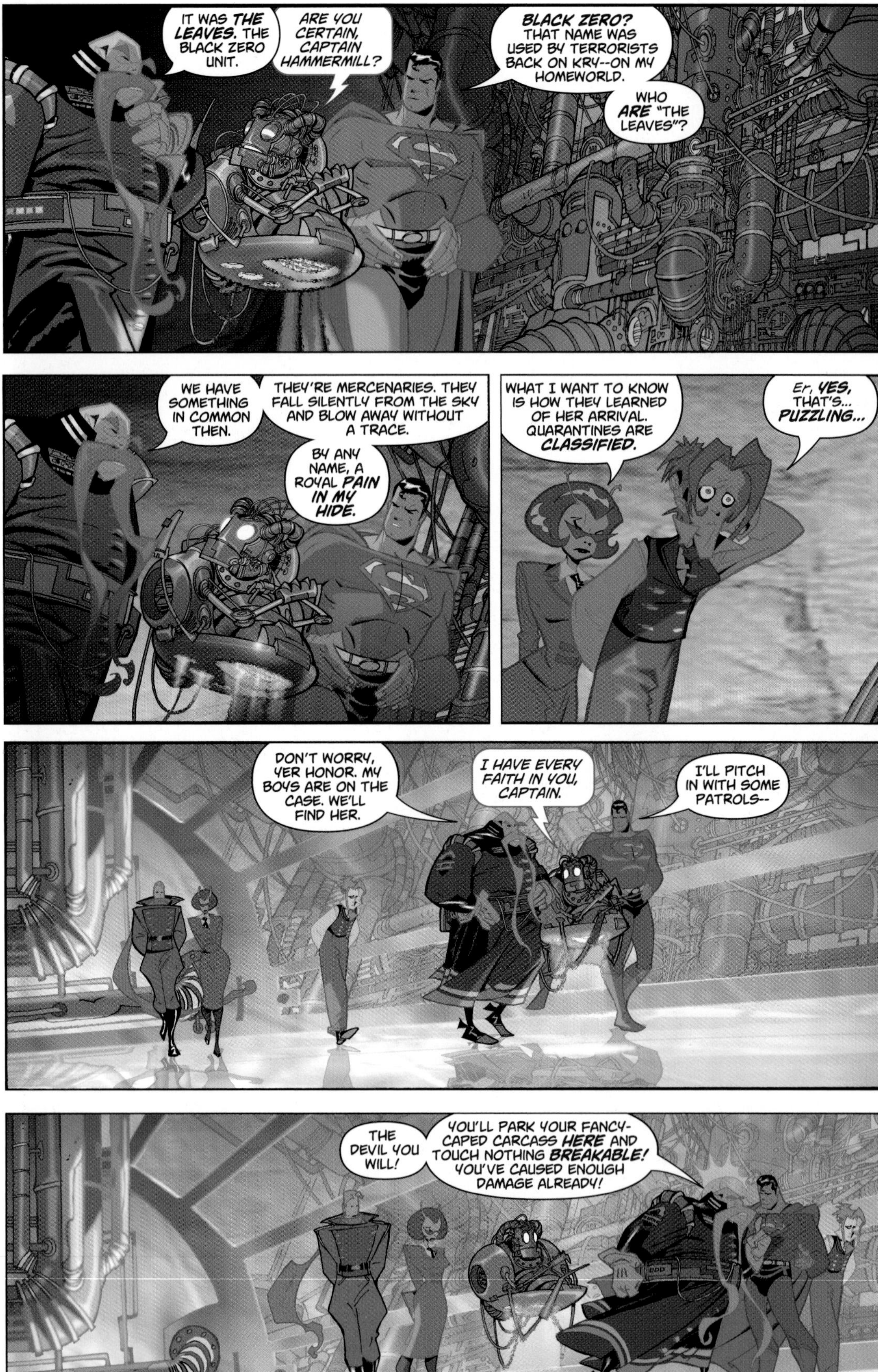

IT WAS THE LEAVES. THE BLACK ZERO UNIT.
ARE YOU CERTAIN, CAPTAIN HAMMERMILL?
BLACK ZERO? THAT NAME WAS USED BY TERRORISTS BACK ON KRY--ON MY HOMEWORLD.
WHO ARE "THE LEAVES"?
WE HAVE SOMETHING IN COMMON THEN.
THEY'RE MERCENARIES. THEY FALL SILENTLY FROM THE SKY AND BLOW AWAY WITHOUT A TRACE.
BY ANY NAME, A ROYAL PAIN IN MY HIDE.
WHAT I WANT TO KNOW IS HOW THEY LEARNED OF HER ARRIVAL. QUARANTINES ARE CLASSIFIED.
Er, YES, THAT'S... PUZZLING...
DON'T WORRY, YER HONOR. MY BOYS ARE ON THE CASE. WE'LL FIND HER.
I HAVE EVERY FAITH IN YOU, CAPTAIN.
I'LL PITCH IN WITH SOME PATROLS--
THE DEVIL YOU WILL!
YOU'LL PARK YOUR FANCY-CAPED CARCASS HERE AND TOUCH NOTHING BREAKABLE! YOU'VE CAUSED ENOUGH DAMAGE ALREADY!

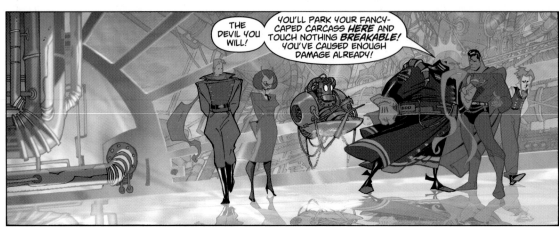

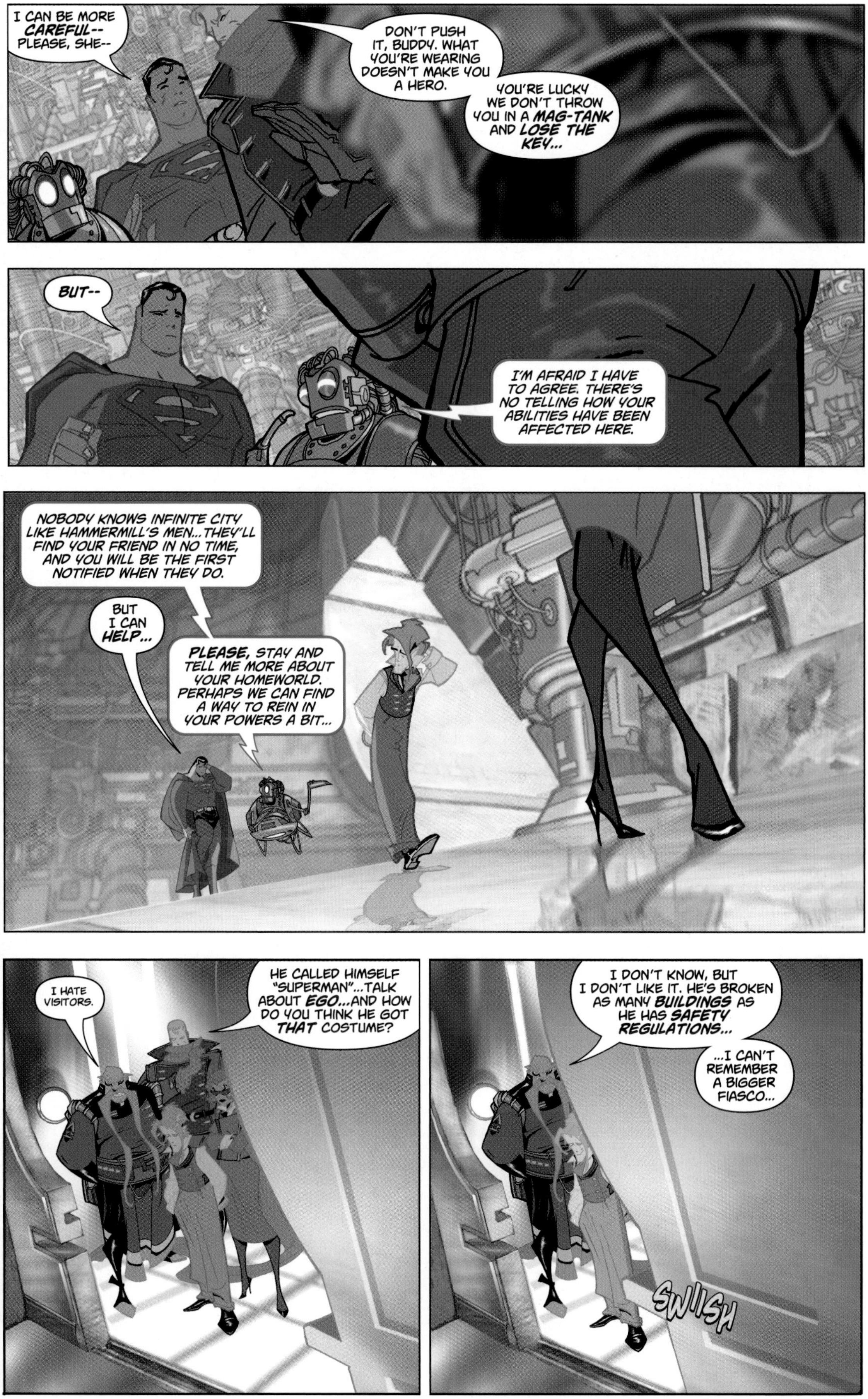
I CAN BE MORE CAREFUL-- PLEASE, SHE--
DON'T PUSH IT, BUDDY. WHAT YOU'RE WEARING DOESN'T MAKE YOU A HERO.
YOU'RE LUCKY WE DON'T THROW YOU IN A MAG-TANK AND LOSE THE KEY...
BUT--
I'M AFRAID I HAVE TO AGREE. THERE'S NO TELLING HOW YOUR ABILITIES HAVE BEEN AFFECTED HERE.
NOBODY KNOWS INFINITE CITY LIKE HAMMERMILL'S MEN...THEY'LL FIND YOUR FRIEND IN NO TIME, AND YOU WILL BE THE FIRST NOTIFIED WHEN THEY DO.
BUT I CAN HELP...
PLEASE, STAY AND TELL ME MORE ABOUT YOUR HOMEWORLD. PERHAPS WE CAN FIND A WAY TO REIN IN YOUR POWERS A BIT...
I HATE VISITORS.
HE CALLED HIMSELF "SUPERMAN"...TALK ABOUT EGO...AND HOW DO YOU THINK HE GOT THAT COSTUME?
I DON'T KNOW, BUT I DON'T LIKE IT. HE'S BROKEN AS MANY BUILDINGS AS HE HAS SAFETY REGULATIONS...
...I CAN'T REMEMBER A BIGGER FIASCO...
SWIISH

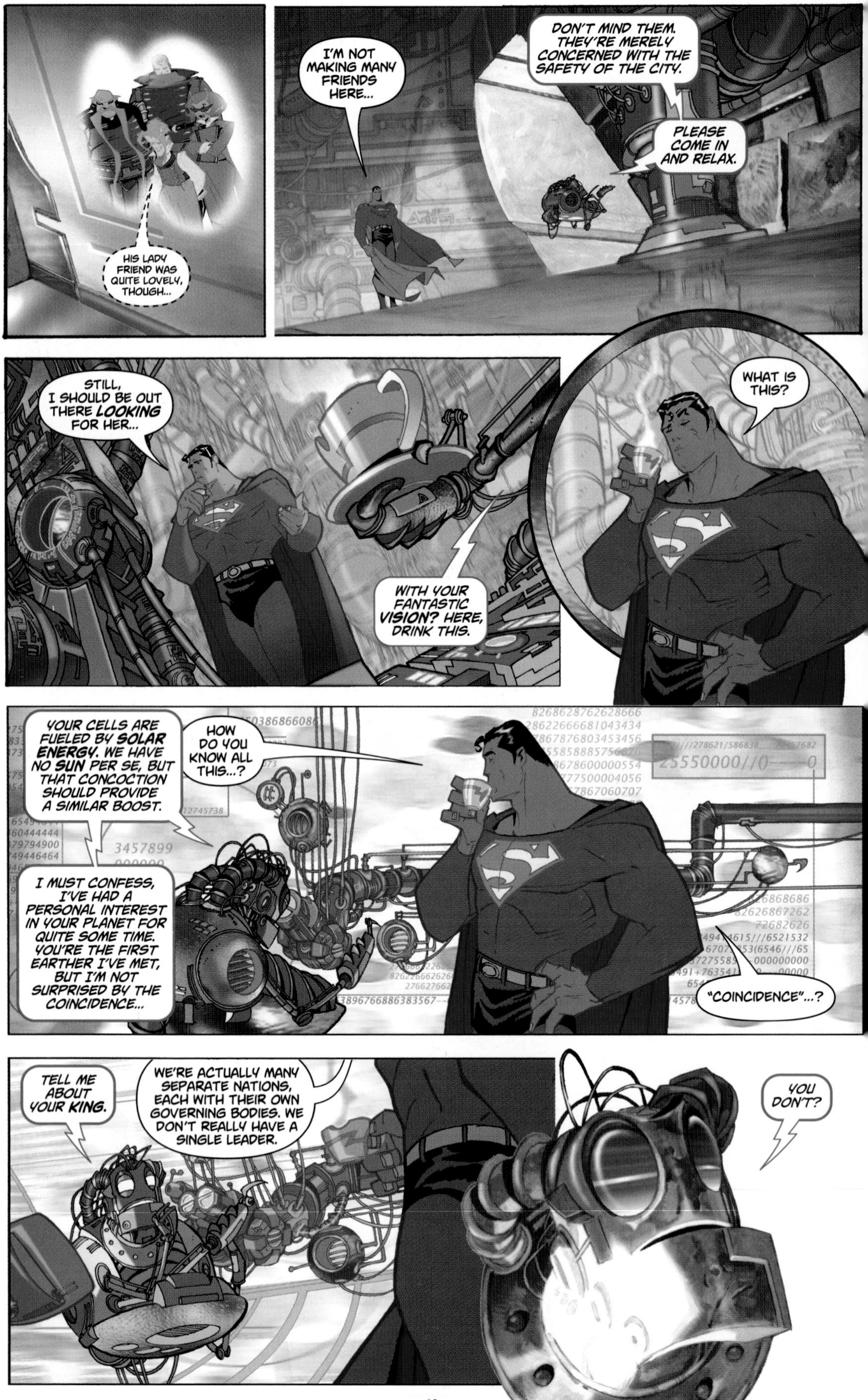
HIS LADY FRIEND WAS QUITE LOVELY, THOUGH...
I'M NOT MAKING MANY FRIENDS HERE...
DON'T MIND THEM. THEY'RE MERELY CONCERNED WITH THE SAFETY OF THE CITY.
PLEASE COME IN AND RELAX.
STILL, I SHOULD BE OUT THERE LOOKING FOR HER...
WITH YOUR FANTASTIC VISION? HERE, DRINK THIS.
WHAT IS THIS?
YOUR CELLS ARE FUELED BY SOLAR ENERGY. WE HAVE NO SUN PER SE, BUT THAT CONCOCTION SHOULD PROVIDE A SIMILAR BOOST.
HOW DO YOU KNOW ALL THIS...?
I MUST CONFESS, I'VE HAD A PERSONAL INTEREST IN YOUR PLANET FOR QUITE SOME TIME. YOU'RE THE FIRST EARTHER I'VE MET, BUT I'M NOT SURPRISED BY THE COINCIDENCE...
"COINCIDENCE"...?
TELL ME ABOUT YOUR KING.
WE'RE ACTUALLY MANY SEPARATE NATIONS, EACH WITH THEIR OWN GOVERNING BODIES. WE DON'T REALLY HAVE A SINGLE LEADER.
YOU DON'T?

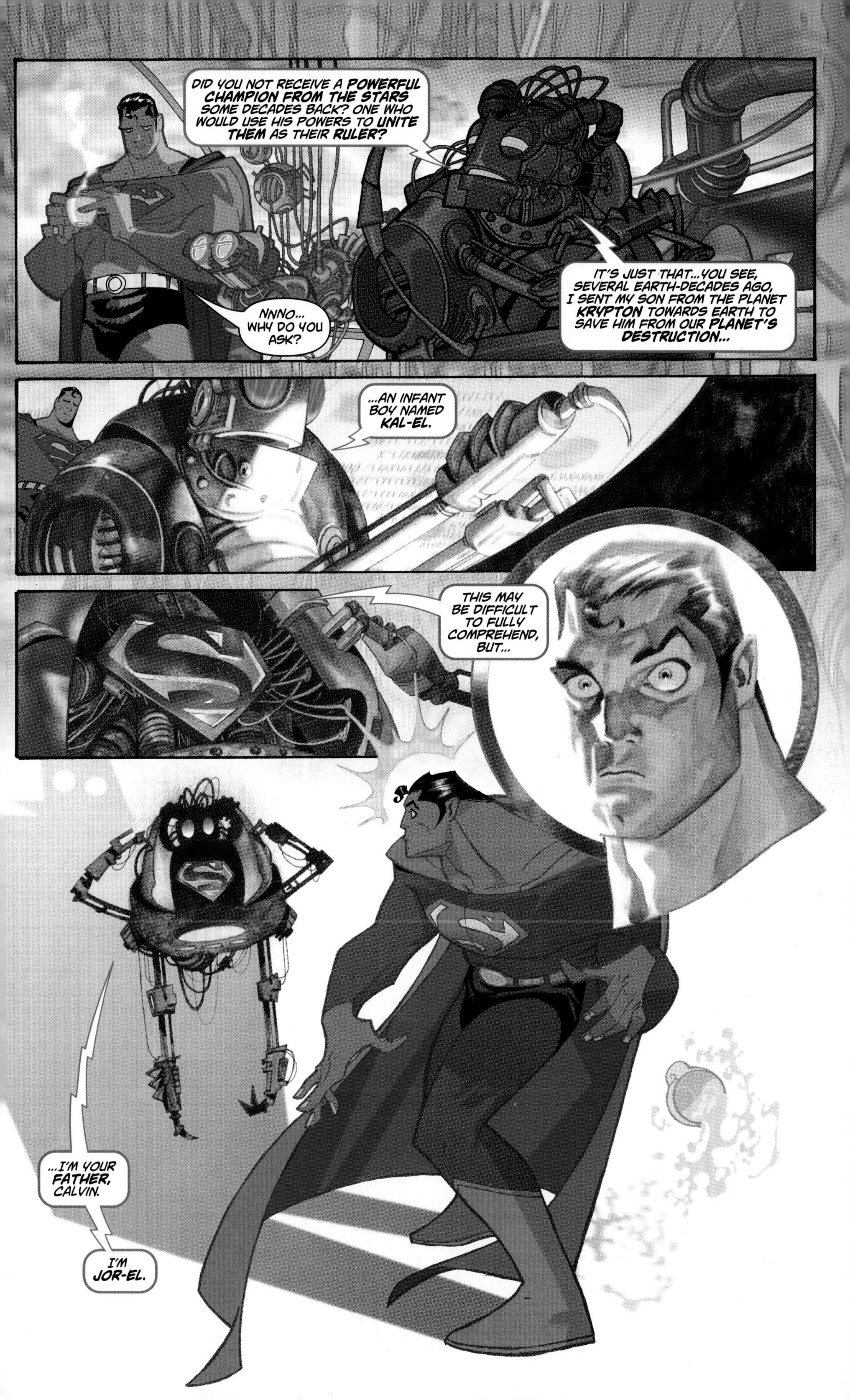
DID YOU NOT RECEIVE A POWERFUL CHAMPION FROM THE STARS SOME DECADES BACK? ONE WHO WOULD USE HIS POWERS TO UNITE THEM AS THEIR RULER?
NNNO... WHY DO YOU ASK?
IT'S JUST THAT...YOU SEE, SEVERAL EARTH-DECADES AGO, I SENT MY SON FROM THE PLANET KRYPTON TOWARDS EARTH TO SAVE HIM FROM OUR PLANET'S DESTRUCTION...
...AN INFANT BOY NAMED KAL-EL.
THIS MAY BE DIFFICULT TO FULLY COMPREHEND, BUT...
...I'M YOUR FATHER, CALVIN.
I'M JOR-EL.

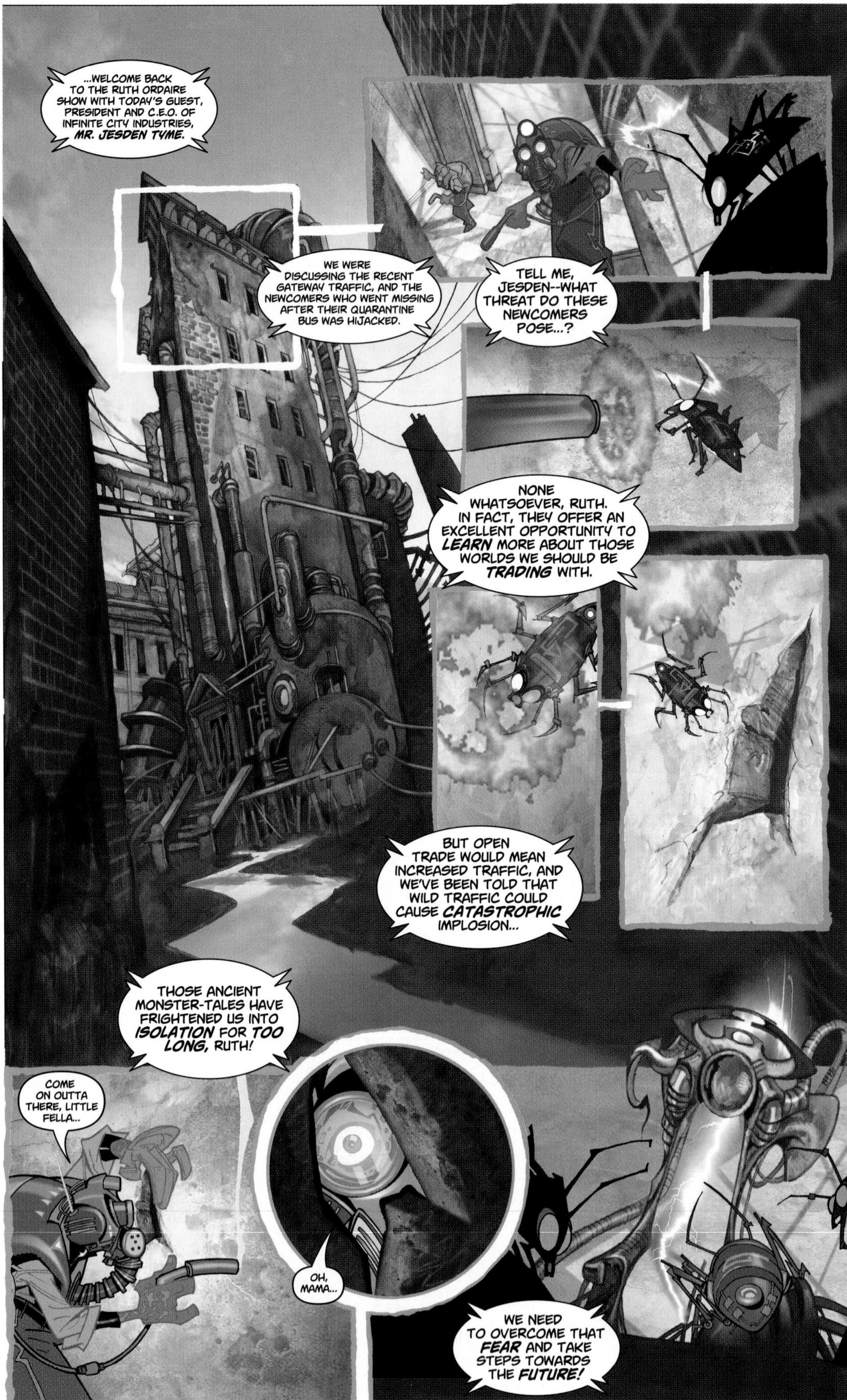
...WELCOME BACK TO THE RUTH ORDAIRE SHOW WITH TODAY'S GUEST, PRESIDENT AND C.E.O. OF INFINITE CITY INDUSTRIES, MR. JESDEN TYME.
WE WERE DISCUSSING THE RECENT GATEWAY TRAFFIC, AND THE NEWCOMERS WHO WENT MISSING AFTER THEIR QUARANTINE BUS WAS HIJACKED.
TELL ME, JESDEN--WHAT THREAT DO THESE NEWCOMERS POSE...?
NONE WHATSOEVER, RUTH. IN FACT, THEY OFFER AN EXCELLENT OPPORTUNITY TO LEARN MORE ABOUT THOSE WORLDS WE SHOULD BE TRADING WITH.
BUT OPEN TRADE WOULD MEAN INCREASED TRAFFIC, AND WE'VE BEEN TOLD THAT WILD TRAFFIC COULD CAUSE CATASTROPHIC IMPLOSION...
THOSE ANCIENT MONSTER-TALES HAVE FRIGHTENED US INTO ISOLATION FOR TOO LONG, RUTH!
COME ON OUTTA THERE, LITTLE FELLA...
OH, MAMA...
WE NEED TO OVERCOME THAT FEAR AND TAKE STEPS TOWARDS THE FUTURE!

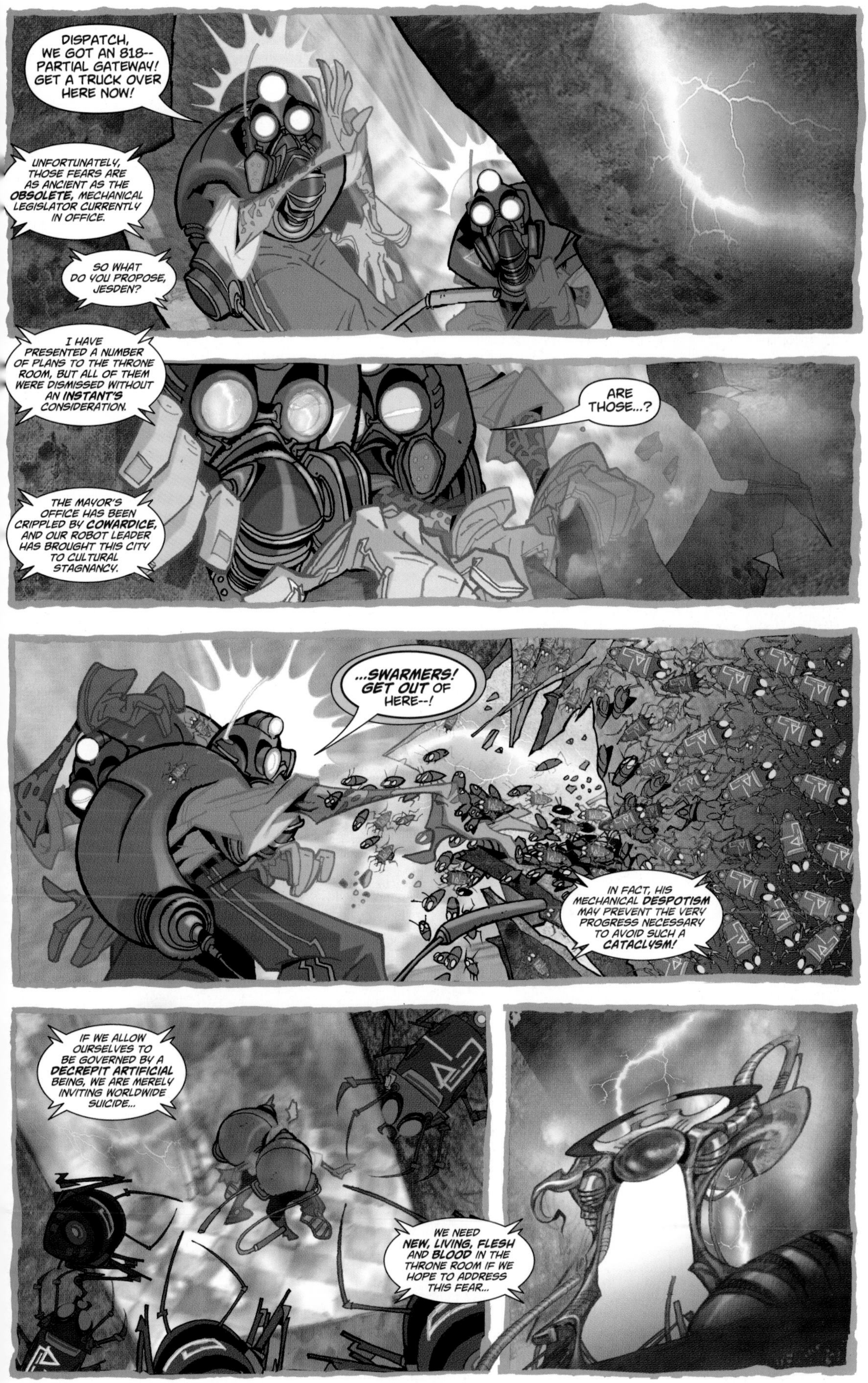
DISPATCH, WE GOT AN 818-- PARTIAL GATEWAY! GET A TRUCK OVER HERE NOW!
UNFORTUNATELY, THOSE FEARS ARE AS ANCIENT AS THE OBSOLETE, MECHANICAL LEGISLATOR CURRENTLY IN OFFICE.
SO WHAT DO YOU PROPOSE, JESDEN?
I HAVE PRESENTED A NUMBER OF PLANS TO THE THRONE ROOM, BUT ALL OF THEM WERE DISMISSED WITHOUT AN INSTANT'S CONSIDERATION.
ARE THOSE...?
THE MAYOR'S OFFICE HAS BEEN CRIPPLED BY COWARDICE, AND OUR ROBOT LEADER HAS BROUGHT THIS CITY TO CULTURAL STAGNANCY.
...SWARMERS! GET OUT OF HERE--!
IN FACT, HIS MECHANICAL DESPOTISM MAY PREVENT THE VERY PROGRESS NECESSARY TO AVOID SUCH A CATACLYSM!
IF WE ALLOW OURSELVES TO BE GOVERNED BY A DECREPIT ARTIFICIAL BEING, WE ARE MERELY INVITING WORLDWIDE SUICIDE...
WE NEED NEW, LIVING, FLESH AND BLOOD IN THE THRONE ROOM IF WE HOPE TO ADDRESS THIS FEAR...

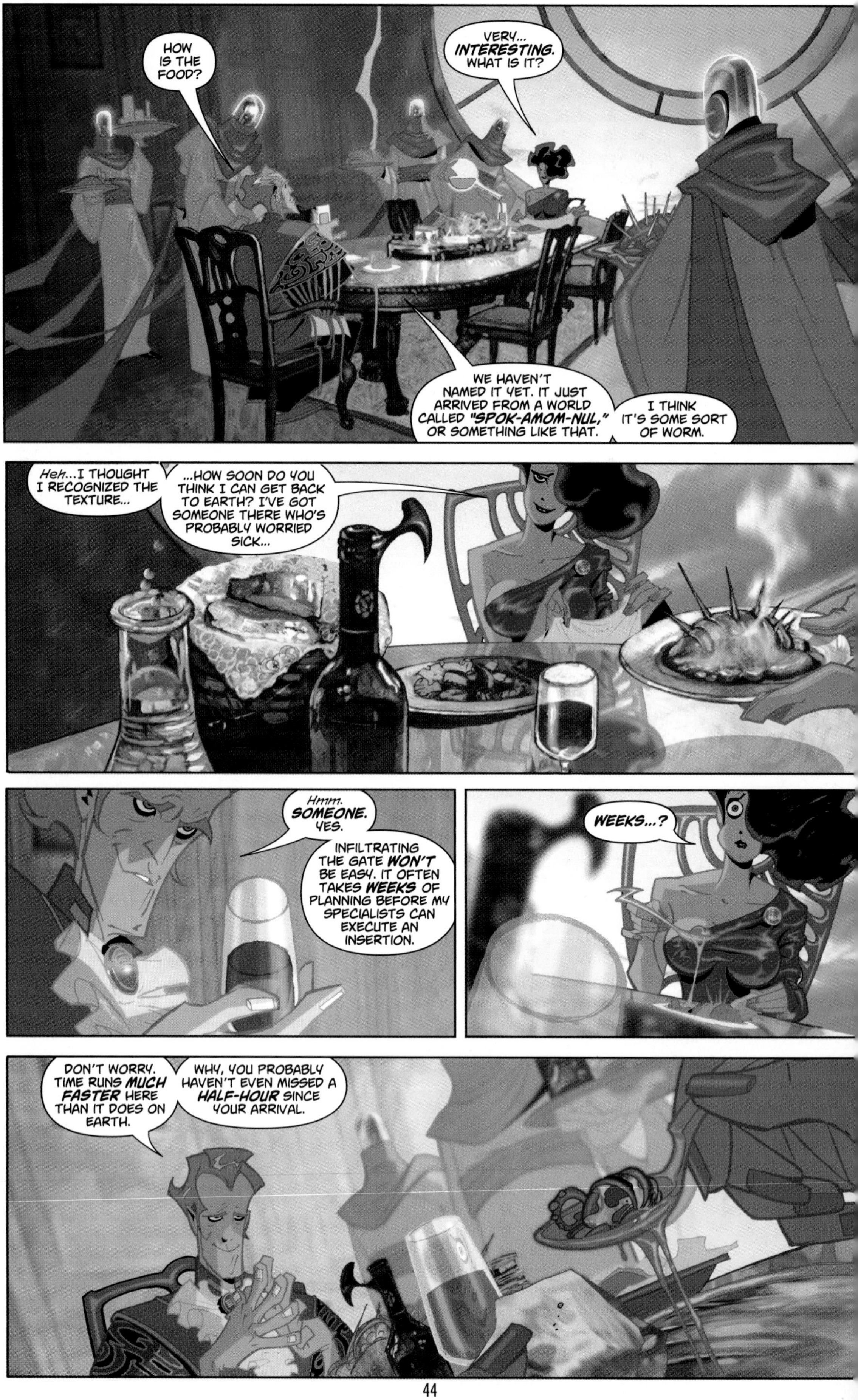
HOW IS THE FOOD?
VERY... INTERESTING. WHAT IS IT?
WE HAVEN'T NAMED IT YET. IT JUST ARRIVED FROM A WORLD CALLED "SPOK-AMOM-NUL," OR SOMETHING LIKE THAT.
I THINK IT'S SOME SORT OF WORM.
Heh...I THOUGHT I RECOGNIZED THE TEXTURE...
...HOW SOON DO YOU THINK I CAN GET BACK TO EARTH? I'VE GOT SOMEONE THERE WHO'S PROBABLY WORRIED SICK...
Hmm. SOMEONE. YES.
INFILTRATING THE GATE WON'T BE EASY. IT OFTEN TAKES WEEKS OF PLANNING BEFORE MY SPECIALISTS CAN EXECUTE AN INSERTION.
WEEKS...?
DON'T WORRY. TIME RUNS MUCH FASTER HERE THAN IT DOES ON EARTH.
WHY, YOU PROBABLY HAVEN'T EVEN MISSED A HALF-HOUR SINCE YOUR ARRIVAL.

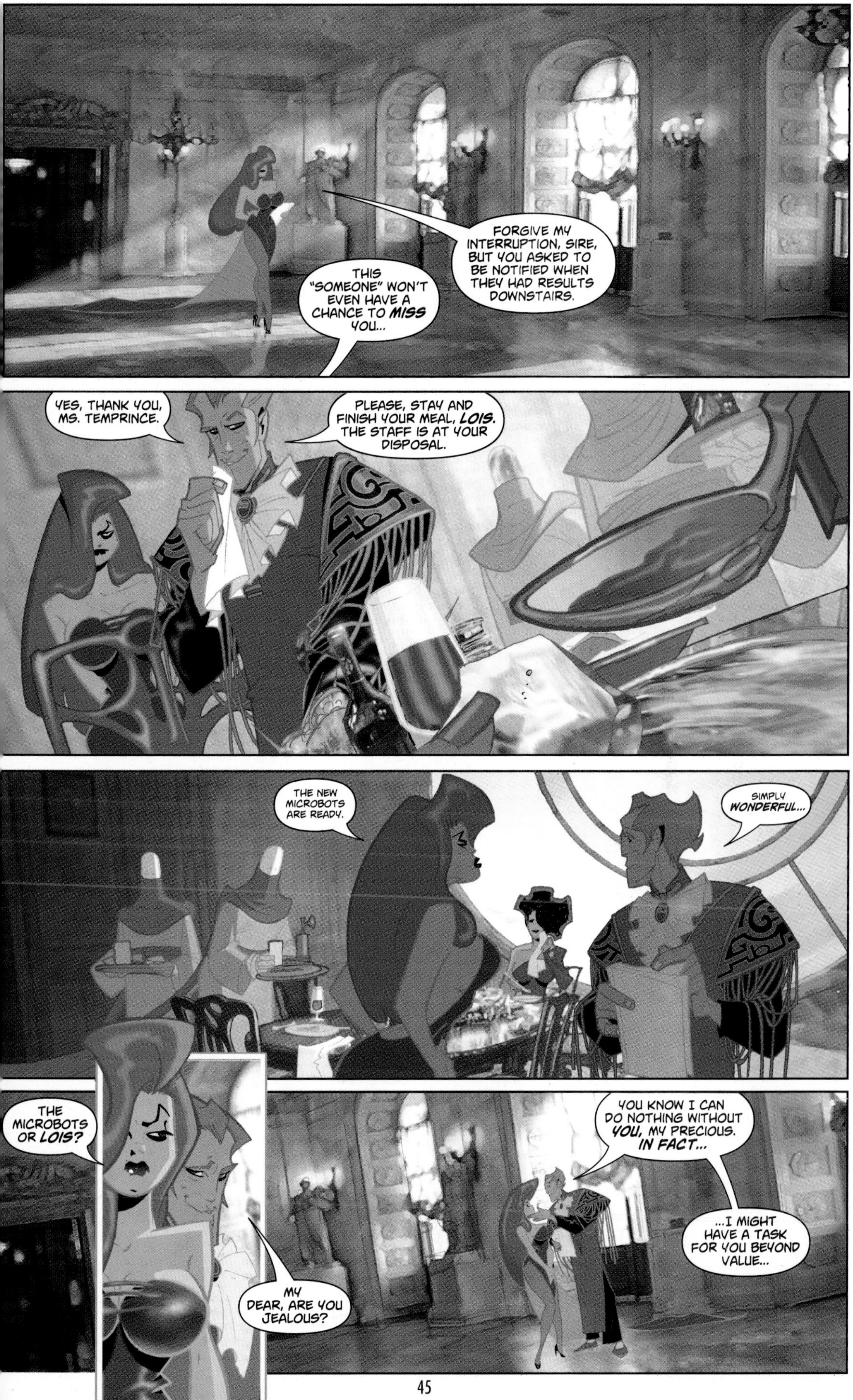
FORGIVE MY INTERRUPTION, SIRE, BUT YOU ASKED TO BE NOTIFIED WHEN THEY HAD RESULTS DOWNSTAIRS.
THIS "SOMEONE" WON'T EVEN HAVE A CHANCE TO MISS YOU...
YES, THANK YOU, MS. TEMPRINCE.
PLEASE, STAY AND FINISH YOUR MEAL, LOIS. THE STAFF IS AT YOUR DISPOSAL.
THE NEW MICROBOTS ARE READY.
SIMPLY WONDERFUL...
THE MICROBOTS OR LOIS?
MY DEAR, ARE YOU JEALOUS?
YOU KNOW I CAN DO NOTHING WITHOUT YOU, MY PRECIOUS. IN FACT...
...I MIGHT HAVE A TASK FOR YOU BEYOND VALUE...

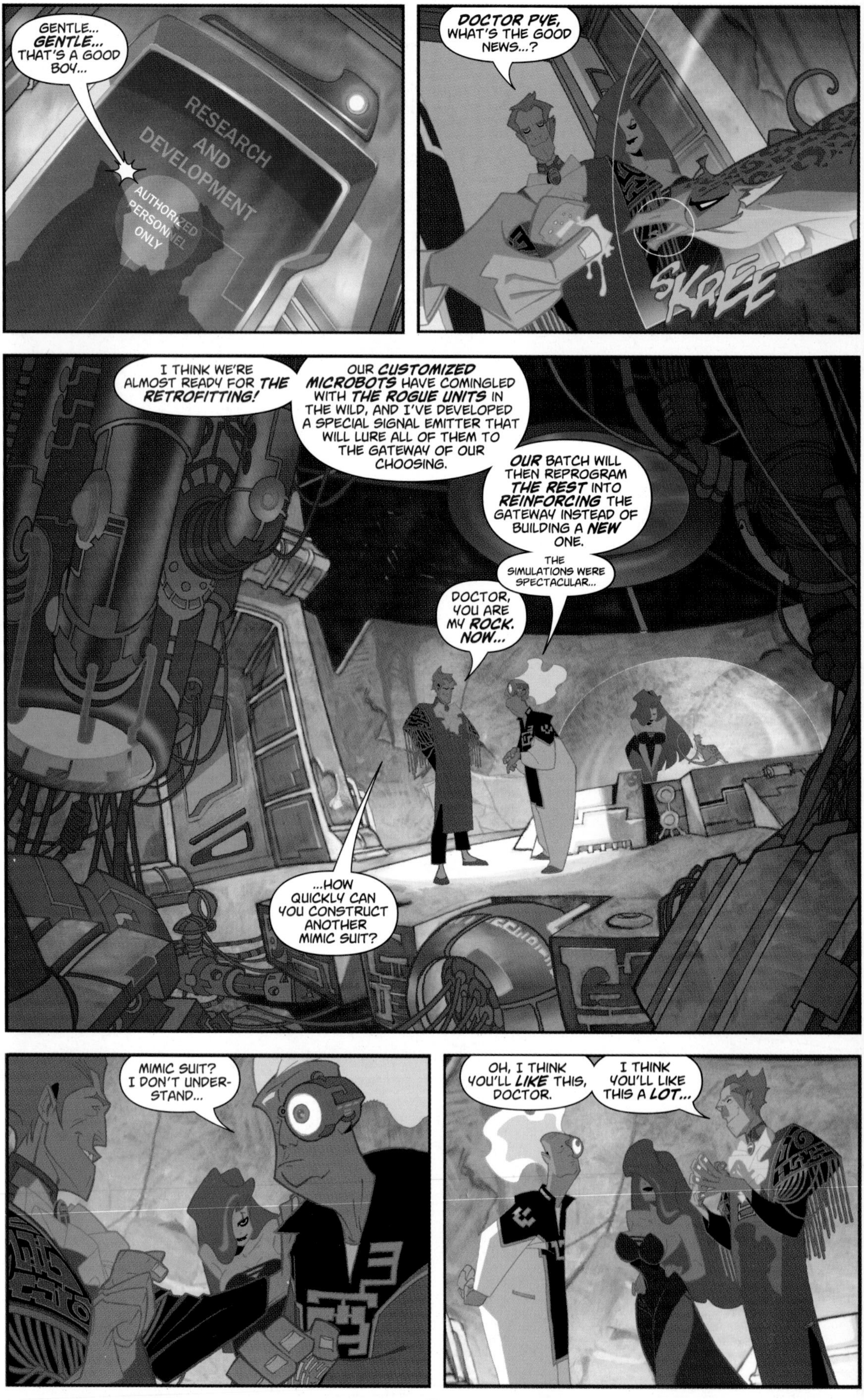
GENTLE... GENTLE... THAT'S A GOOD BOY...
RESEARCH AND DEVELOPMENT
AUTHORIZED PERSONNEL ONLY
DOCTOR PYE, WHAT'S THE GOOD NEWS...?
SKREE
I THINK WE'RE ALMOST READY FOR THE RETROFITTING!
OUR CUSTOMIZED MICROBOTS HAVE COMINGLED WITH THE ROGUE UNITS IN THE WILD, AND I'VE DEVELOPED A SPECIAL SIGNAL EMITTER THAT WILL LURE ALL OF THEM TO THE GATEWAY OF OUR CHOOSING.
OUR BATCH WILL THEN REPROGRAM THE REST INTO REINFORCING THE GATEWAY INSTEAD OF BUILDING A NEW ONE.
THE SIMULATIONS WERE SPECTACULAR...
DOCTOR, YOU ARE MY ROCK. NOW...
...HOW QUICKLY CAN YOU CONSTRUCT ANOTHER MIMIC SUIT?
MIMIC SUIT? I DON'T UNDER-STAND...
OH, I THINK YOU'LL LIKE THIS, DOCTOR.
I THINK YOU'LL LIKE THIS A LOT...

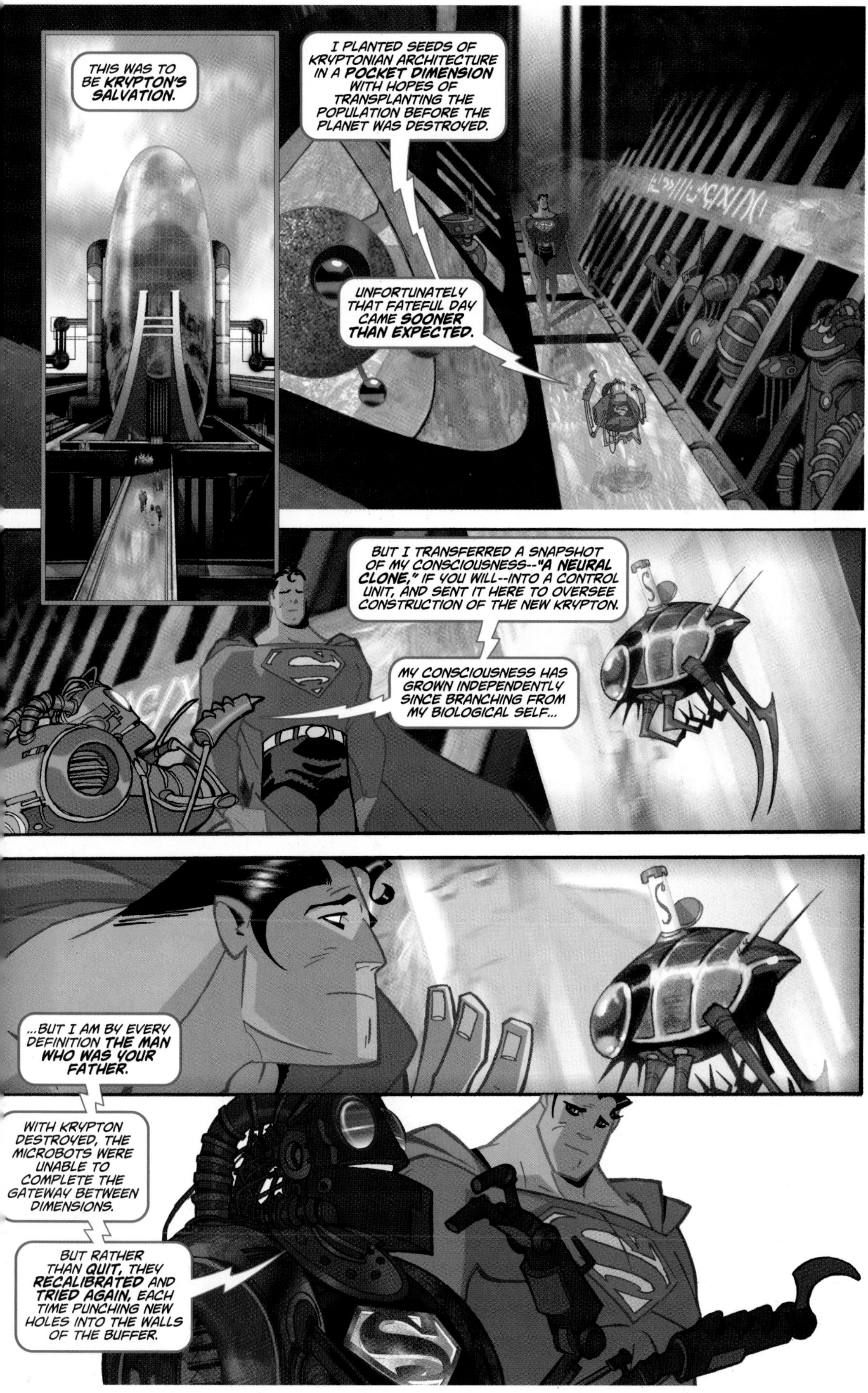
THIS WAS TO BE KRYPTON'S SALVATION.
I PLANTED SEEDS OF KRYPTONIAN ARCHITECTURE IN A POCKET DIMENSION WITH HOPES OF TRANSPLANTING THE POPULATION BEFORE THE PLANET WAS DESTROYED.
UNFORTUNATELY THAT FATEFUL DAY CAME SOONER THAN EXPECTED.
BUT I TRANSFERRED A SNAPSHOT OF MY CONSCIOUSNESS--"A NEURAL CLONE," IF YOU WILL--INTO A CONTROL UNIT, AND SENT IT HERE TO OVERSEE CONSTRUCTION OF THE NEW KRYPTON.
MY CONSCIOUSNESS HAS GROWN INDEPENDENTLY SINCE BRANCHING FROM MY BIOLOGICAL SELF...
...BUT I AM BY EVERY DEFINITION THE MAN WHO WAS YOUR FATHER.
WITH KRYPTON DESTROYED, THE MICROBOTS WERE UNABLE TO COMPLETE THE GATEWAY BETWEEN DIMENSIONS.
BUT RATHER THAN QUIT, THEY RECALIBRATED AND TRIED AGAIN, EACH TIME PUNCHING NEW HOLES INTO THE WALLS OF THE BUFFER.

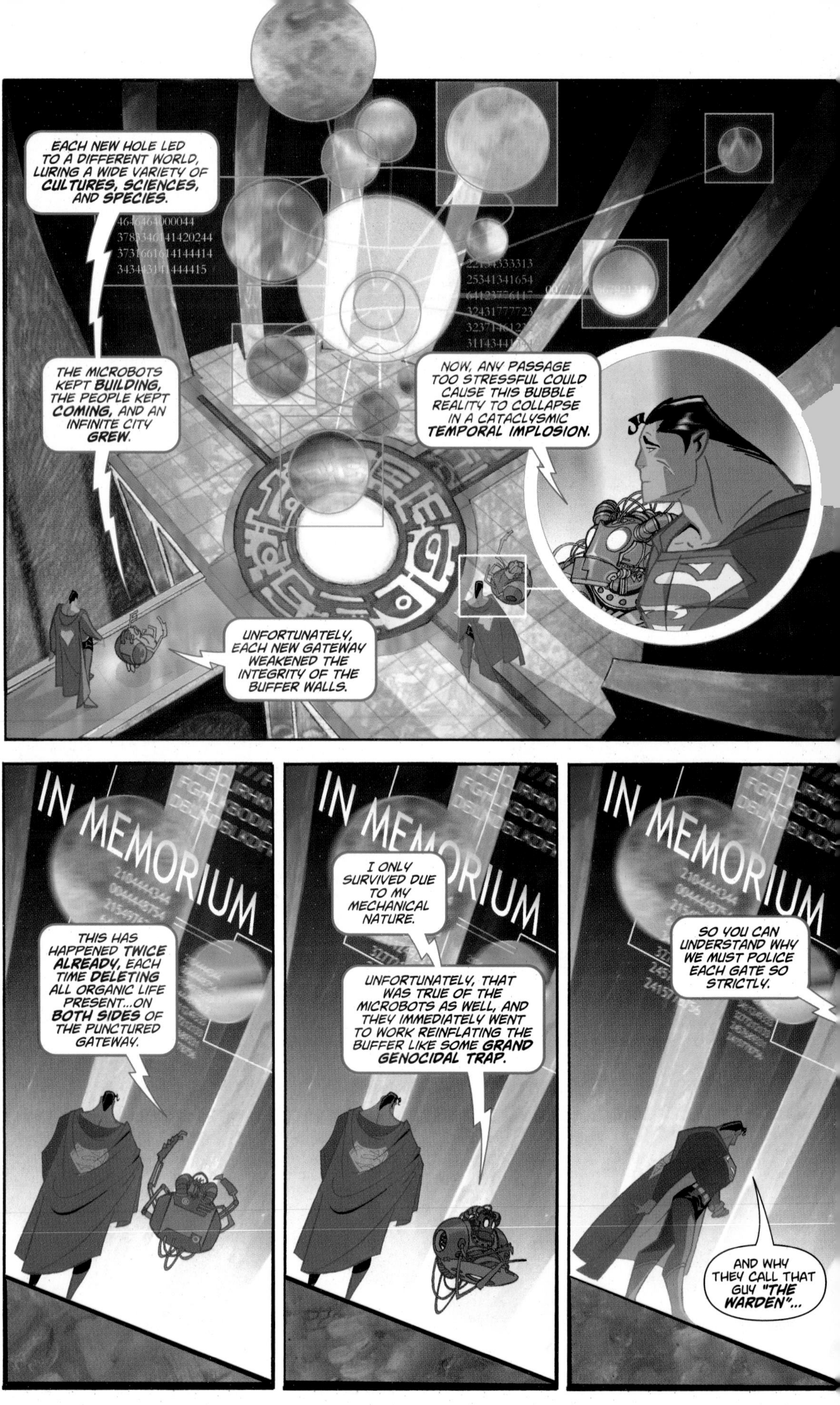
EACH NEW HOLE LED TO A DIFFERENT WORLD, LURING A WIDE VARIETY OF CULTURES, SCIENCES, AND SPECIES.
THE MICROBOTS KEPT BUILDING, THE PEOPLE KEPT COMING, AND AN INFINITE CITY GREW.
UNFORTUNATELY, EACH NEW GATEWAY WEAKENED THE INTEGRITY OF THE BUFFER WALLS.
NOW, ANY PASSAGE TOO STRESSFUL COULD CAUSE THIS BUBBLE REALITY TO COLLAPSE IN A CATACLYSMIC TEMPORAL IMPLOSION.
IN MEMORIUM
THIS HAS HAPPENED TWICE ALREADY, EACH TIME DELETING ALL ORGANIC LIFE PRESENT...ON BOTH SIDES OF THE PUNCTURED GATEWAY.
IN MEMORIUM
I ONLY SURVIVED DUE TO MY MECHANICAL NATURE.
UNFORTUNATELY, THAT WAS TRUE OF THE MICROBOTS AS WELL, AND THEY IMMEDIATELY WENT TO WORK REINFLATING THE BUFFER LIKE SOME GRAND GENOCIDAL TRAP.
IN MEMORIUM
SO YOU CAN UNDERSTAND WHY WE MUST POLICE EACH GATE SO STRICTLY.
AND WHY THEY CALL THAT GUY "THE WARDEN"...

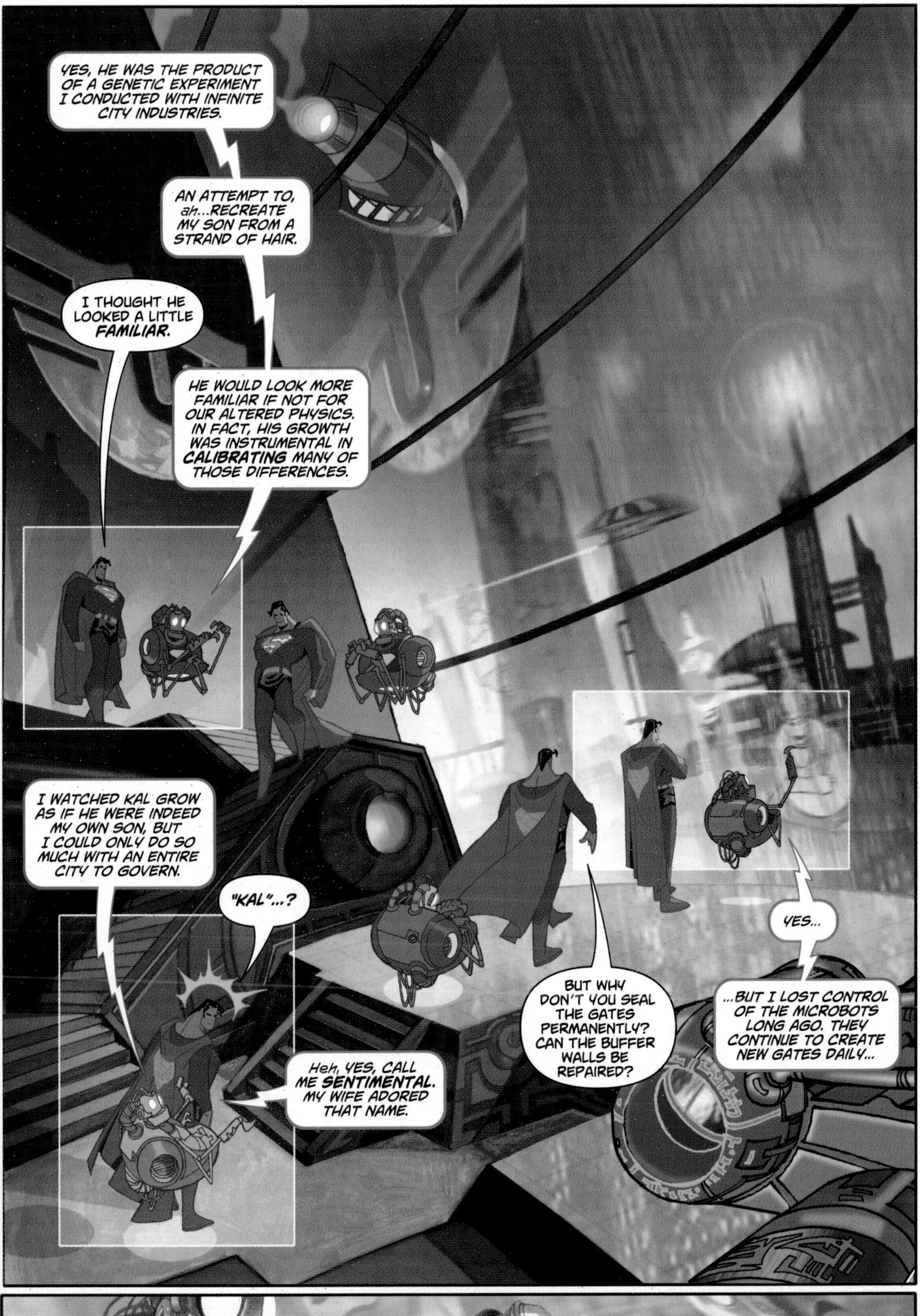
YES, HE WAS THE PRODUCT OF A GENETIC EXPERIMENT I CONDUCTED WITH INFINITE CITY INDUSTRIES.
AN ATTEMPT TO, ah...RECREATE MY SON FROM A STRAND OF HAIR.
I THOUGHT HE LOOKED A LITTLE FAMILIAR.
HE WOULD LOOK MORE FAMILIAR IF NOT FOR OUR ALTERED PHYSICS. IN FACT, HIS GROWTH WAS INSTRUMENTAL IN CALIBRATING MANY OF THOSE DIFFERENCES.
I WATCHED KAL GROW AS IF HE WERE INDEED MY OWN SON, BUT I COULD ONLY DO SO MUCH WITH AN ENTIRE CITY TO GOVERN.
"KAL"...?
Heh, YES, CALL ME SENTIMENTAL. MY WIFE ADORED THAT NAME.
BUT WHY DON'T YOU SEAL THE GATES PERMANENTLY? CAN THE BUFFER WALLS BE REPAIRED?
YES...
...BUT I LOST CONTROL OF THE MICROBOTS LONG AGO. THEY CONTINUE TO CREATE NEW GATES DAILY...

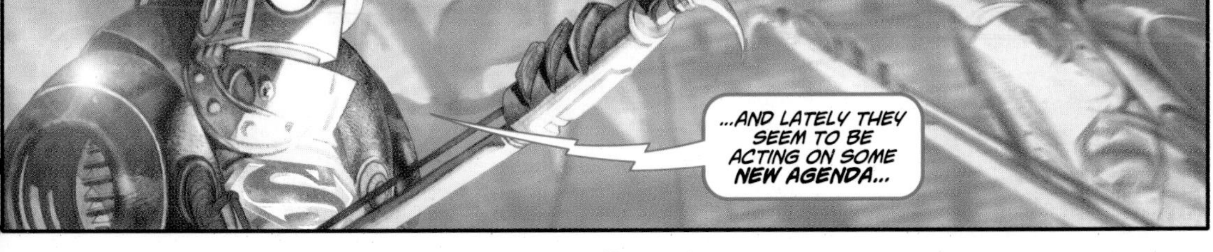
...AND LATELY THEY SEEM TO BE ACTING ON SOME NEW AGENDA...

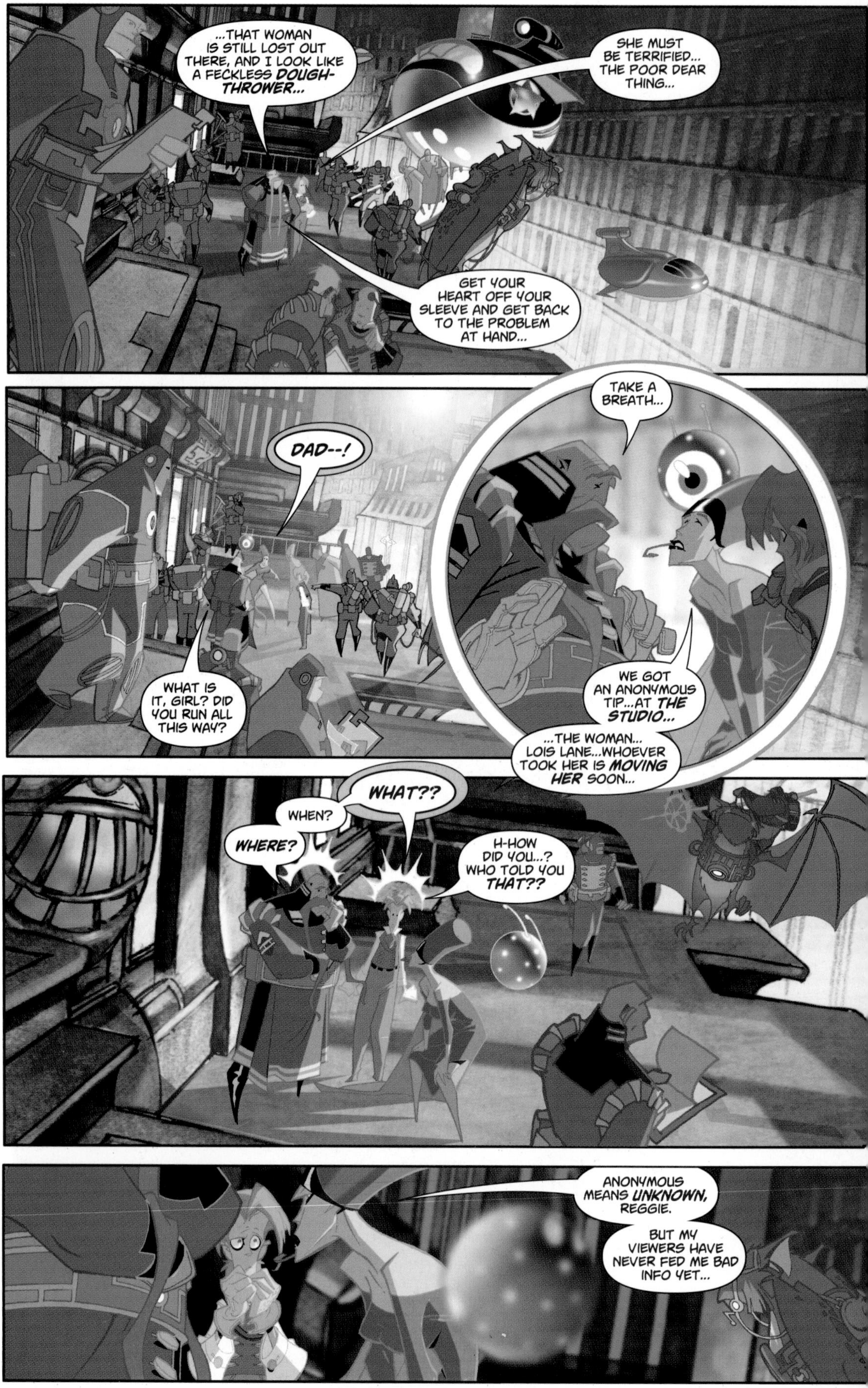

...THAT WOMAN IS STILL LOST OUT THERE, AND I LOOK LIKE A FECKLESS DOUGH-THROWER...
SHE MUST BE TERRIFIED... THE POOR DEAR THING...
GET YOUR HEART OFF YOUR SLEEVE AND GET BACK TO THE PROBLEM AT HAND...
DAD--!
WHAT IS IT, GIRL? DID YOU RUN ALL THIS WAY?
TAKE A BREATH...
WE GOT AN ANONYMOUS TIP...AT THE STUDIO...
...THE WOMAN... LOIS LANE...WHOEVER TOOK HER IS MOVING HER SOON...
WHAT??
WHEN?
WHERE?
H-HOW DID YOU...? WHO TOLD YOU THAT??
ANONYMOUS MEANS UNKNOWN, REGGIE.
BUT MY VIEWERS HAVE NEVER FED ME BAD INFO YET...

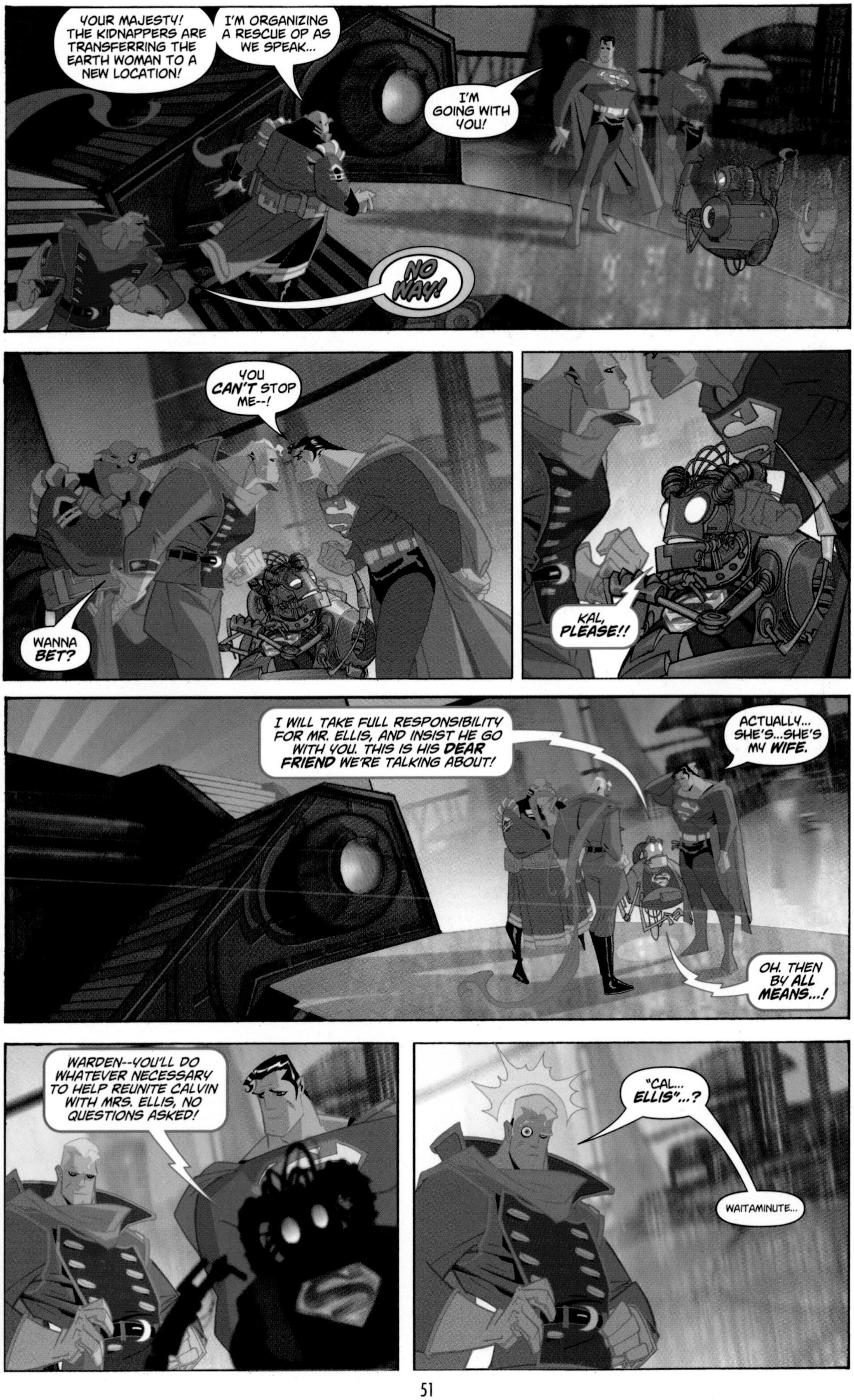
YOUR MAJESTY! THE KIDNAPPERS ARE TRANSFERRING THE EARTH WOMAN TO A NEW LOCATION!
I'M ORGANIZING A RESCUE OP AS WE SPEAK...
I'M GOING WITH YOU!
NO WAY!
YOU CAN'T STOP ME--!
WANNA BET?
KAL, PLEASE!!
I WILL TAKE FULL RESPONSIBILITY FOR MR. ELLIS, AND INSIST HE GO WITH YOU. THIS IS HIS DEAR FRIEND WE'RE TALKING ABOUT!
ACTUALLY... SHE'S...SHE'S MY WIFE.
OH. THEN BY ALL MEANS...!
WARDEN--YOU'LL DO WHATEVER NECESSARY TO HELP REUNITE CALVIN WITH MRS. ELLIS, NO QUESTIONS ASKED!
"CAL... ELLIS"...?
WAITAMINUTE...

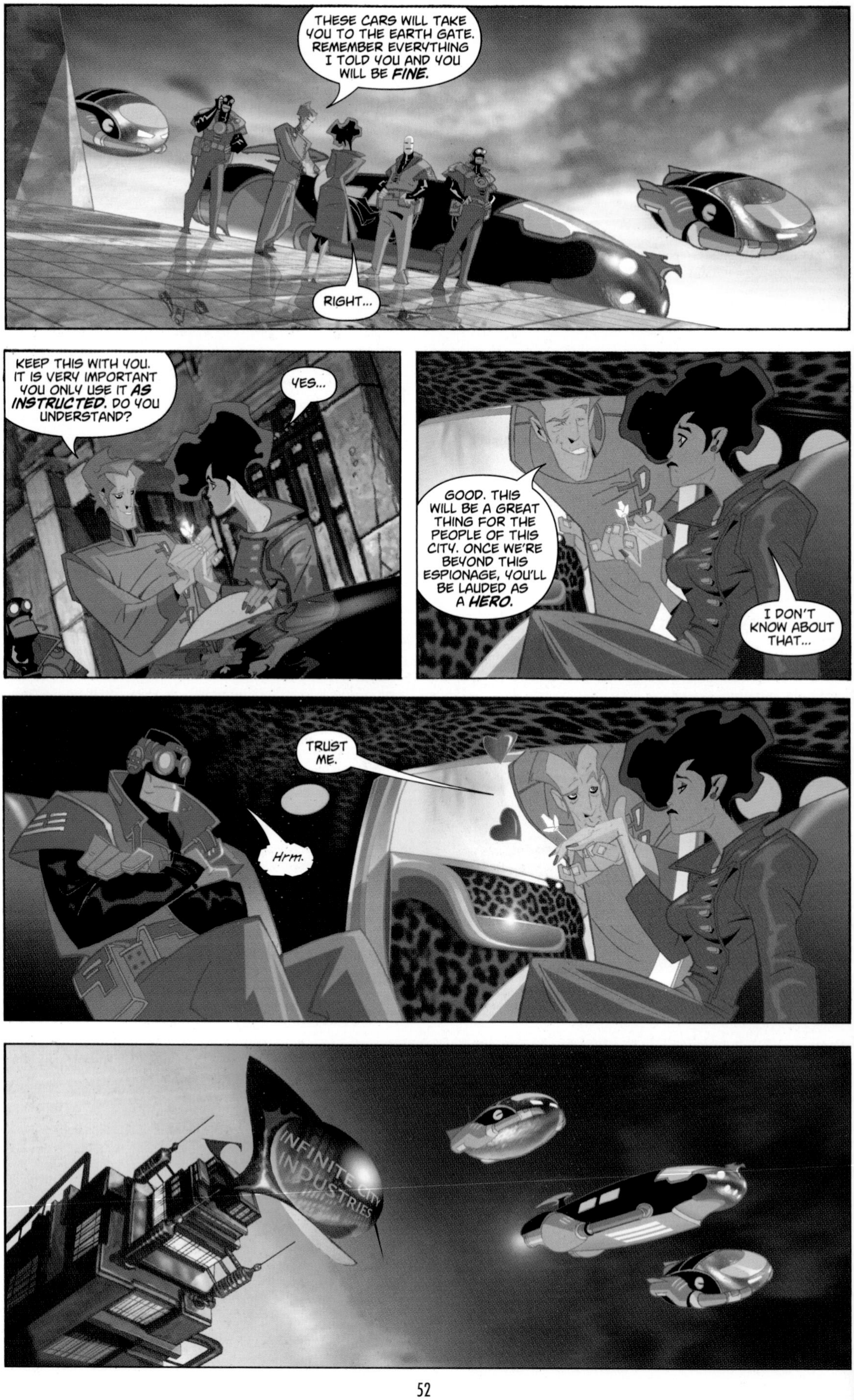

THESE CARS WILL TAKE YOU TO THE EARTH GATE. REMEMBER EVERYTHING I TOLD YOU AND YOU WILL BE FINE.
RIGHT...
KEEP THIS WITH YOU. IT IS VERY IMPORTANT YOU ONLY USE IT AS INSTRUCTED. DO YOU UNDERSTAND?
YES...
GOOD. THIS WILL BE A GREAT THING FOR THE PEOPLE OF THIS CITY. ONCE WE'RE BEYOND THIS ESPIONAGE, YOU'LL BE LAUDED AS A HERO.
I DON'T KNOW ABOUT THAT...
TRUST ME.
Hrm.
INFINITE CITY INDUSTRIES

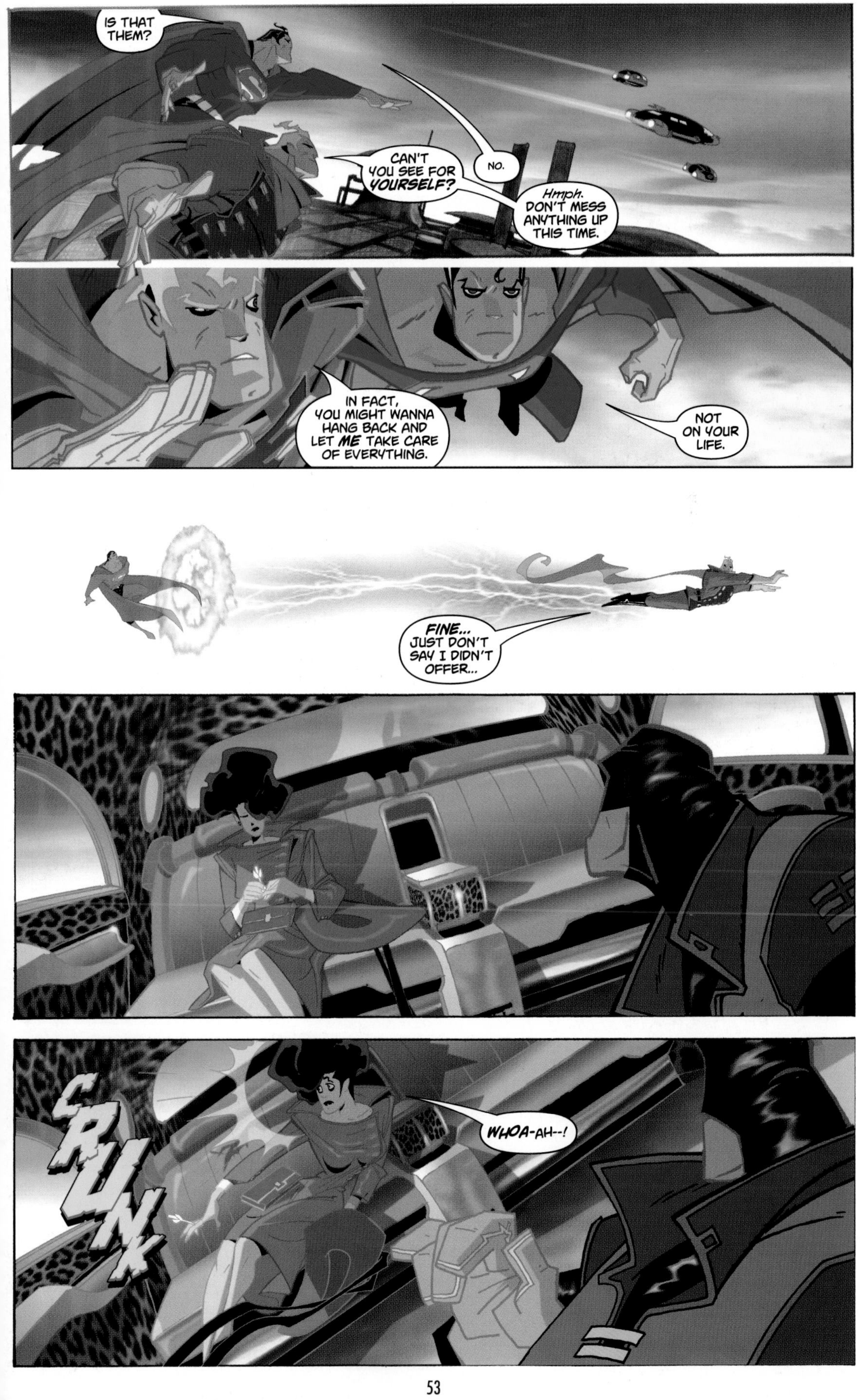
IS THAT THEM?
CAN'T YOU SEE FOR *YOURSELF?*
NO.
*Hmph.* DON'T MESS ANYTHING UP THIS TIME.
IN FACT, YOU MIGHT WANNA HANG BACK AND LET *ME* TAKE CARE OF EVERYTHING.
NOT ON YOUR LIFE.
*FINE...* JUST DON'T SAY I DIDN'T OFFER...
CRUNK
*WHOA*-AH--!

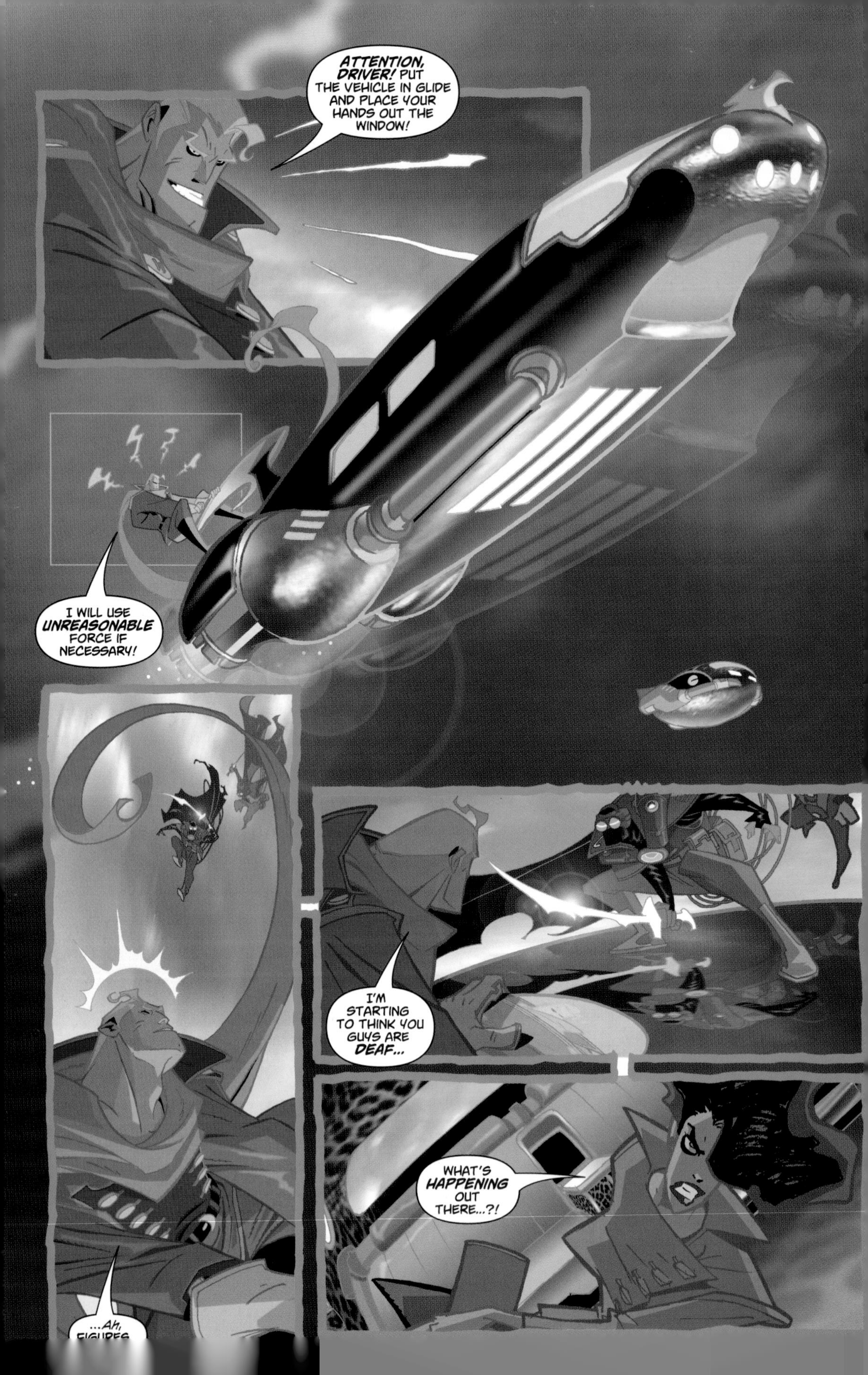

ATTENTION, DRIVER! PUT THE VEHICLE IN GLIDE AND PLACE YOUR HANDS OUT THE WINDOW!
I WILL USE UNREASONABLE FORCE IF NECESSARY!
I'M STARTING TO THINK YOU GUYS ARE DEAF...
WHAT'S HAPPENING OUT THERE...?!
...Ah,

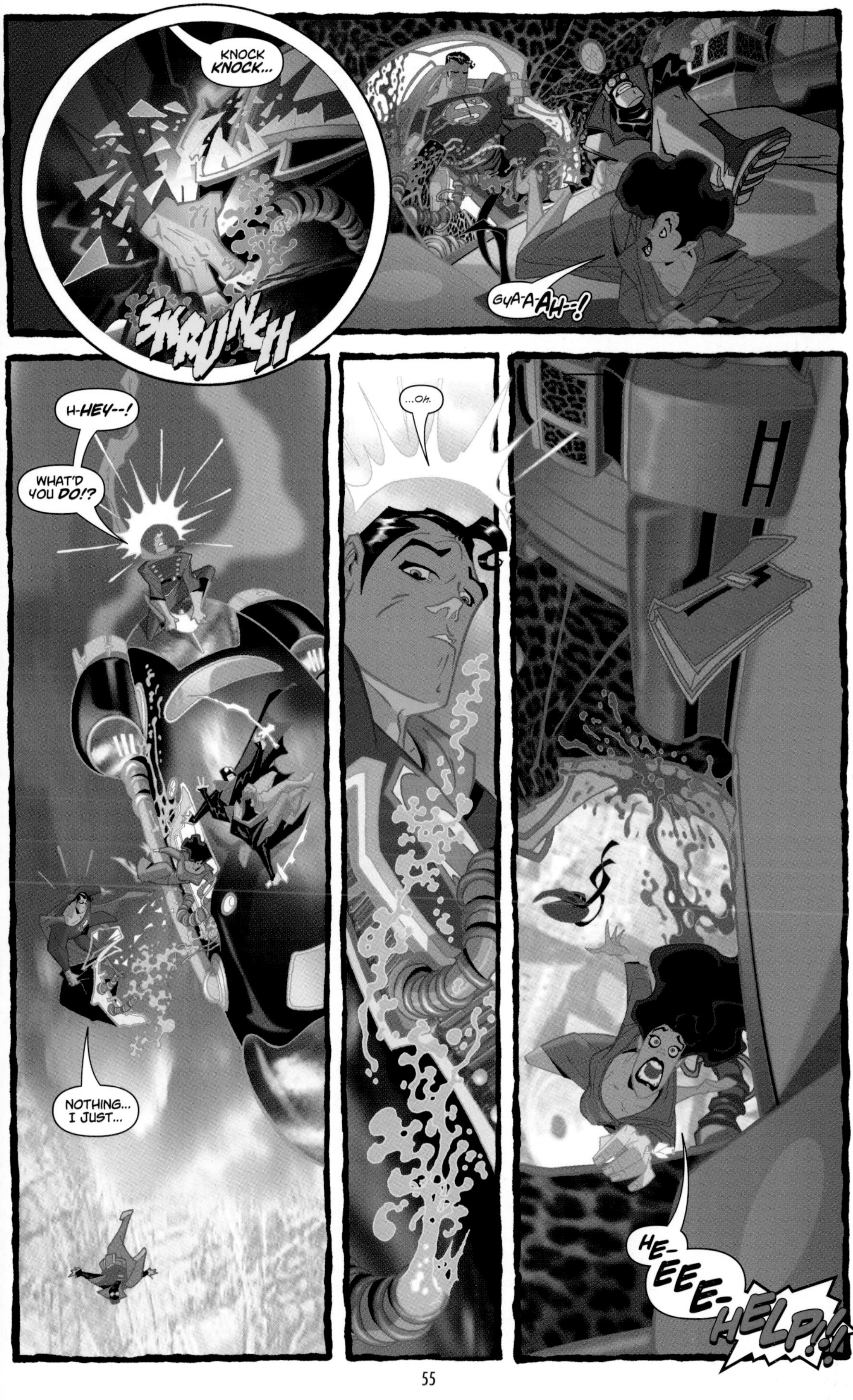
KNOCK
KNOCK...
SKRUNCH
GYA-A-AH--!
H-HEY--!
WHAT'D YOU DO!?
NOTHING... I JUST...
...Oh.
HE-EEE-HELP!!!

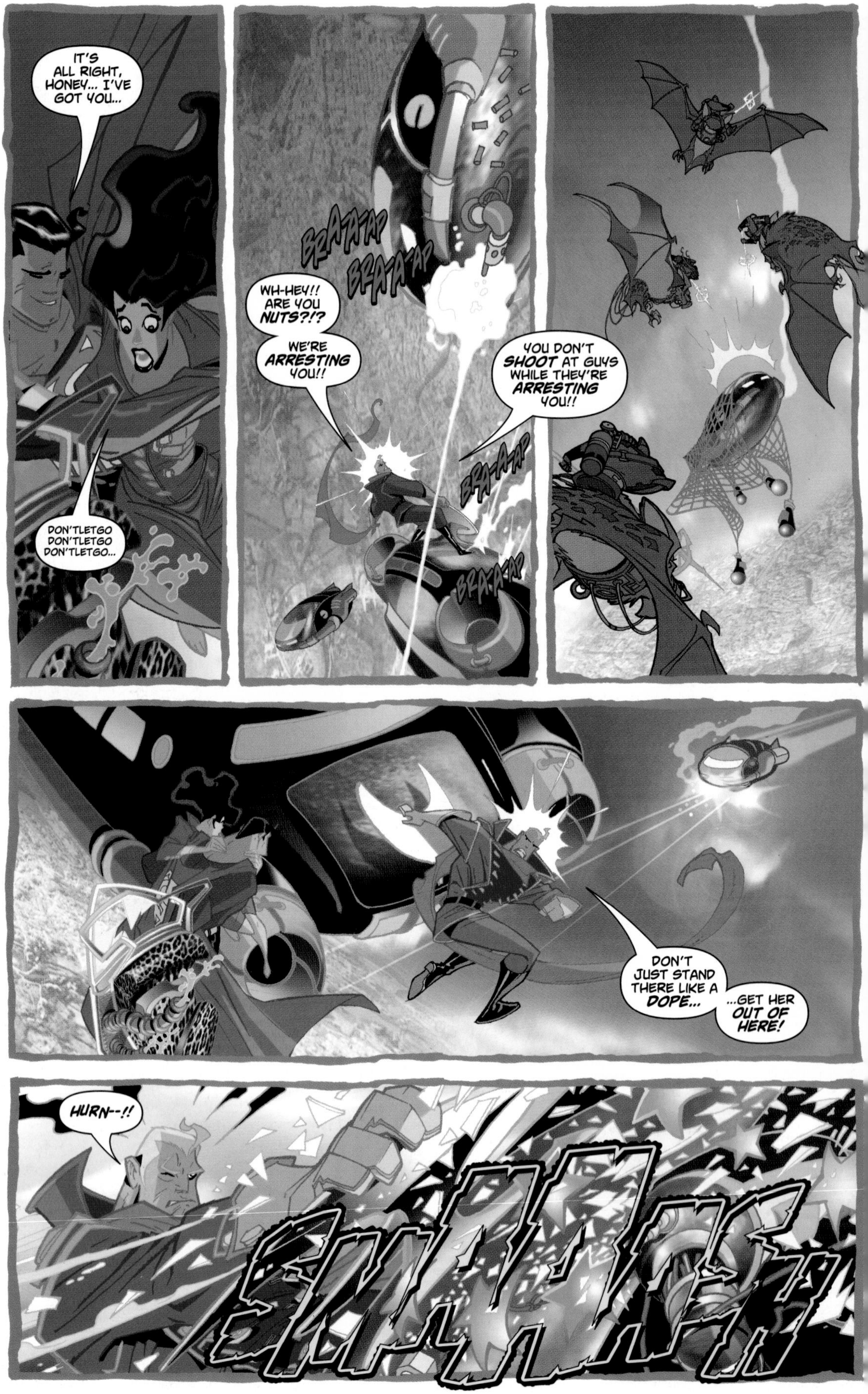
IT'S ALL RIGHT, HONEY... I'VE GOT YOU...
DON'TLETGO DON'TLETGO DON'TLETGO...
BRA-A-A-AP
BRA-A-A-AP
WH-HEY!! ARE YOU NUTS?!?
WE'RE ARRESTING YOU!!
YOU DON'T SHOOT AT GUYS WHILE THEY'RE ARRESTING YOU!!
BRA-A-AP
BRA-A-AP
DON'T JUST STAND THERE LIKE A DOPE...
...GET HER OUT OF HERE!
HURN--!!

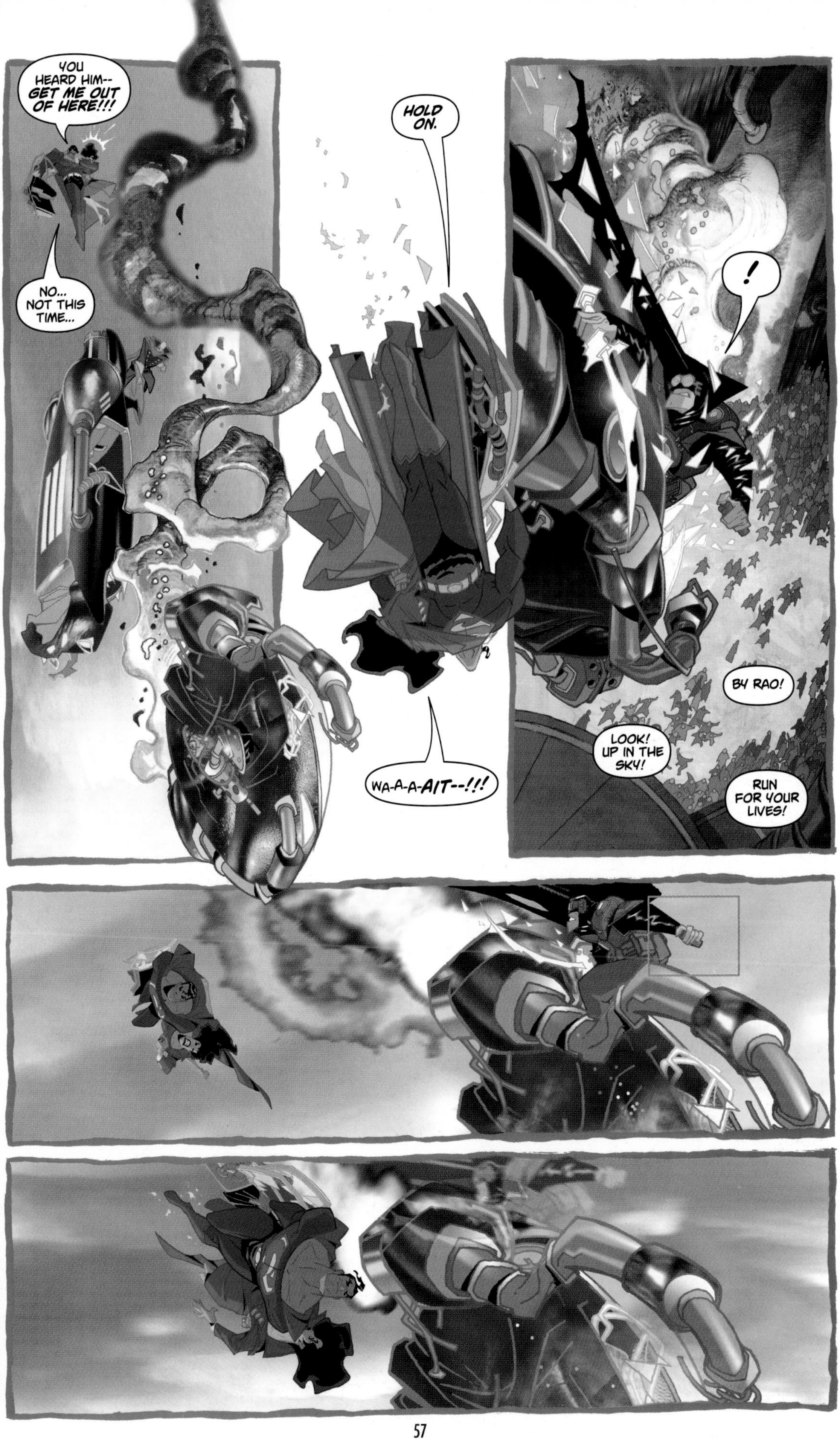
YOU HEARD HIM-- GET ME OUT OF HERE!!!
NO... NOT THIS TIME...
HOLD ON.
WA-A-A-AIT--!!!
!
BY RAO!
LOOK! UP IN THE SKY!
RUN FOR YOUR LIVES!

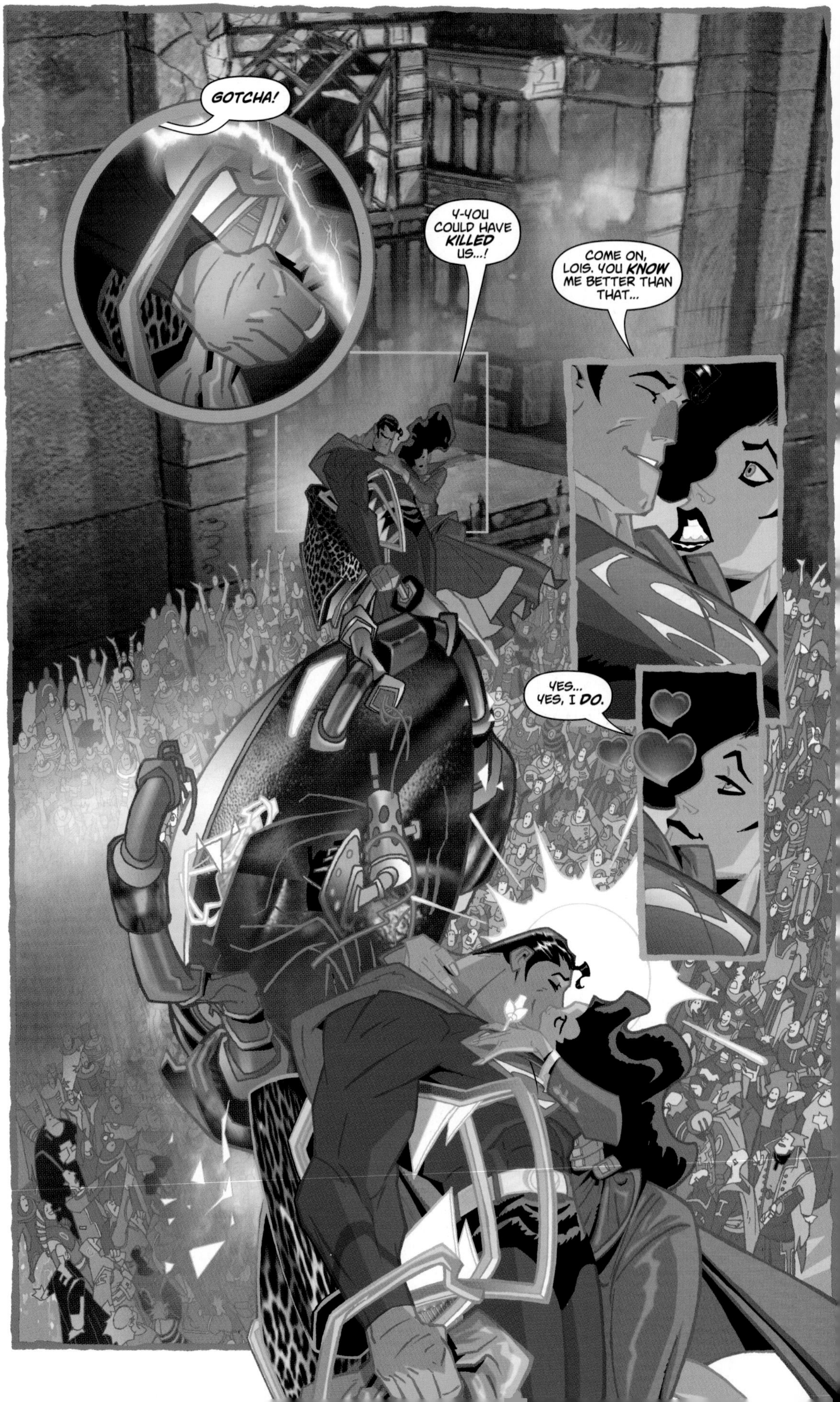
GOTCHA!
Y-YOU COULD HAVE KILLED US...!
COME ON, LOIS. YOU KNOW ME BETTER THAN THAT...
YES... YES, I DO.

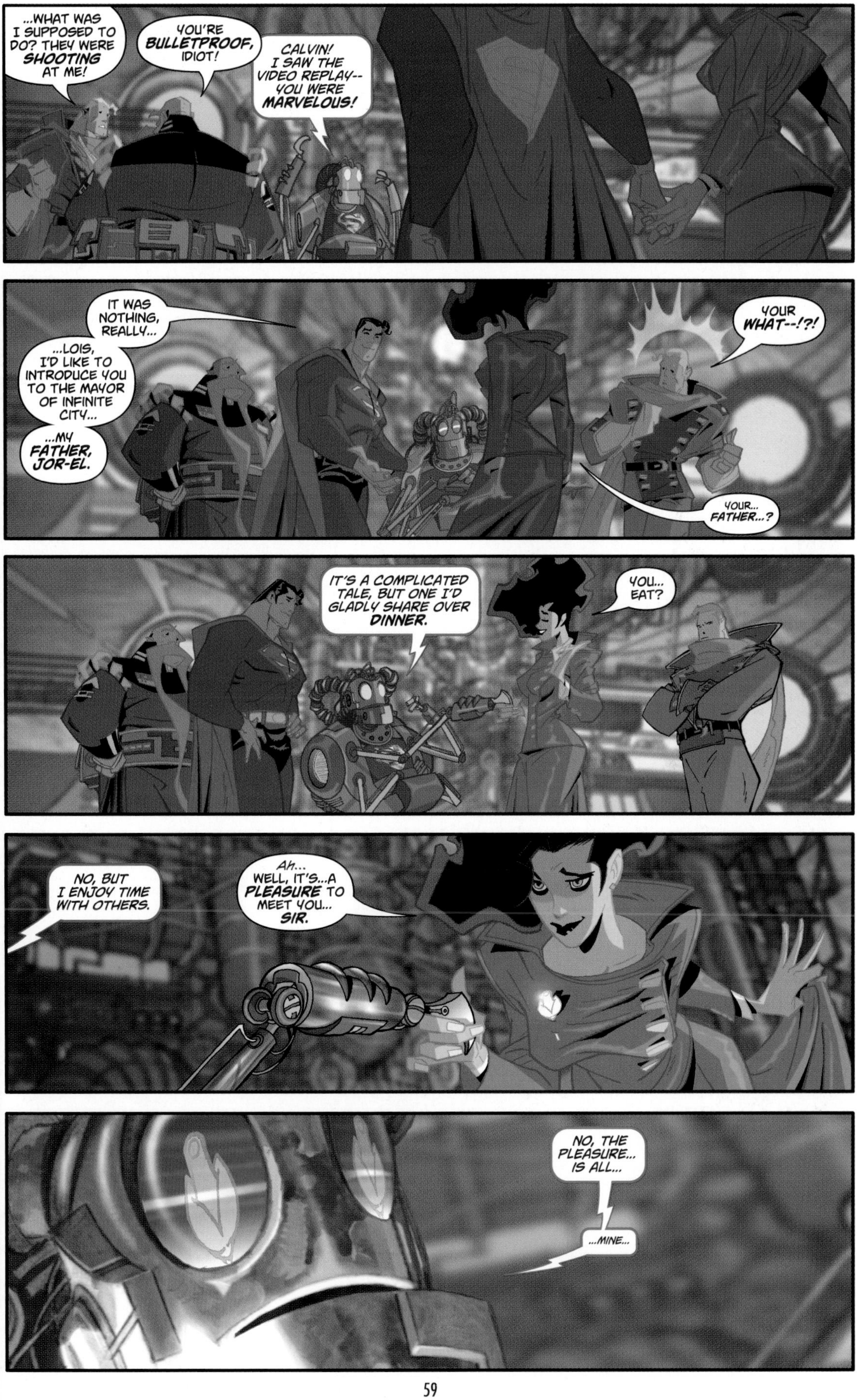
...WHAT WAS I SUPPOSED TO DO? THEY WERE SHOOTING AT ME!
YOU'RE BULLETPROOF, IDIOT!
CALVIN! I SAW THE VIDEO REPLAY-- YOU WERE MARVELOUS!
IT WAS NOTHING, REALLY...
...LOIS, I'D LIKE TO INTRODUCE YOU TO THE MAYOR OF INFINITE CITY...
...MY FATHER, JOR-EL.
YOUR WHAT--!?!
YOUR... FATHER...?
IT'S A COMPLICATED TALE, BUT ONE I'D GLADLY SHARE OVER DINNER.
YOU... EAT?
NO, BUT I ENJOY TIME WITH OTHERS.
Ah... WELL, IT'S...A PLEASURE TO MEET YOU... SIR.
NO, THE PLEASURE... IS ALL...
...MINE...

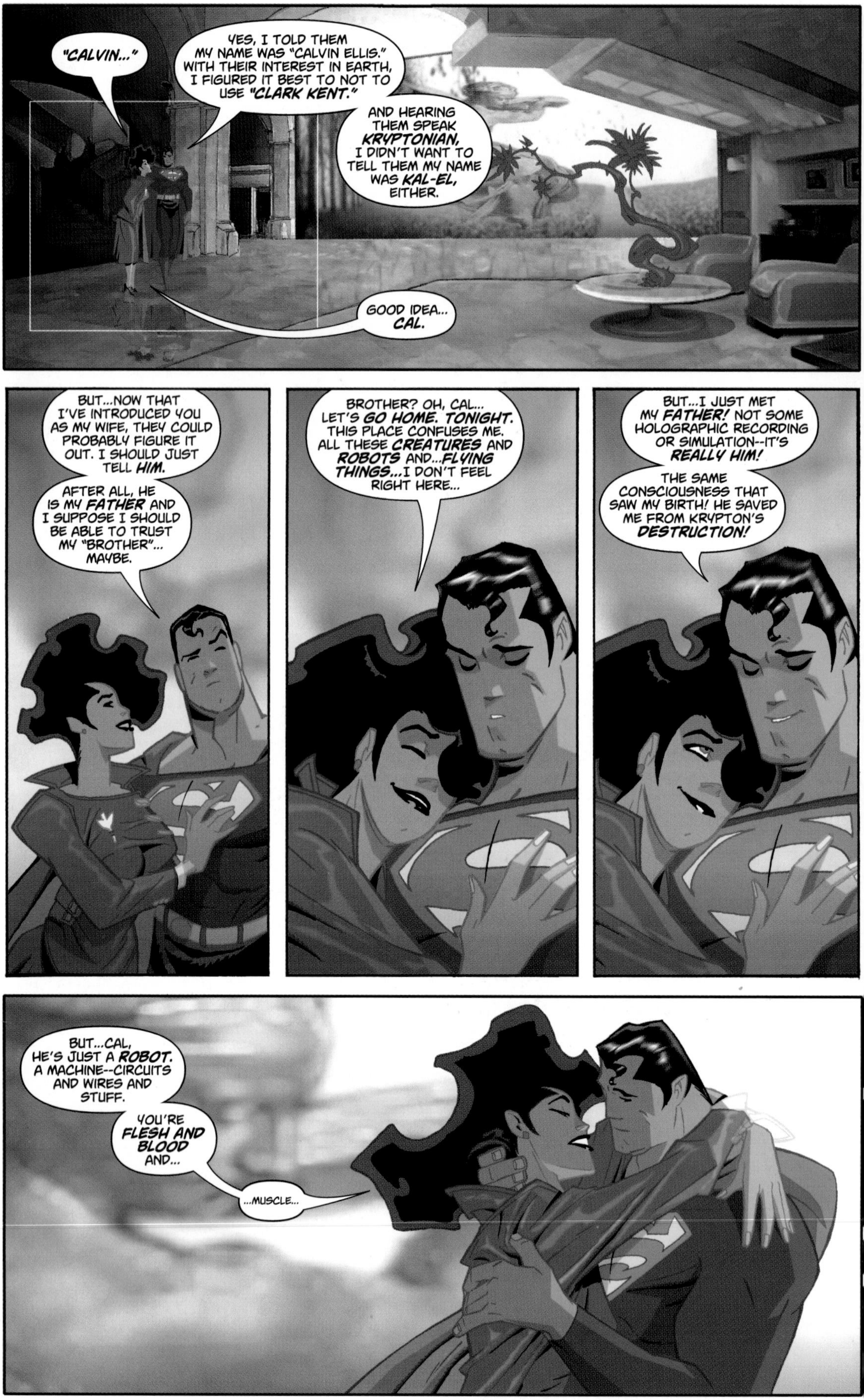
"CALVIN..."
YES, I TOLD THEM MY NAME WAS "CALVIN ELLIS." WITH THEIR INTEREST IN EARTH, I FIGURED IT BEST TO NOT TO USE "CLARK KENT."
AND HEARING THEM SPEAK KRYPTONIAN, I DIDN'T WANT TO TELL THEM MY NAME WAS KAL-EL, EITHER.
GOOD IDEA... CAL.
BUT...NOW THAT I'VE INTRODUCED YOU AS MY WIFE, THEY COULD PROBABLY FIGURE IT OUT. I SHOULD JUST TELL HIM.
AFTER ALL, HE IS MY FATHER AND I SUPPOSE I SHOULD BE ABLE TO TRUST MY "BROTHER"... MAYBE.
BROTHER? OH, CAL... LET'S GO HOME. TONIGHT. THIS PLACE CONFUSES ME. ALL THESE CREATURES AND ROBOTS AND...FLYING THINGS...I DON'T FEEL RIGHT HERE...
BUT...I JUST MET MY FATHER! NOT SOME HOLOGRAPHIC RECORDING OR SIMULATION--IT'S REALLY HIM!
THE SAME CONSCIOUSNESS THAT SAW MY BIRTH! HE SAVED ME FROM KRYPTON'S DESTRUCTION!
BUT...CAL, HE'S JUST A ROBOT. A MACHINE--CIRCUITS AND WIRES AND STUFF.
YOU'RE FLESH AND BLOOD AND...
...MUSCLE...

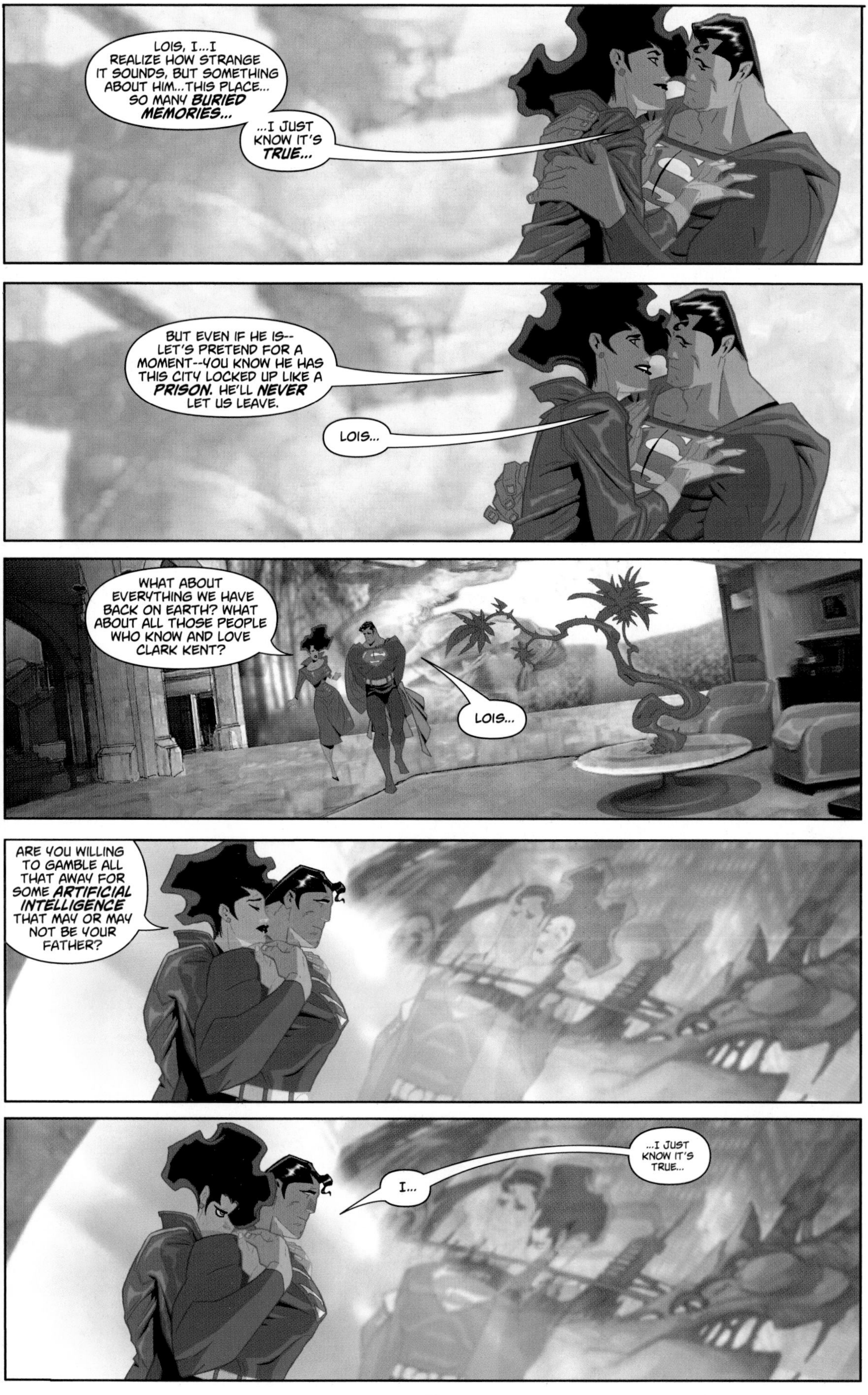
LOIS, I...I REALIZE HOW STRANGE IT SOUNDS, BUT SOMETHING ABOUT HIM...THIS PLACE... SO MANY BURIED MEMORIES...
...I JUST KNOW IT'S TRUE...
BUT EVEN IF HE IS-- LET'S PRETEND FOR A MOMENT--YOU KNOW HE HAS THIS CITY LOCKED UP LIKE A PRISON. HE'LL NEVER LET US LEAVE.
LOIS...
WHAT ABOUT EVERYTHING WE HAVE BACK ON EARTH? WHAT ABOUT ALL THOSE PEOPLE WHO KNOW AND LOVE CLARK KENT?
LOIS...
ARE YOU WILLING TO GAMBLE ALL THAT AWAY FOR SOME ARTIFICIAL INTELLIGENCE THAT MAY OR MAY NOT BE YOUR FATHER?
I...
...I JUST KNOW IT'S TRUE...

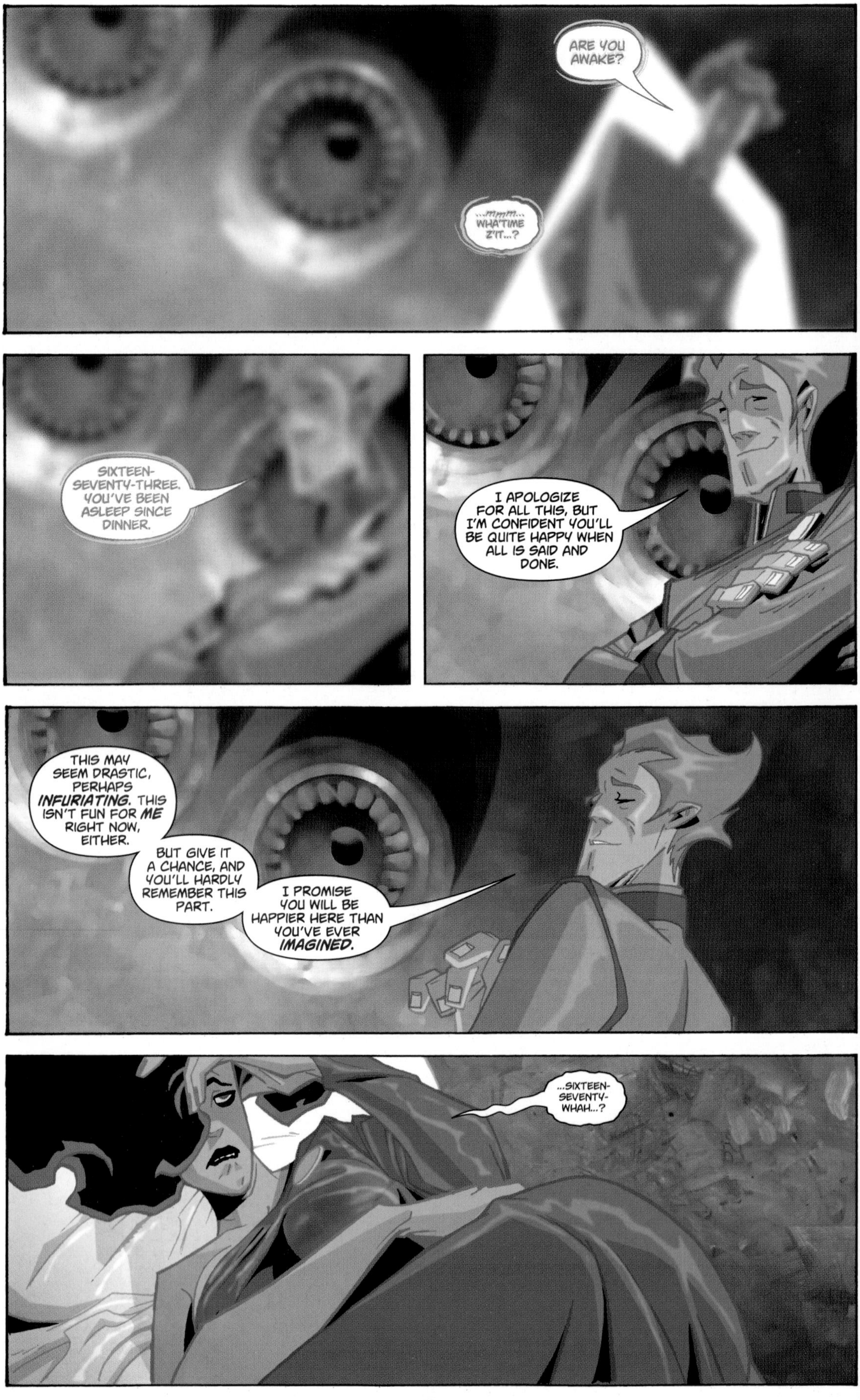
ARE YOU AWAKE?
...mmm... WHA'TIME Z'IT...?
SIXTEEN-SEVENTY-THREE. YOU'VE BEEN ASLEEP SINCE DINNER.
I APOLOGIZE FOR ALL THIS, BUT I'M CONFIDENT YOU'LL BE QUITE HAPPY WHEN ALL IS SAID AND DONE.
THIS MAY SEEM DRASTIC, PERHAPS *INFURIATING.* THIS ISN'T FUN FOR *ME* RIGHT NOW, EITHER.
BUT GIVE IT A CHANCE, AND YOU'LL HARDLY REMEMBER THIS PART.
I PROMISE YOU WILL BE HAPPIER HERE THAN YOU'VE EVER *IMAGINED.*
...SIXTEEN-SEVENTY-WHAH...?

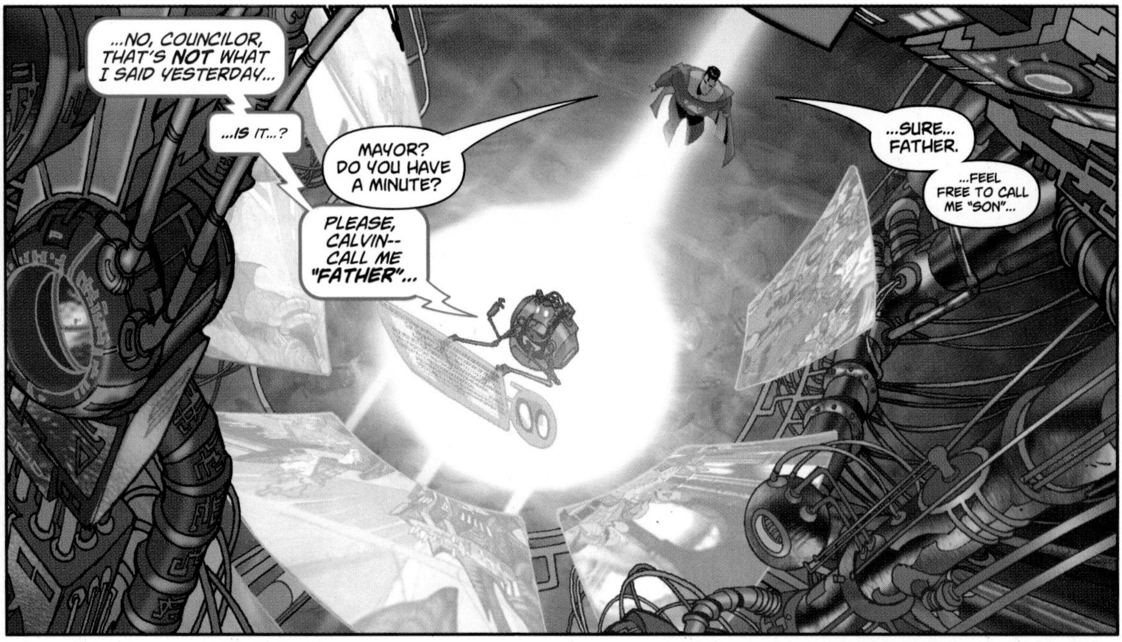
...NO, COUNCILOR, THAT'S NOT WHAT I SAID YESTERDAY...
...IS IT...?
MAYOR? DO YOU HAVE A MINUTE?
PLEASE, CALVIN-- CALL ME "FATHER"...
...SURE... FATHER.
...FEEL FREE TO CALL ME "SON"...

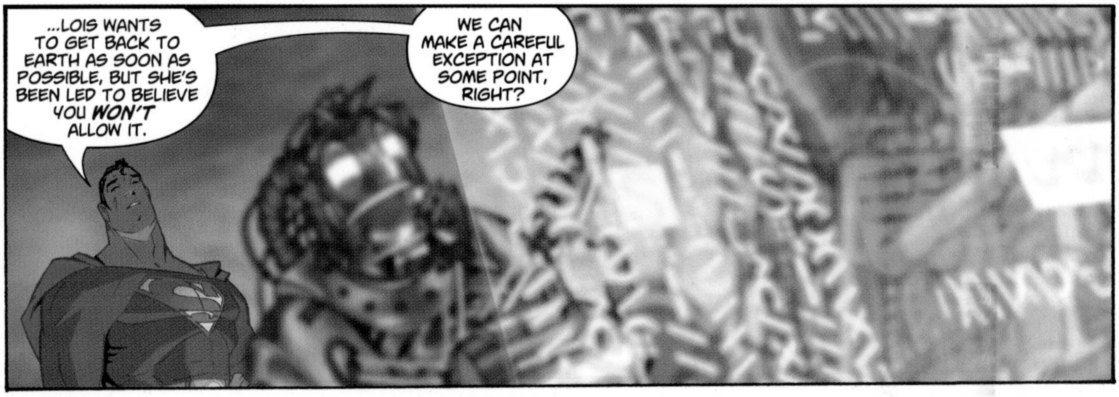
...LOIS WANTS TO GET BACK TO EARTH AS SOON AS POSSIBLE, BUT SHE'S BEEN LED TO BELIEVE YOU WON'T ALLOW IT.
WE CAN MAKE A CAREFUL EXCEPTION AT SOME POINT, RIGHT?

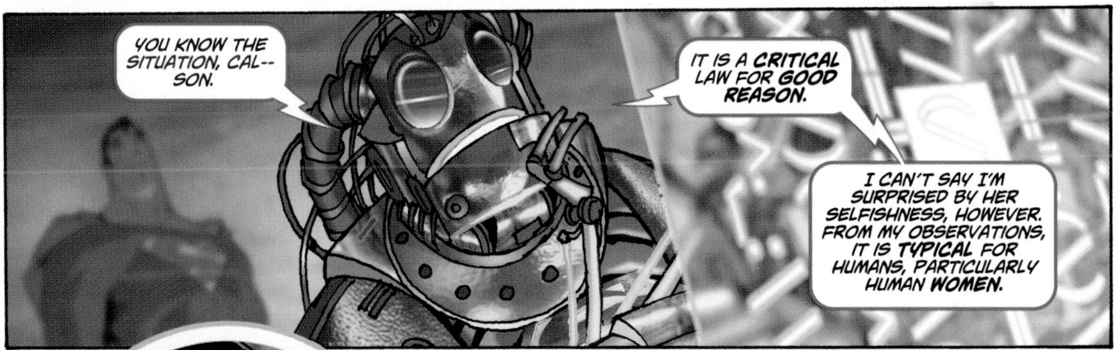
YOU KNOW THE SITUATION, CAL-- SON.
IT IS A CRITICAL LAW FOR GOOD REASON.
I CAN'T SAY I'M SURPRISED BY HER SELFISHNESS, HOWEVER. FROM MY OBSERVATIONS, IT IS TYPICAL FOR HUMANS, PARTICULARLY HUMAN WOMEN.

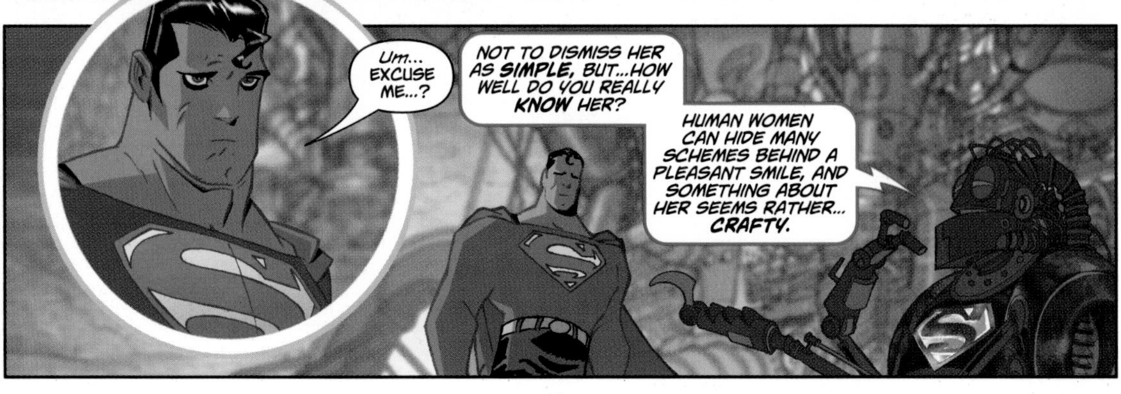
Um... EXCUSE ME...?
NOT TO DISMISS HER AS SIMPLE, BUT...HOW WELL DO YOU REALLY KNOW HER?
HUMAN WOMEN CAN HIDE MANY SCHEMES BEHIND A PLEASANT SMILE, AND SOMETHING ABOUT HER SEEMS RATHER... CRAFTY.

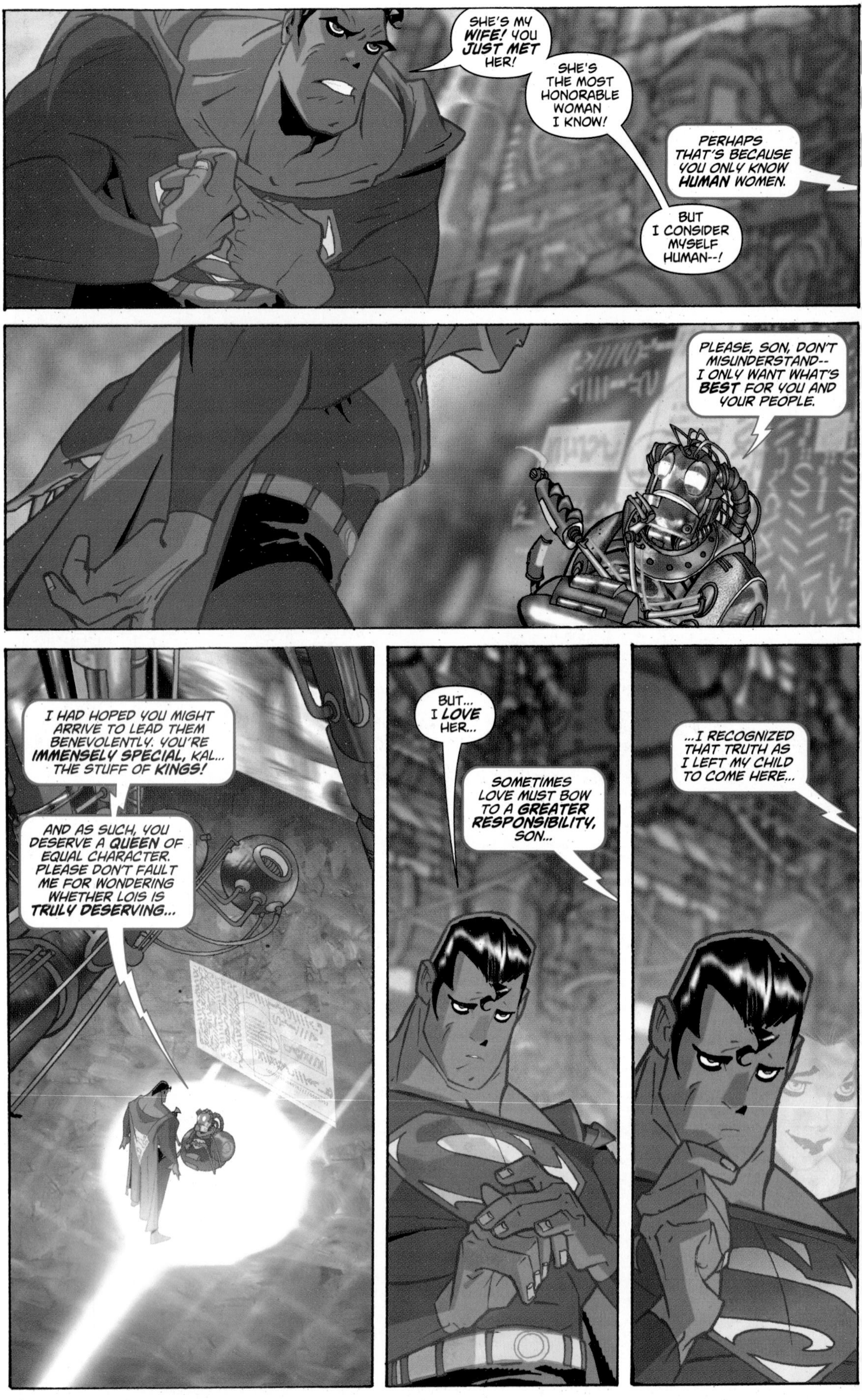
SHE'S MY WIFE! YOU JUST MET HER!
SHE'S THE MOST HONORABLE WOMAN I KNOW!
PERHAPS THAT'S BECAUSE YOU ONLY KNOW HUMAN WOMEN.
BUT I CONSIDER MYSELF HUMAN--!
PLEASE, SON, DON'T MISUNDERSTAND-- I ONLY WANT WHAT'S BEST FOR YOU AND YOUR PEOPLE.
I HAD HOPED YOU MIGHT ARRIVE TO LEAD THEM BENEVOLENTLY. YOU'RE IMMENSELY SPECIAL, KAL... THE STUFF OF KINGS!
AND AS SUCH, YOU DESERVE A QUEEN OF EQUAL CHARACTER. PLEASE DON'T FAULT ME FOR WONDERING WHETHER LOIS IS TRULY DESERVING...
BUT... I LOVE HER...
SOMETIMES LOVE MUST BOW TO A GREATER RESPONSIBILITY, SON...
...I RECOGNIZED THAT TRUTH AS I LEFT MY CHILD TO COME HERE...

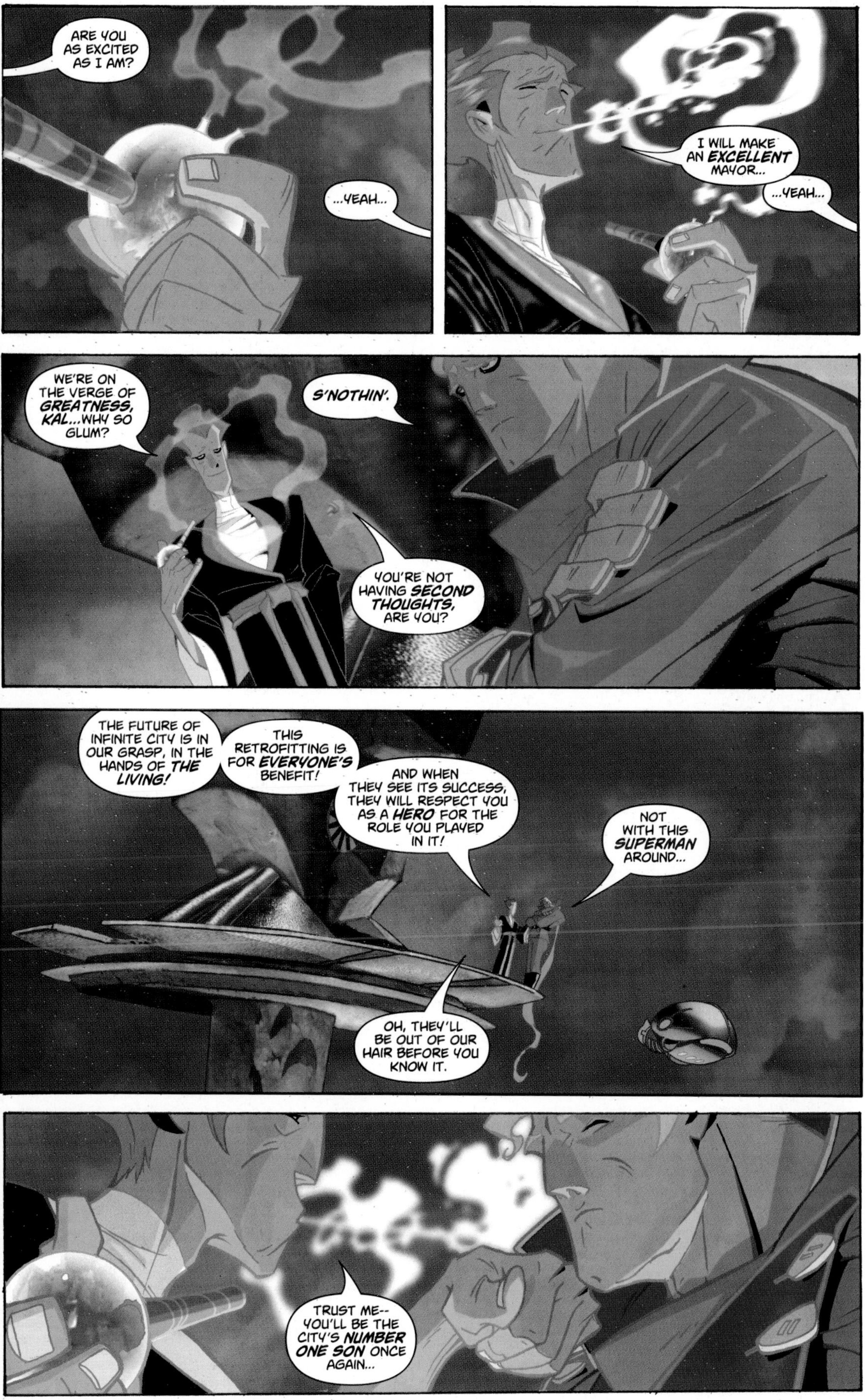
ARE YOU AS EXCITED AS I AM?
...YEAH...
I WILL MAKE AN EXCELLENT MAYOR...
...YEAH...
WE'RE ON THE VERGE OF GREATNESS, KAL...WHY SO GLUM?
S'NOTHIN'.
YOU'RE NOT HAVING SECOND THOUGHTS, ARE YOU?
THE FUTURE OF INFINITE CITY IS IN OUR GRASP, IN THE HANDS OF THE LIVING!
THIS RETROFITTING IS FOR EVERYONE'S BENEFIT!
AND WHEN THEY SEE ITS SUCCESS, THEY WILL RESPECT YOU AS A HERO FOR THE ROLE YOU PLAYED IN IT!
NOT WITH THIS SUPERMAN AROUND...
OH, THEY'LL BE OUT OF OUR HAIR BEFORE YOU KNOW IT.
TRUST ME-- YOU'LL BE THE CITY'S NUMBER ONE SON ONCE AGAIN...

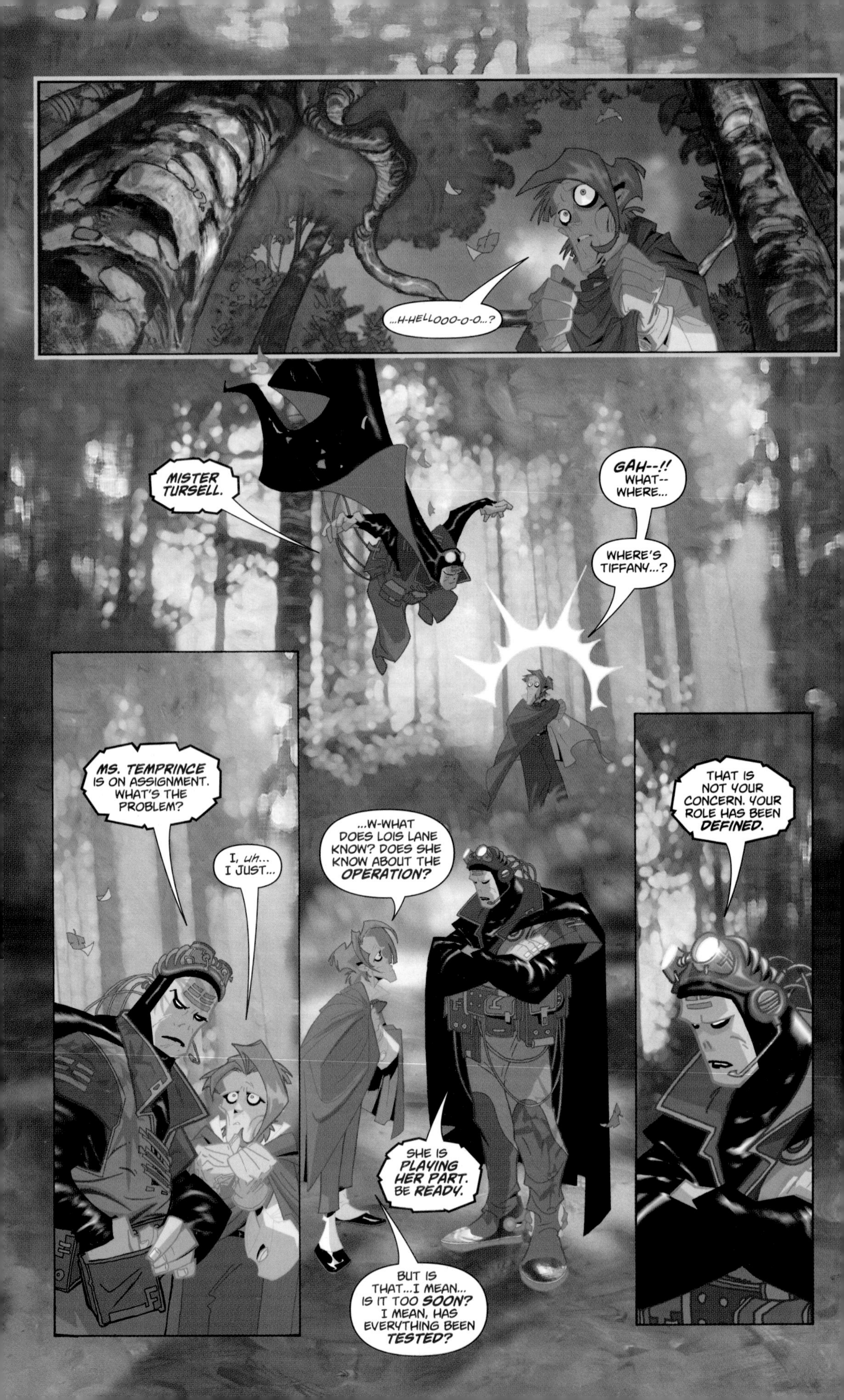
...H-HELLOOO-O-O...?
MISTER TURSELL.
GAH--!! WHAT-- WHERE...
WHERE'S TIFFANY...?
MS. TEMPRINCE IS ON ASSIGNMENT. WHAT'S THE PROBLEM?
I, uh... I JUST...
...W-WHAT DOES LOIS LANE KNOW? DOES SHE KNOW ABOUT THE OPERATION?
SHE IS PLAYING HER PART. BE READY.
BUT IS THAT...I MEAN... IS IT TOO SOON? I MEAN, HAS EVERYTHING BEEN TESTED?
THAT IS NOT YOUR CONCERN. YOUR ROLE HAS BEEN DEFINED.

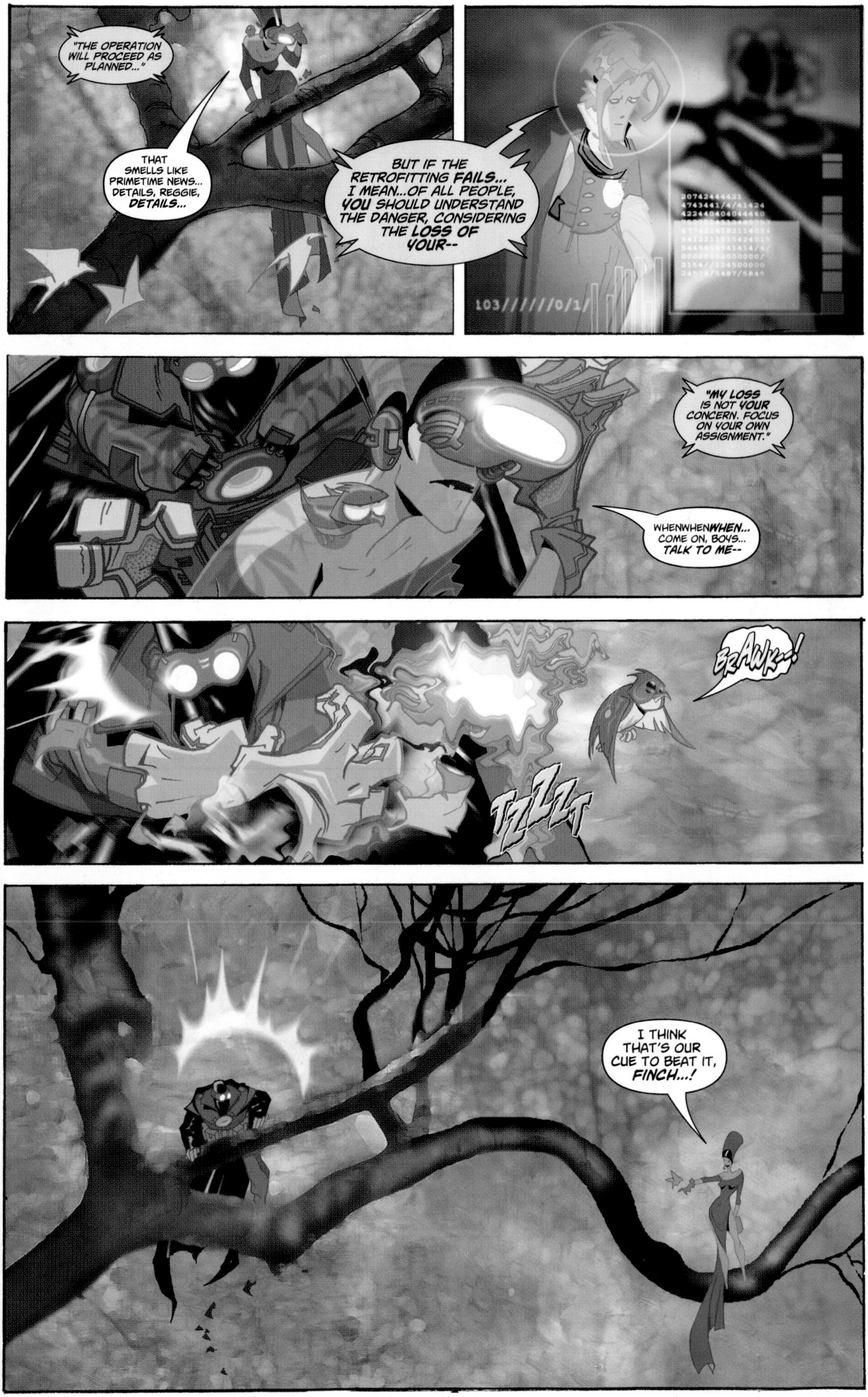
"THE OPERATION WILL PROCEED AS PLANNED..."
THAT SMELLS LIKE PRIMETIME NEWS... DETAILS, REGGIE, DETAILS...
BUT IF THE RETROFITTING FAILS... I MEAN...OF ALL PEOPLE, YOU SHOULD UNDERSTAND THE DANGER, CONSIDERING THE LOSS OF YOUR--
"MY LOSS IS NOT YOUR CONCERN. FOCUS ON YOUR OWN ASSIGNMENT."
WHENWHENWHEN... COME ON, BOYS... TALK TO ME--
BRAWK--!
TZZZZT
I THINK THAT'S OUR CUE TO BEAT IT, FINCH...!

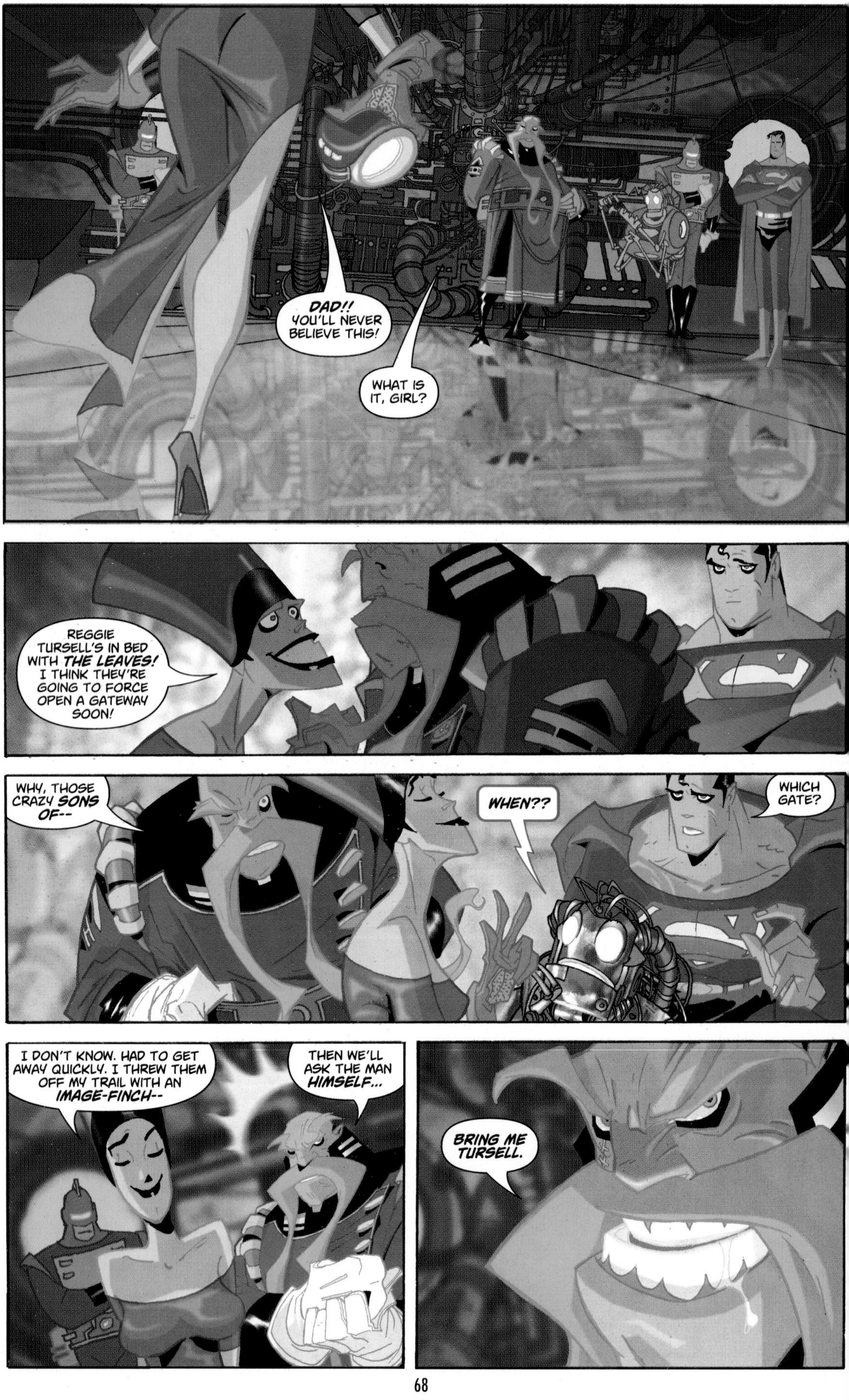
DAD!! YOU'LL NEVER BELIEVE THIS!
WHAT IS IT, GIRL?
REGGIE TURSELL'S IN BED WITH THE LEAVES! I THINK THEY'RE GOING TO FORCE OPEN A GATEWAY SOON!
WHY, THOSE CRAZY SONS OF--
WHEN??
WHICH GATE?
I DON'T KNOW. HAD TO GET AWAY QUICKLY. I THREW THEM OFF MY TRAIL WITH AN IMAGE-FINCH--
THEN WE'LL ASK THE MAN HIMSELF...
BRING ME TURSELL.

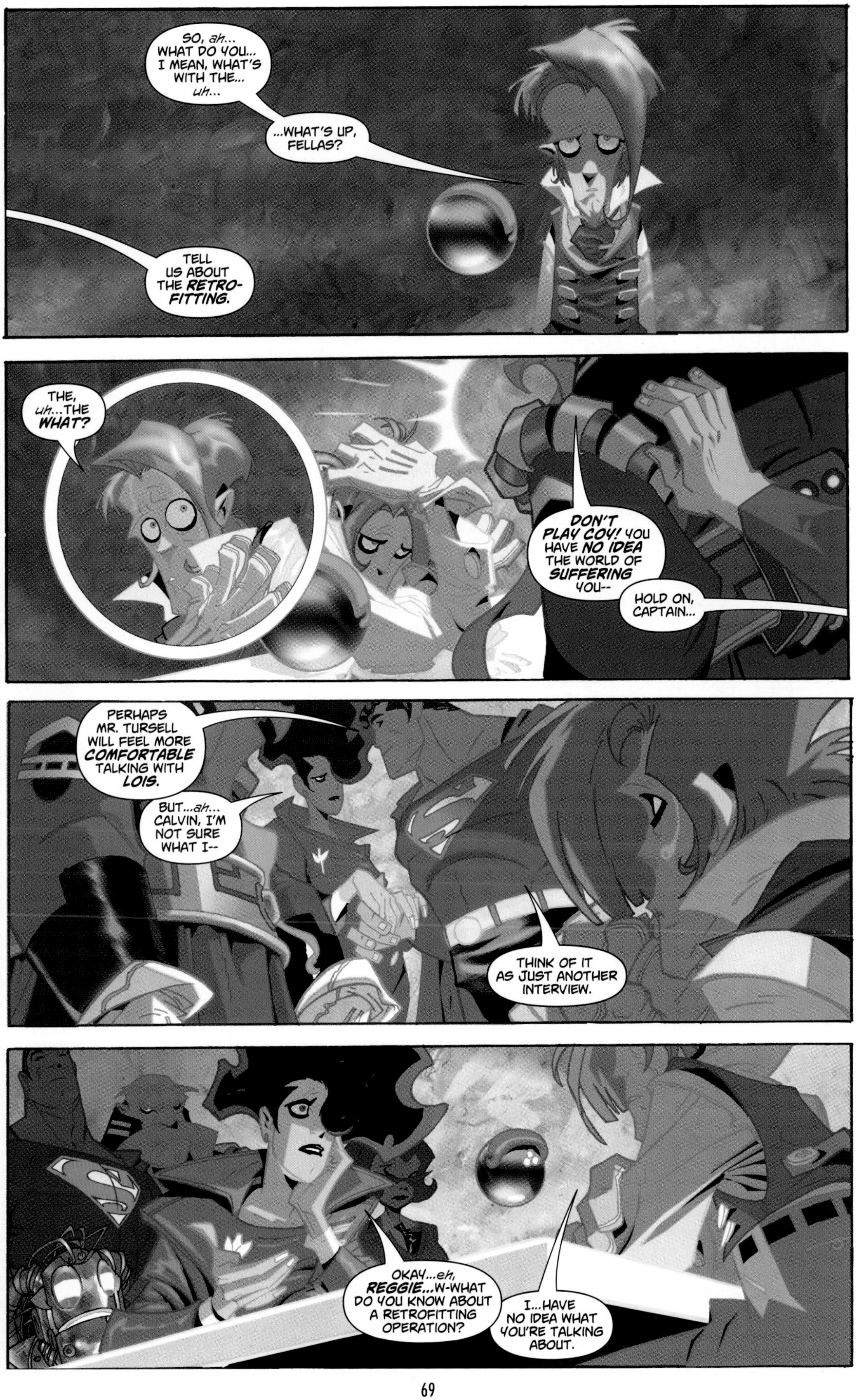

SO, *ah*... WHAT DO YOU... I MEAN, WHAT'S WITH THE... *uh*...
...WHAT'S UP, FELLAS?
TELL US ABOUT THE ***RETRO-FITTING.***
THE, *uh*...THE ***WHAT?***
***DON'T PLAY COY!*** YOU HAVE ***NO IDEA*** THE WORLD OF ***SUFFERING*** YOU--
HOLD ON, CAPTAIN...
PERHAPS MR. TURSELL WILL FEEL MORE ***COMFORTABLE*** TALKING WITH ***LOIS.***
BUT...*ah*... CALVIN, I'M NOT SURE WHAT I--
THINK OF IT AS JUST ANOTHER INTERVIEW.
OKAY...*eh*, ***REGGIE...*** W-WHAT DO YOU KNOW ABOUT A RETROFITTING OPERATION?
I...HAVE NO IDEA WHAT YOU'RE TALKING ABOUT.

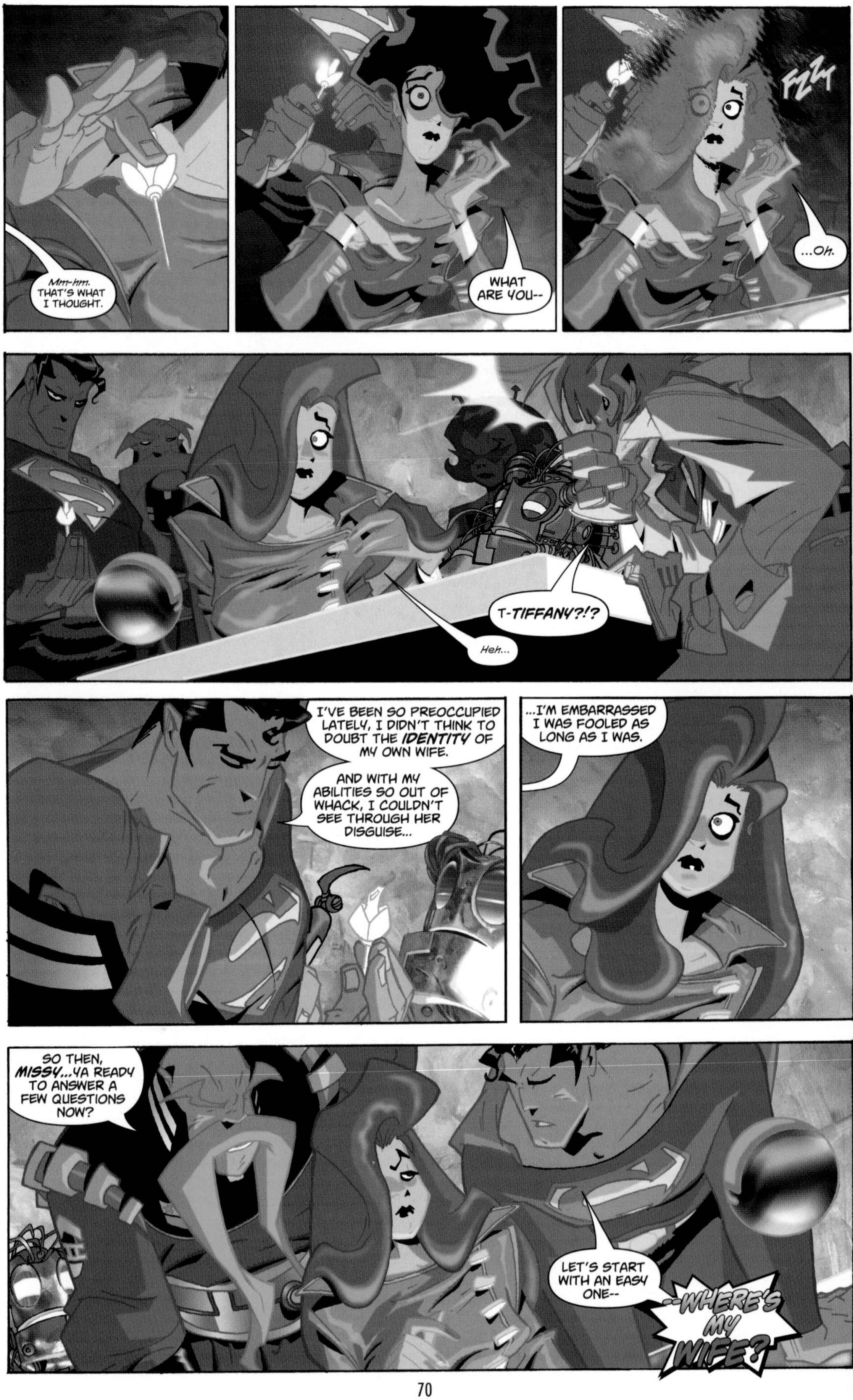

Mm-hm. THAT'S WHAT I THOUGHT.
WHAT ARE YOU--
FZZZT
...Oh.
T-TIFFANY?!?
Heh...
I'VE BEEN SO PREOCCUPIED LATELY, I DIDN'T THINK TO DOUBT THE IDENTITY OF MY OWN WIFE.
AND WITH MY ABILITIES SO OUT OF WHACK, I COULDN'T SEE THROUGH HER DISGUISE...
...I'M EMBARRASSED I WAS FOOLED AS LONG AS I WAS.
SO THEN, MISSY...YA READY TO ANSWER A FEW QUESTIONS NOW?
LET'S START WITH AN EASY ONE--
--WHERE'S MY WIFE?

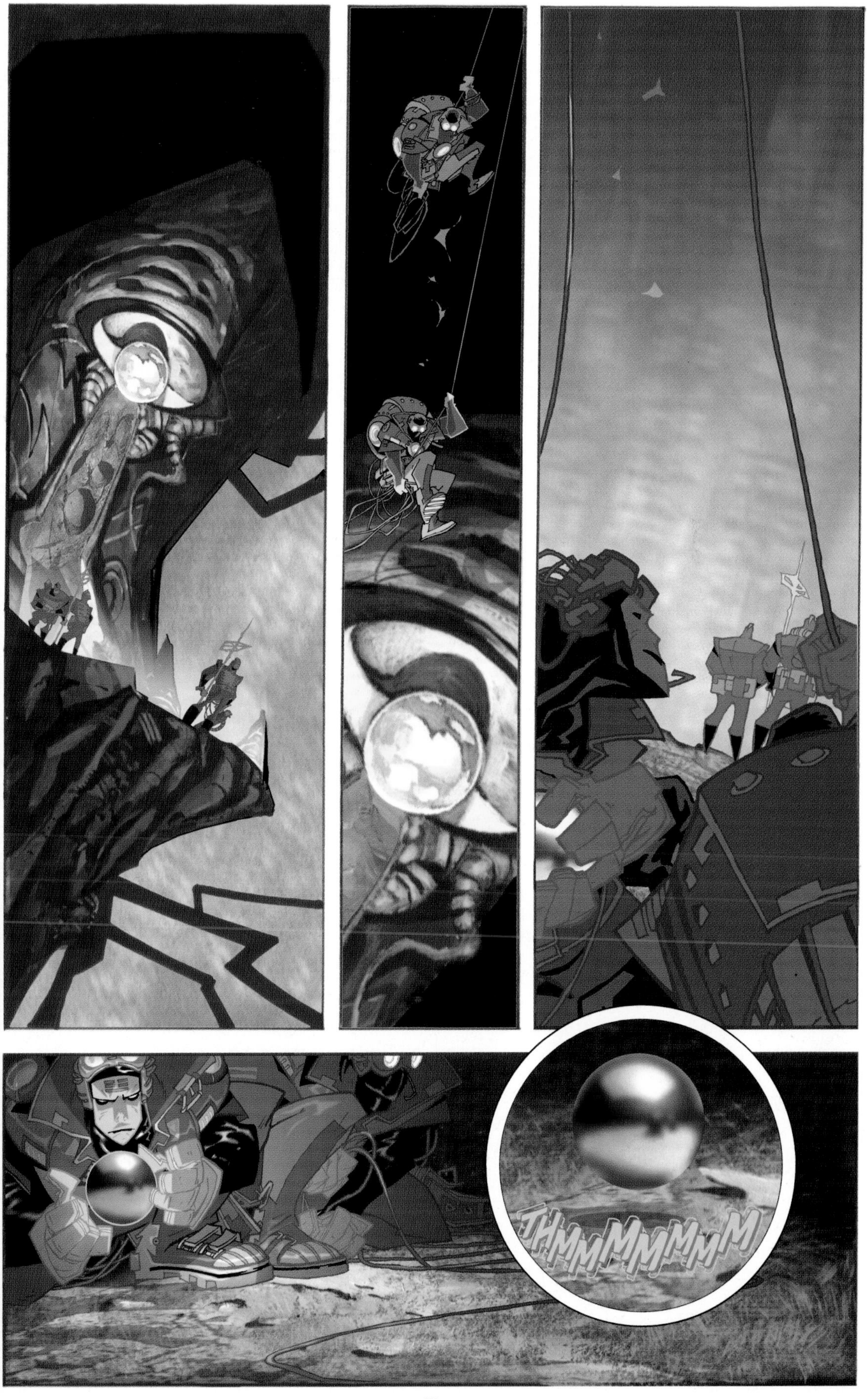
THMMMMMMMM

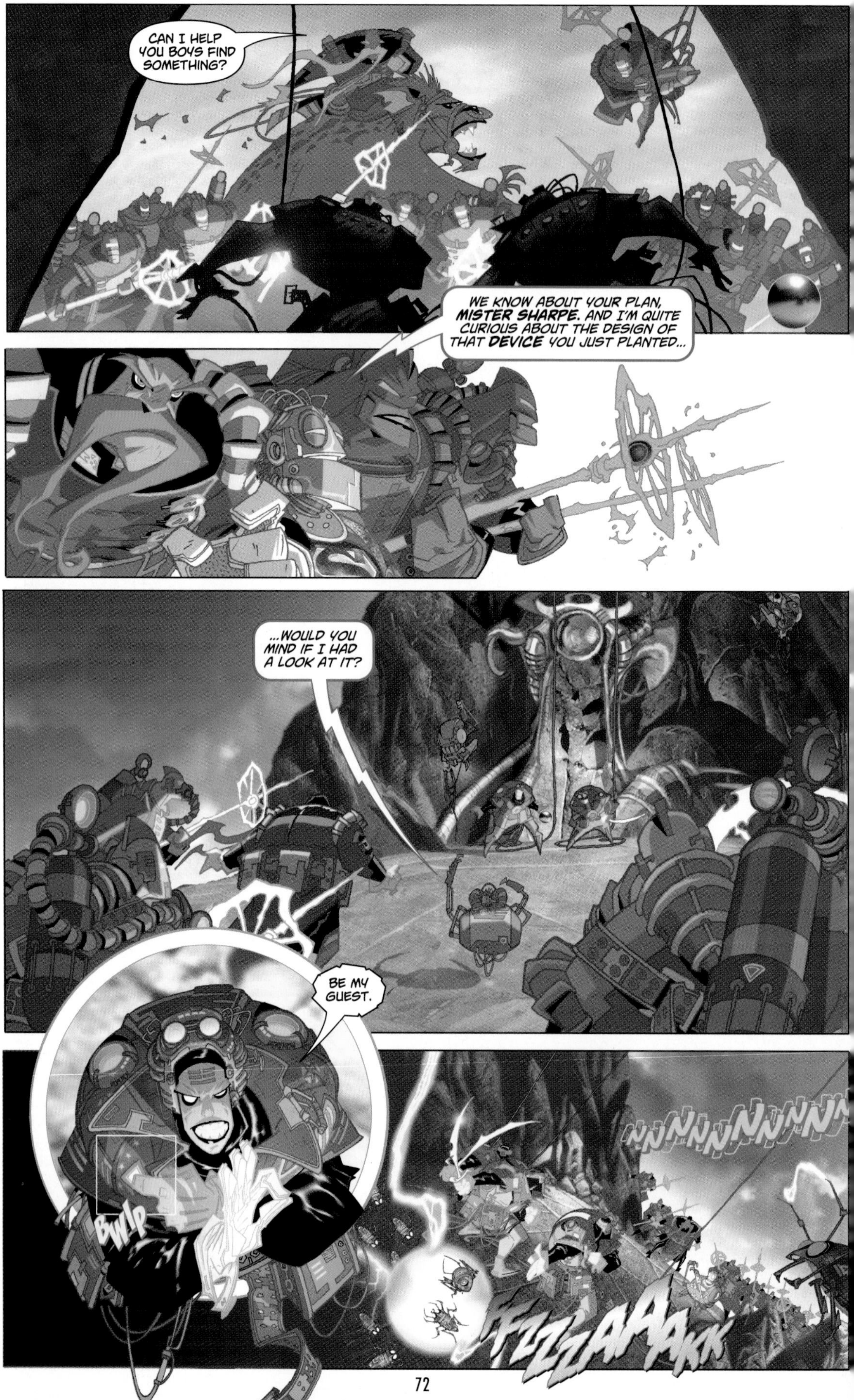
CAN I HELP YOU BOYS FIND SOMETHING?
WE KNOW ABOUT YOUR PLAN, MISTER SHARPE. AND I'M QUITE CURIOUS ABOUT THE DESIGN OF THAT DEVICE YOU JUST PLANTED...
...WOULD YOU MIND IF I HAD A LOOK AT IT?
BE MY GUEST.
BWIP
NNNNNNNNNNN
FZZZAAAAKK

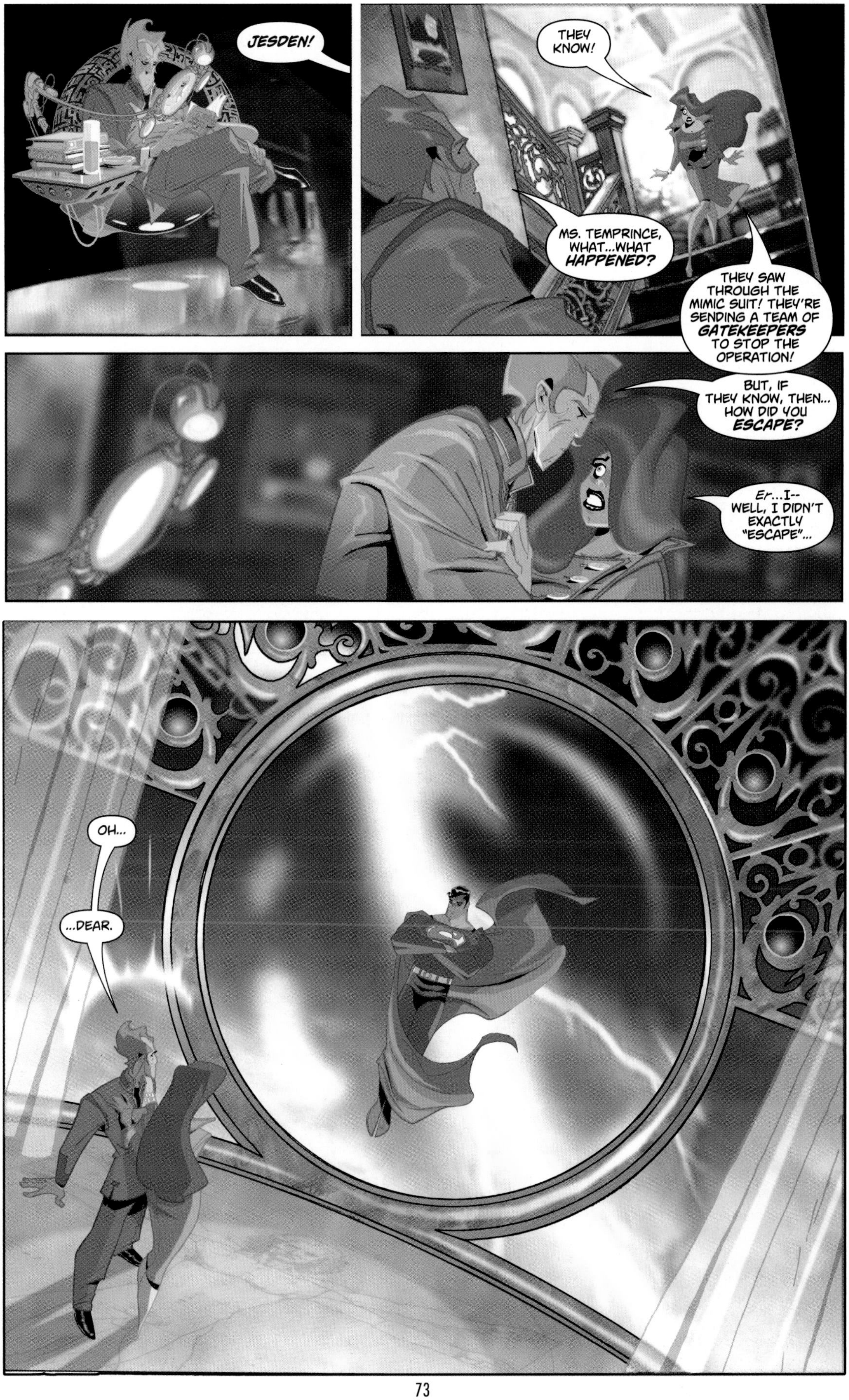
JESDEN!
THEY KNOW!
MS. TEMPRINCE, WHAT...WHAT HAPPENED?
THEY SAW THROUGH THE MIMIC SUIT! THEY'RE SENDING A TEAM OF GATEKEEPERS TO STOP THE OPERATION!
BUT, IF THEY KNOW, THEN... HOW DID YOU ESCAPE?
Er...I-- WELL, I DIDN'T EXACTLY "ESCAPE"...
OH...
...DEAR.

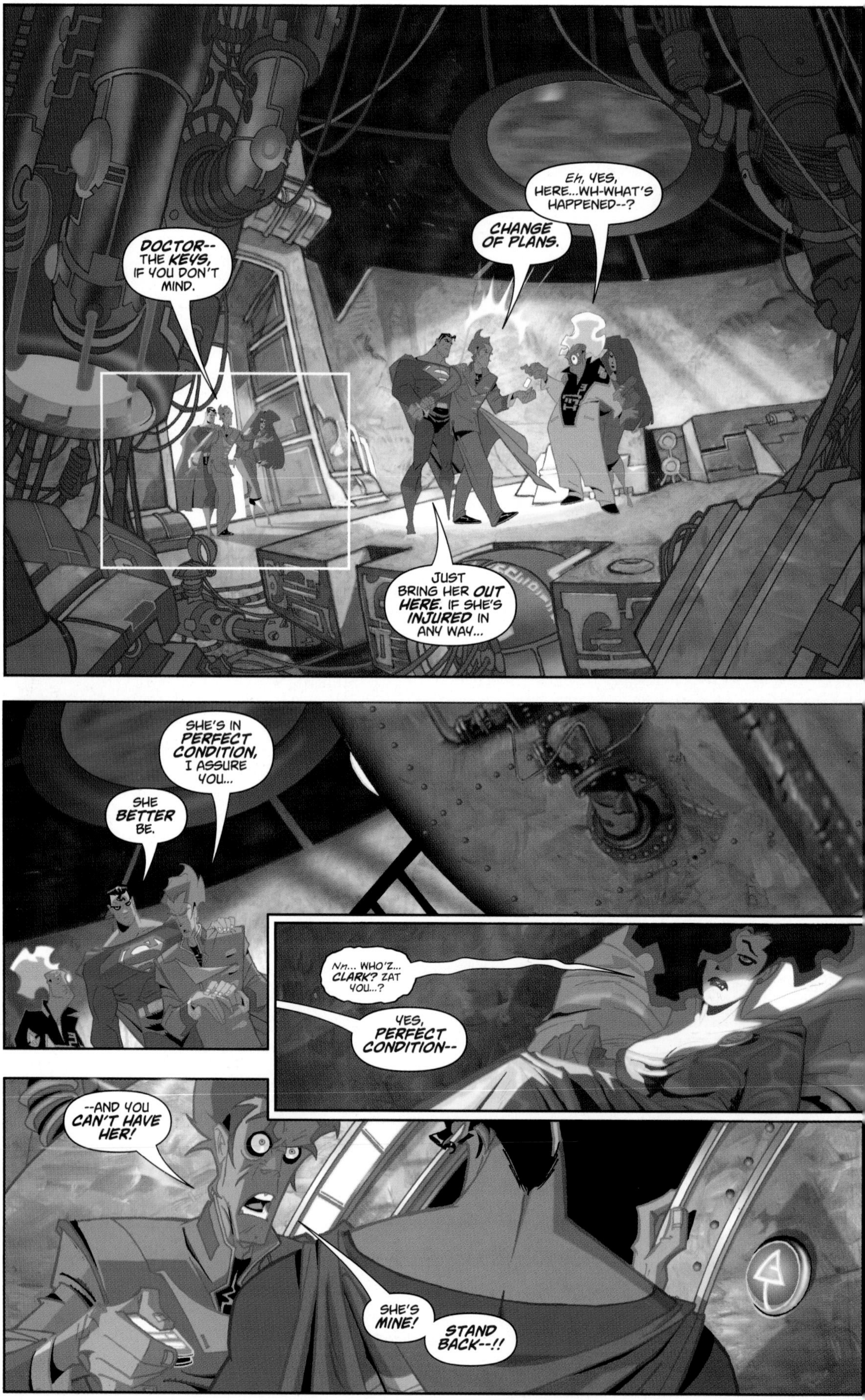
DOCTOR-- THE KEYS, IF YOU DON'T MIND.
CHANGE OF PLANS.
Eh, YES, HERE...WH-WHAT'S HAPPENED--?
JUST BRING HER OUT HERE. IF SHE'S INJURED IN ANY WAY...
SHE'S IN PERFECT CONDITION, I ASSURE YOU...
SHE BETTER BE.
Nn... WHO'Z... CLARK? ZAT YOU...?
YES, PERFECT CONDITION--
--AND YOU CAN'T HAVE HER!
SHE'S MINE!
STAND BACK--!!

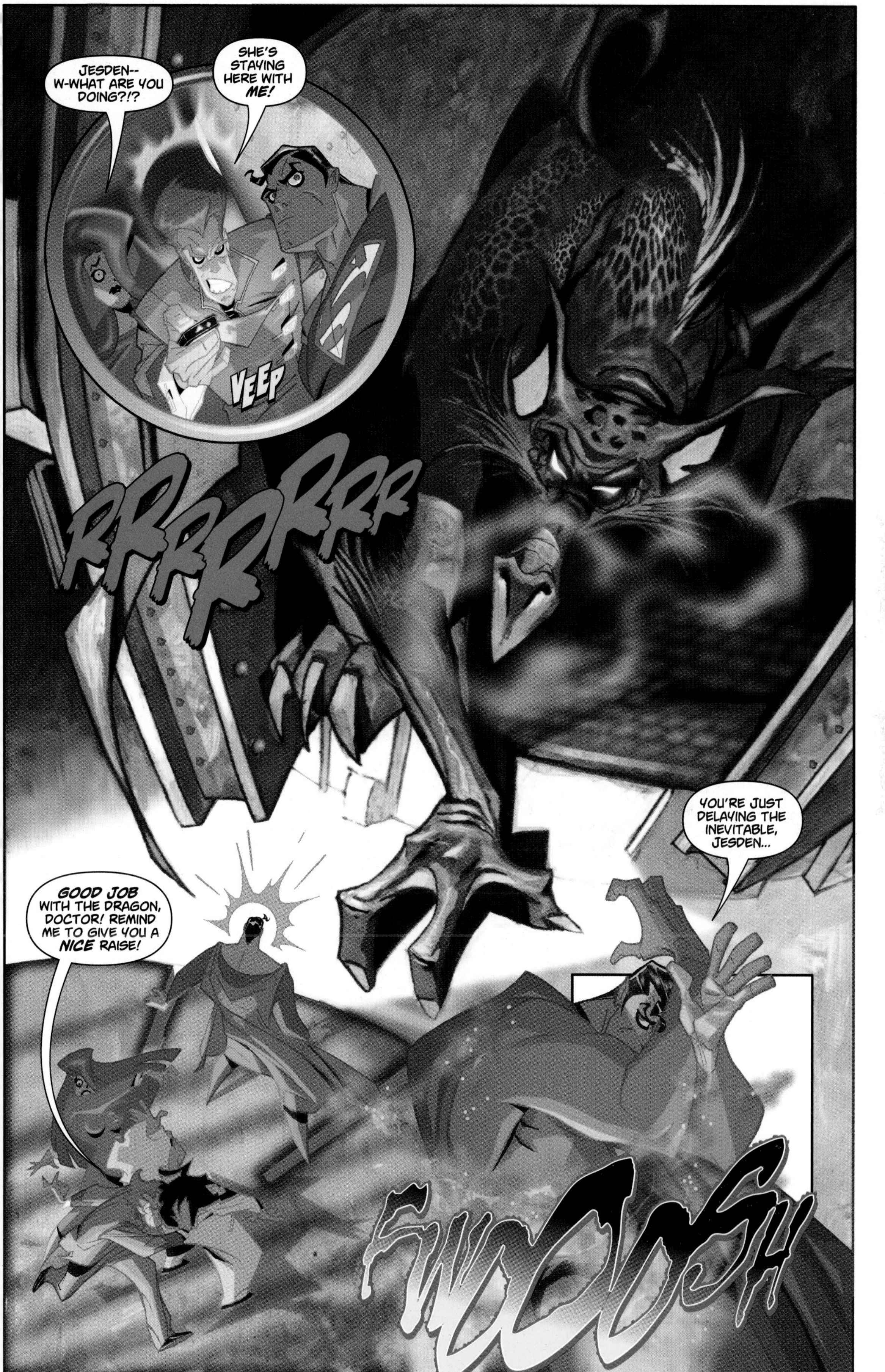
JESDEN--
W-WHAT ARE YOU
DOING?!?
SHE'S
STAYING
HERE WITH
ME!
VEEP
RRRRRRR
YOU'RE JUST
DELAYING THE
INEVITABLE,
JESDEN...
GOOD JOB
WITH THE DRAGON,
DOCTOR! REMIND
ME TO GIVE YOU A
NICE RAISE!
FWOOOSH

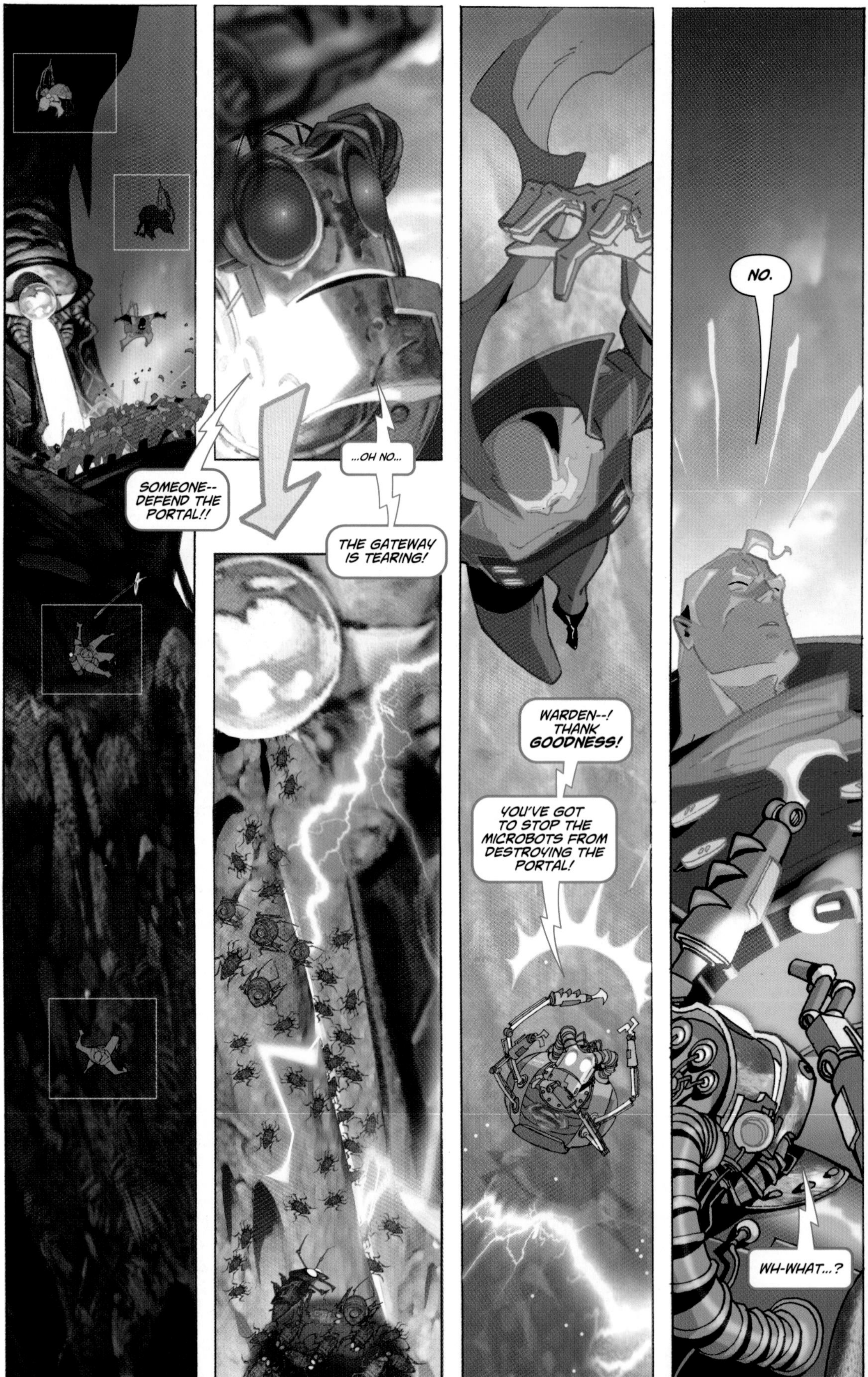
SOMEONE--
DEFEND THE PORTAL!!
...OH NO...
THE GATEWAY IS TEARING!
WARDEN--! THANK GOODNESS!
YOU'VE GOT TO STOP THE MICROBOTS FROM DESTROYING THE PORTAL!
NO.
WH-WHAT...?

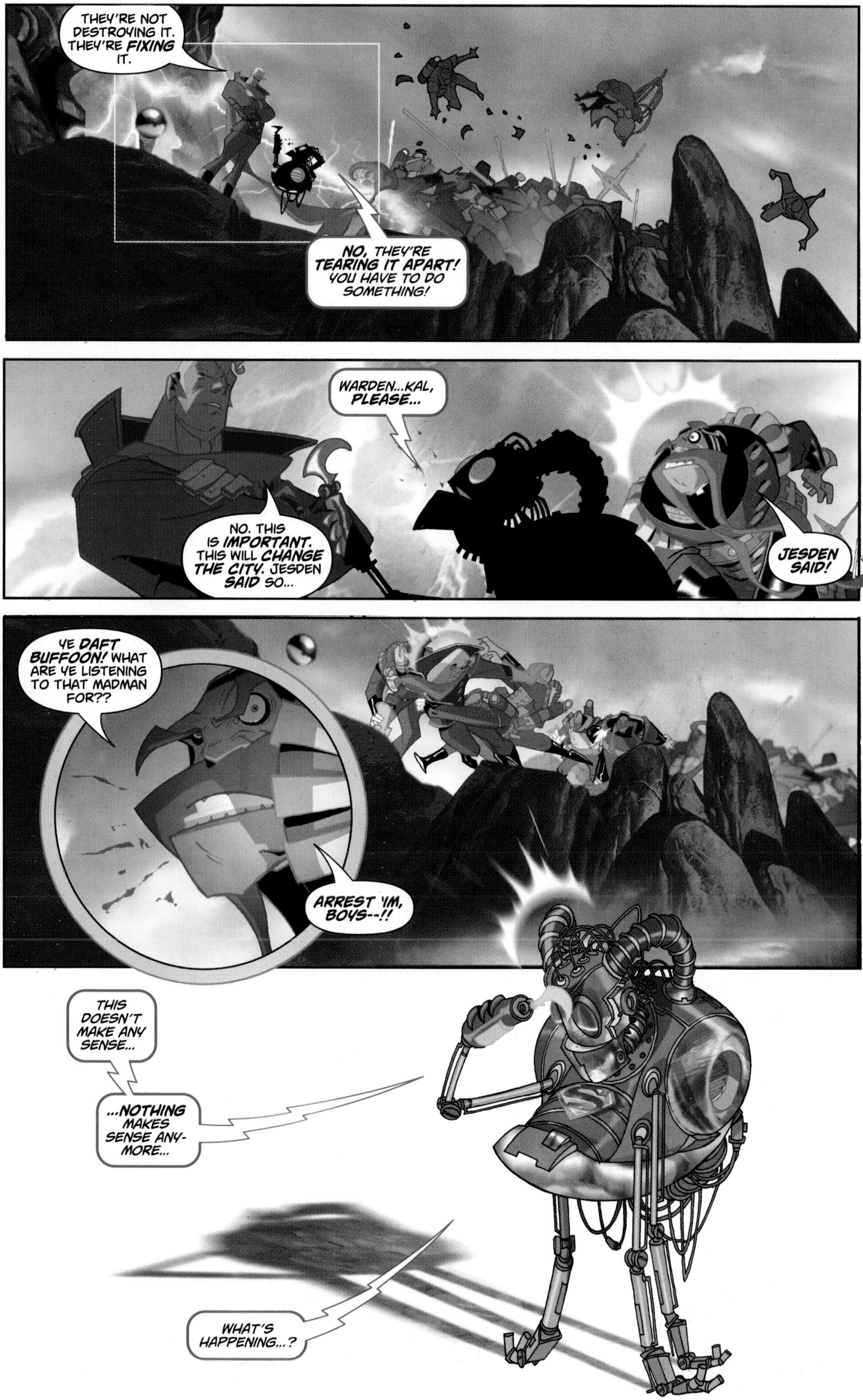
THEY'RE NOT DESTROYING IT. THEY'RE FIXING IT.
NO, THEY'RE TEARING IT APART! YOU HAVE TO DO SOMETHING!
WARDEN...KAL, PLEASE...
NO. THIS IS IMPORTANT. THIS WILL CHANGE THE CITY. JESDEN SAID SO...
JESDEN SAID!
YE DAFT BUFFOON! WHAT ARE YE LISTENING TO THAT MADMAN FOR??
ARREST 'IM, BOYS--!!
THIS DOESN'T MAKE ANY SENSE...
...NOTHING MAKES SENSE ANY-MORE...
WHAT'S HAPPENING...?

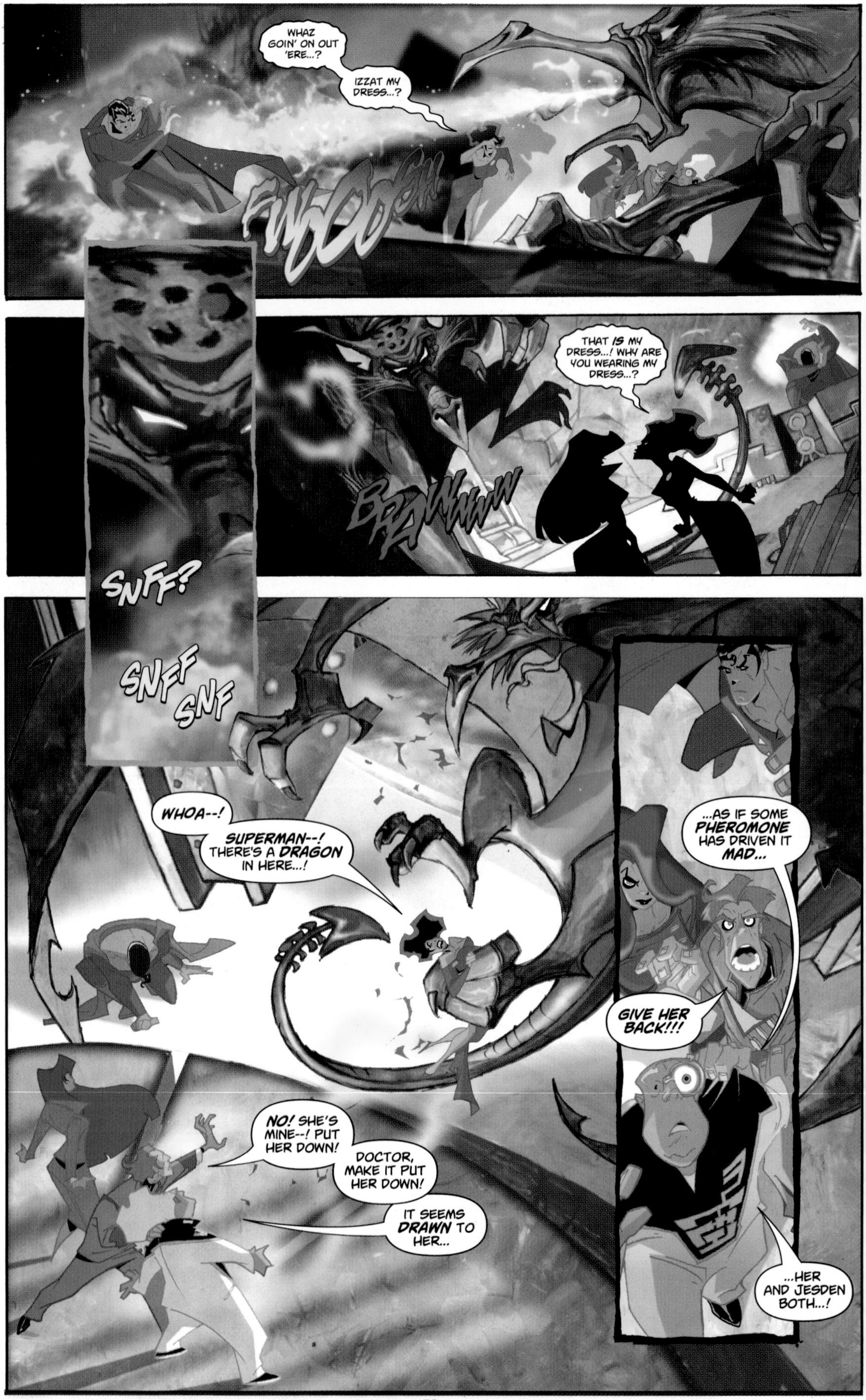
WHAZ GOIN' ON OUT 'ERE...?
IZZAT MY DRESS...?
FWOOOSH!
THAT IS MY DRESS...! WHY ARE YOU WEARING MY DRESS...?
BRAWWWW
SNFF?
SNFF SNF
WHOA--! SUPERMAN--! THERE'S A DRAGON IN HERE...!
...AS IF SOME PHEROMONE HAS DRIVEN IT MAD...
GIVE HER BACK!!!
NO! SHE'S MINE--! PUT HER DOWN!
DOCTOR, MAKE IT PUT HER DOWN!
IT SEEMS DRAWN TO HER...
...HER AND JESDEN BOTH...!

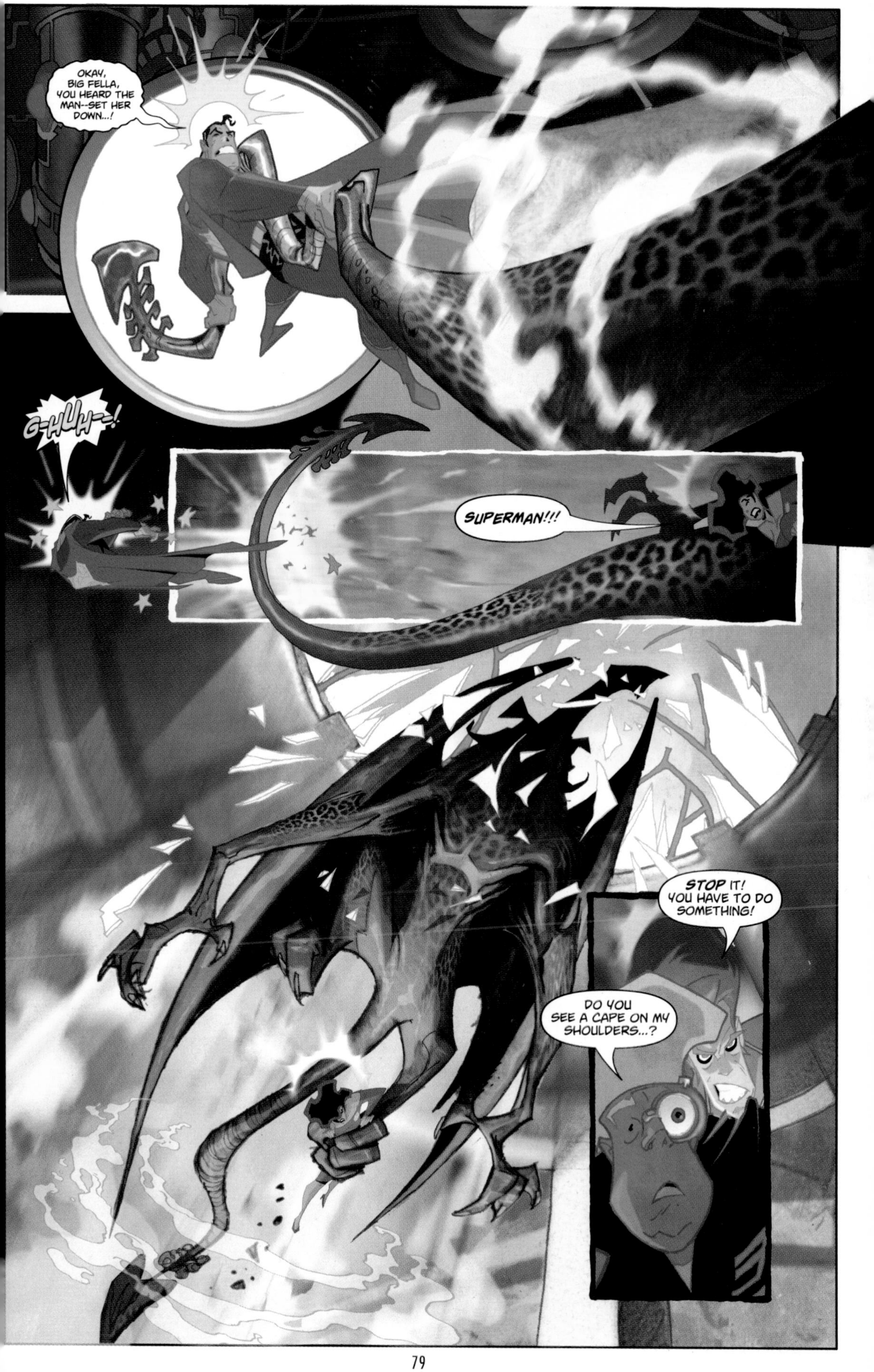
OKAY, BIG FELLA, YOU HEARD THE MAN--SET HER DOWN...!
G-HUH--!
SUPERMAN!!!
STOP IT! YOU HAVE TO DO SOMETHING!
DO YOU SEE A CAPE ON MY SHOULDERS...?

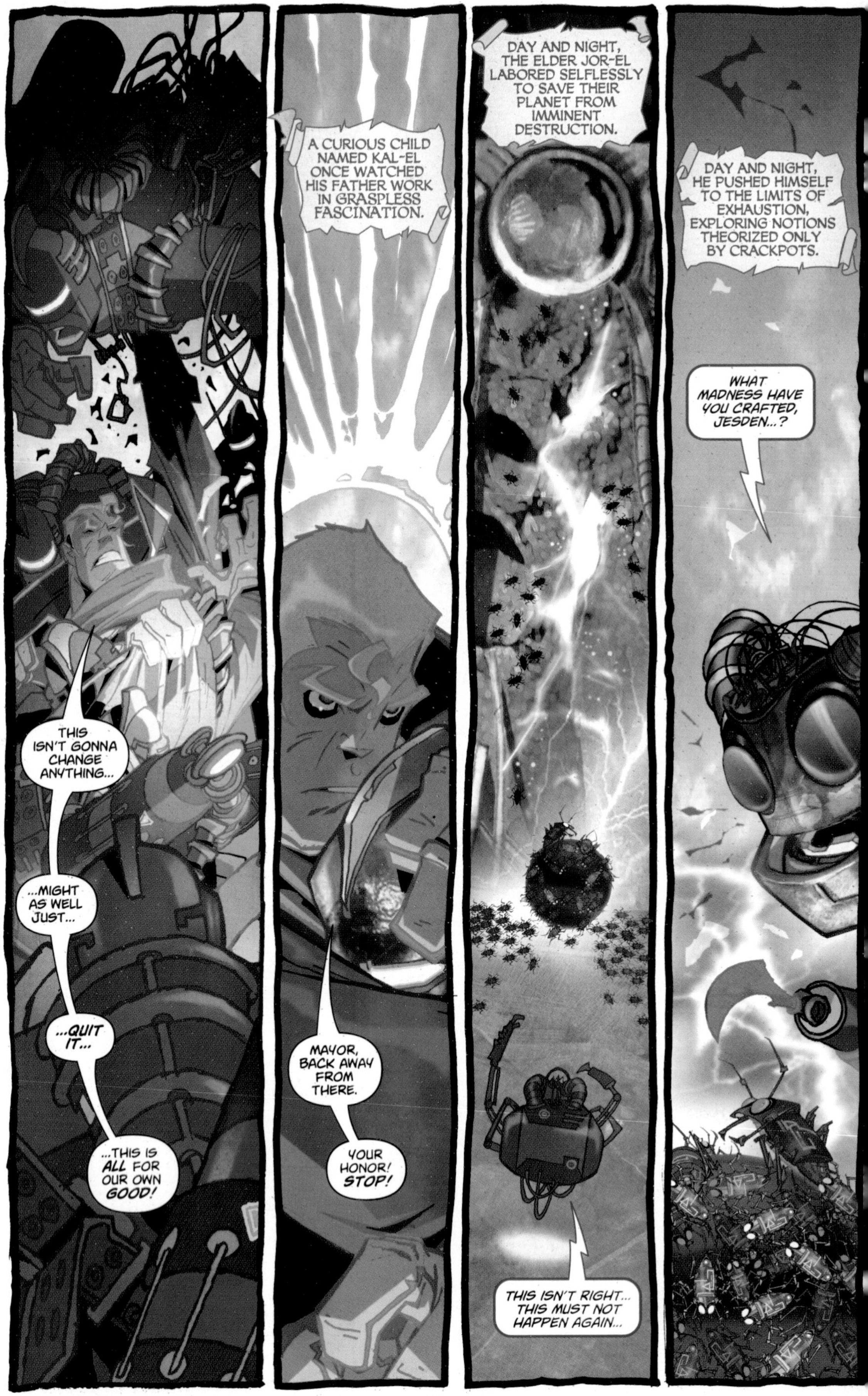
THIS ISN'T GONNA CHANGE ANYTHING...
...MIGHT AS WELL JUST...
...QUIT IT...
...THIS IS ALL FOR OUR OWN GOOD!
A CURIOUS CHILD NAMED KAL-EL ONCE WATCHED HIS FATHER WORK IN GRASPLESS FASCINATION.
MAYOR, BACK AWAY FROM THERE.
YOUR HONOR! STOP!
DAY AND NIGHT, THE ELDER JOR-EL LABORED SELFLESSLY TO SAVE THEIR PLANET FROM IMMINENT DESTRUCTION.
THIS ISN'T RIGHT... THIS MUST NOT HAPPEN AGAIN...
DAY AND NIGHT, HE PUSHED HIMSELF TO THE LIMITS OF EXHAUSTION, EXPLORING NOTIONS THEORIZED ONLY BY CRACKPOTS.
WHAT MADNESS HAVE YOU CRAFTED, JESDEN...?

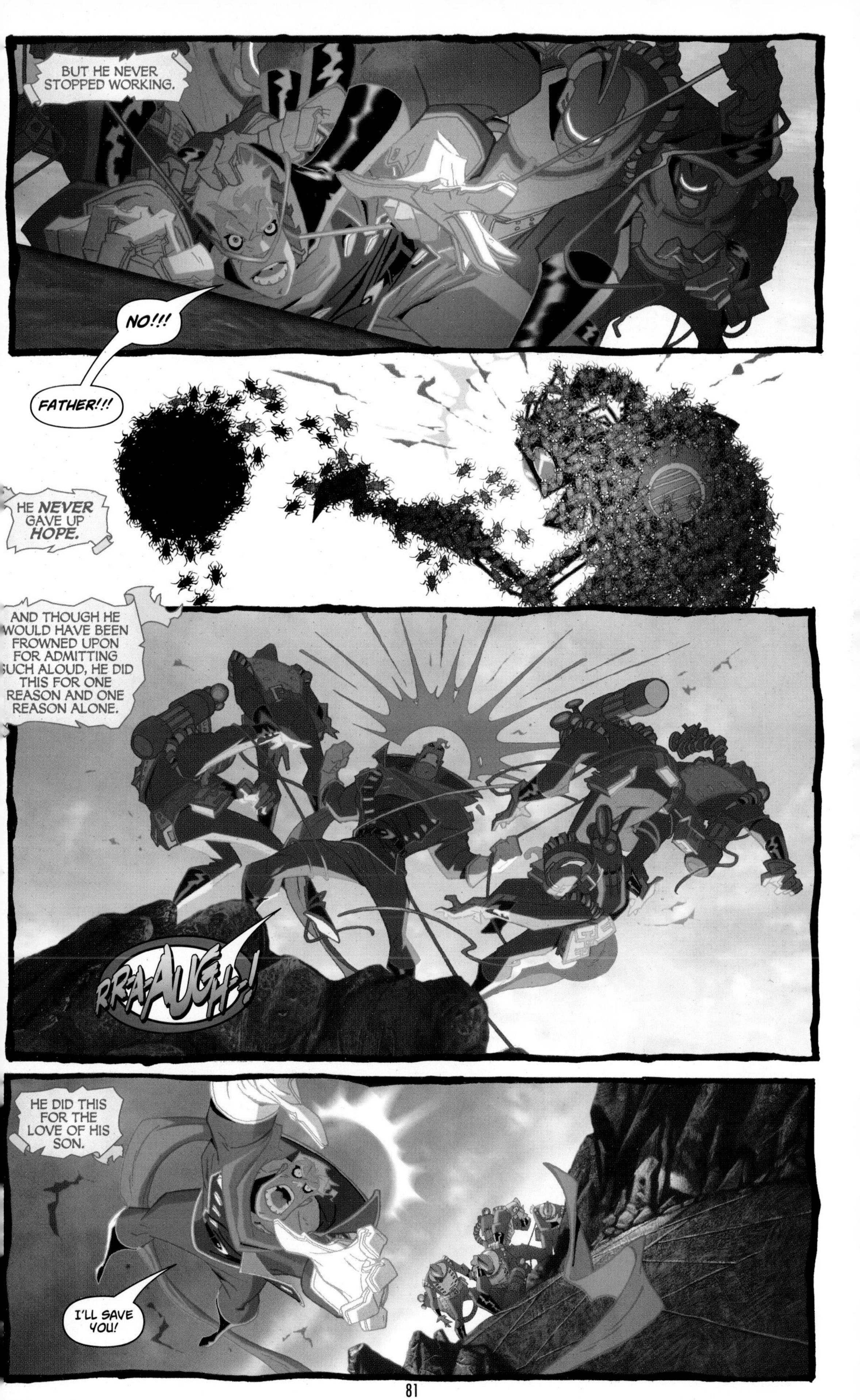
BUT HE NEVER STOPPED WORKING.
NO!!!
FATHER!!!
HE NEVER GAVE UP HOPE.
AND THOUGH HE WOULD HAVE BEEN FROWNED UPON FOR ADMITTING SUCH ALOUD, HE DID THIS FOR ONE REASON AND ONE REASON ALONE.
RRA-AUGH-!
HE DID THIS FOR THE LOVE OF HIS SON.
I'LL SAVE YOU!

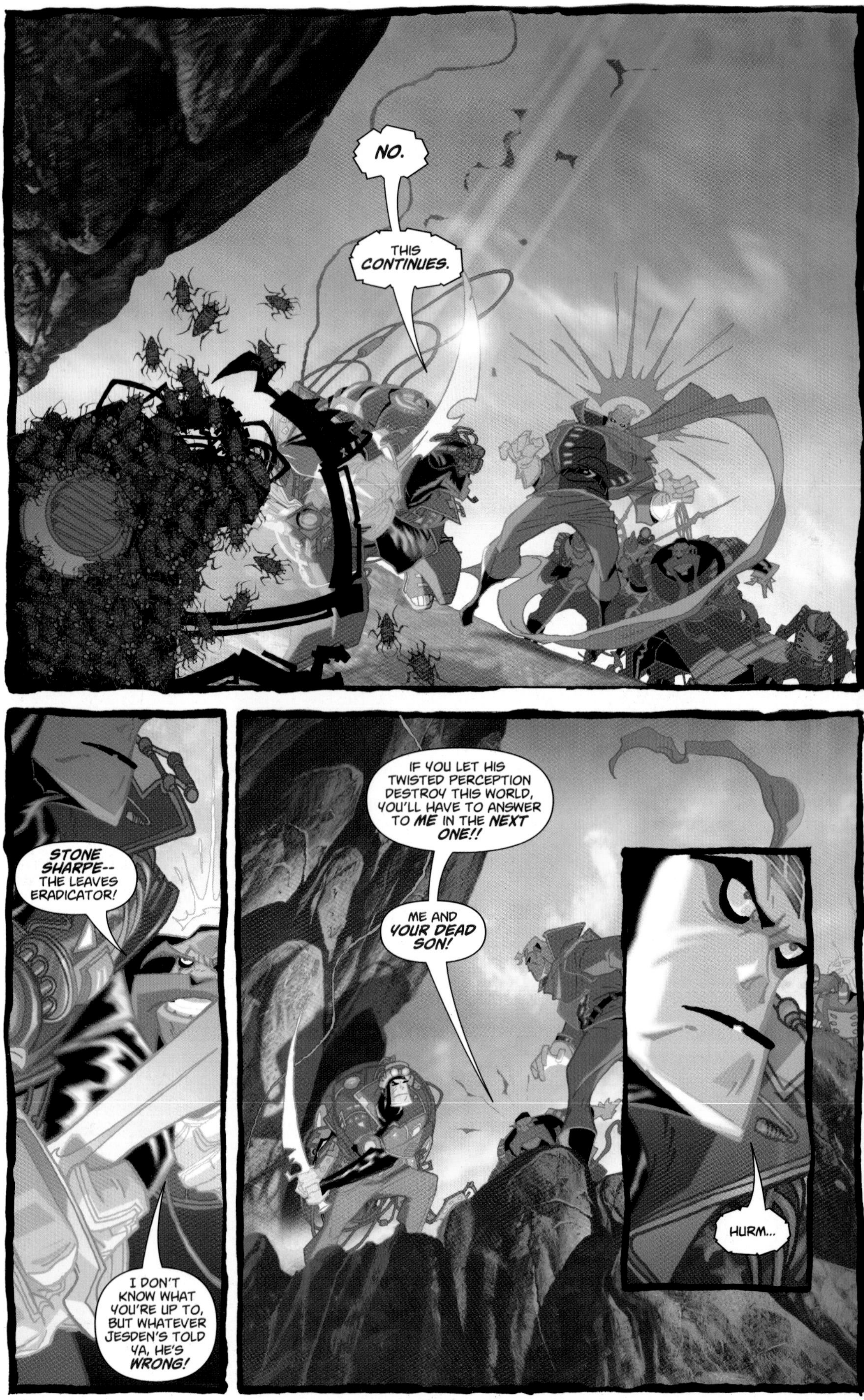
NO.
THIS CONTINUES.
STONE SHARPE-- THE LEAVES ERADICATOR!
I DON'T KNOW WHAT YOU'RE UP TO, BUT WHATEVER JESDEN'S TOLD YA, HE'S WRONG!
IF YOU LET HIS TWISTED PERCEPTION DESTROY THIS WORLD, YOU'LL HAVE TO ANSWER TO ME IN THE NEXT ONE!!
ME AND YOUR DEAD SON!
HURM...

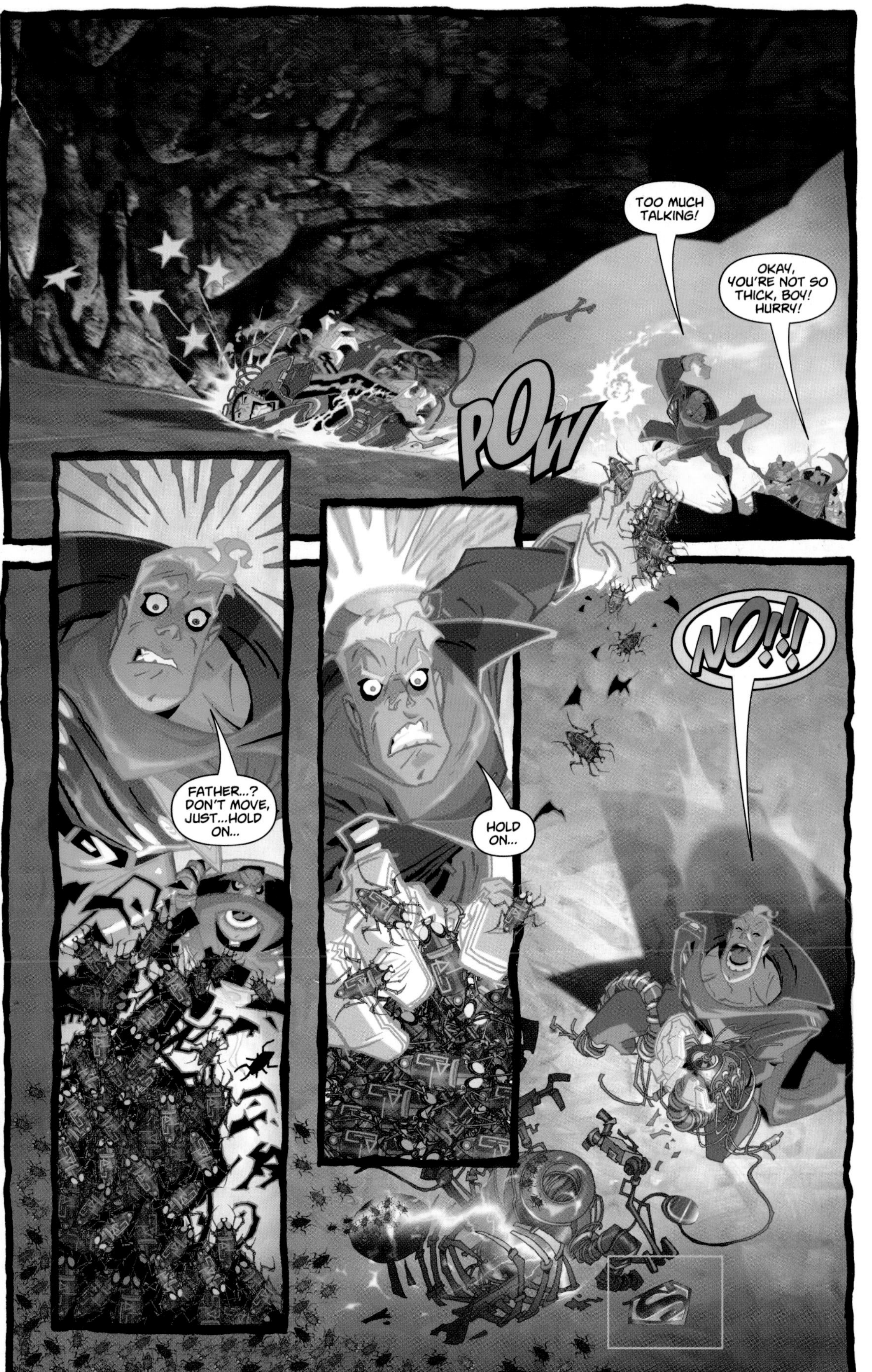
TOO MUCH TALKING!
OKAY, YOU'RE NOT SO THICK, BOY! HURRY!
POW
FATHER...? DON'T MOVE, JUST...HOLD ON...
HOLD ON...
NO!!!

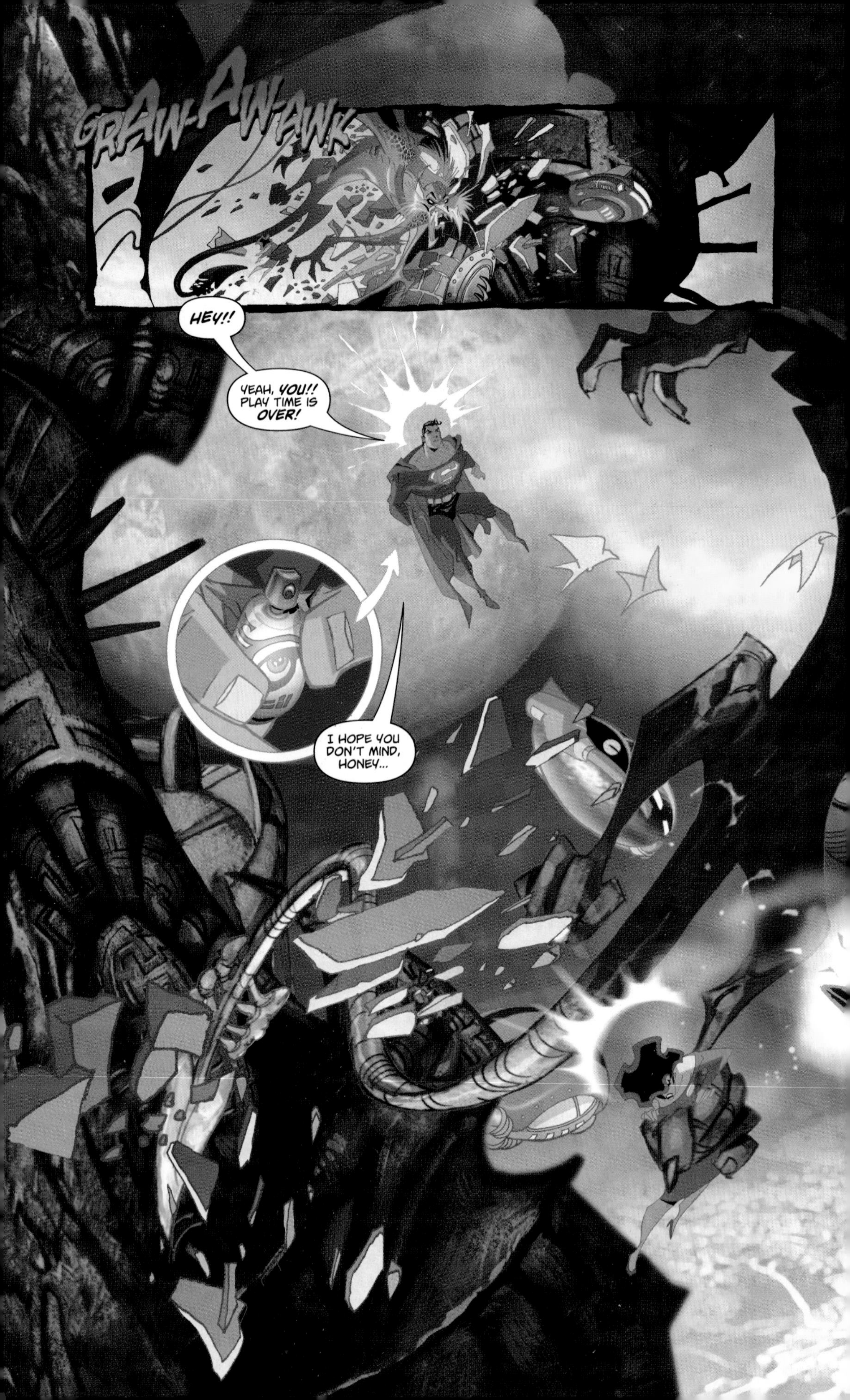
GRAW-AW-AWK
HEY!!
YEAH, YOU!! PLAY TIME IS OVER!
I HOPE YOU DON'T MIND, HONEY...

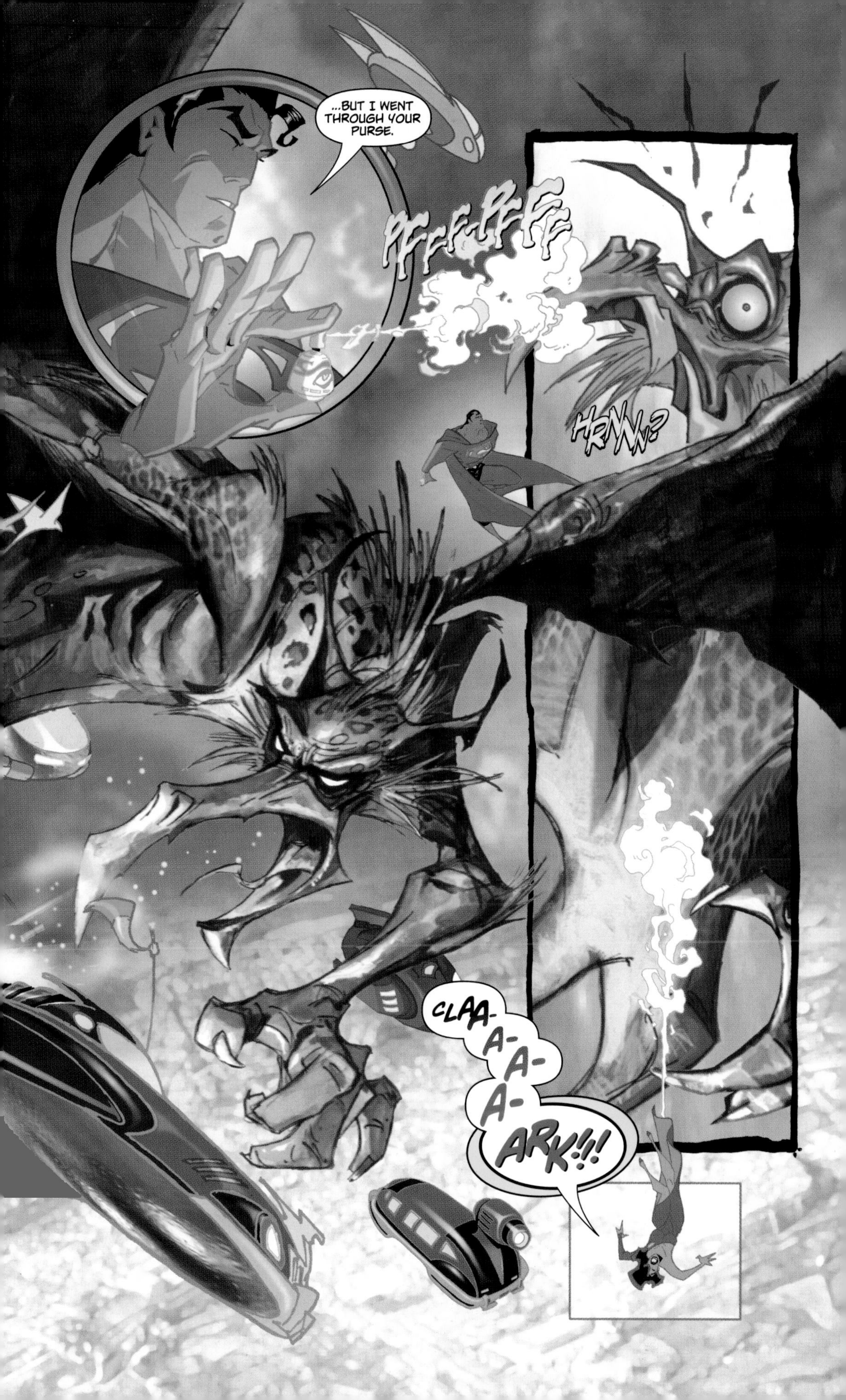
...BUT I WENT THROUGH YOUR PURSE.
PFFF-PFFF
HRNNN?
CLAA-A-A-A-ARK!!!

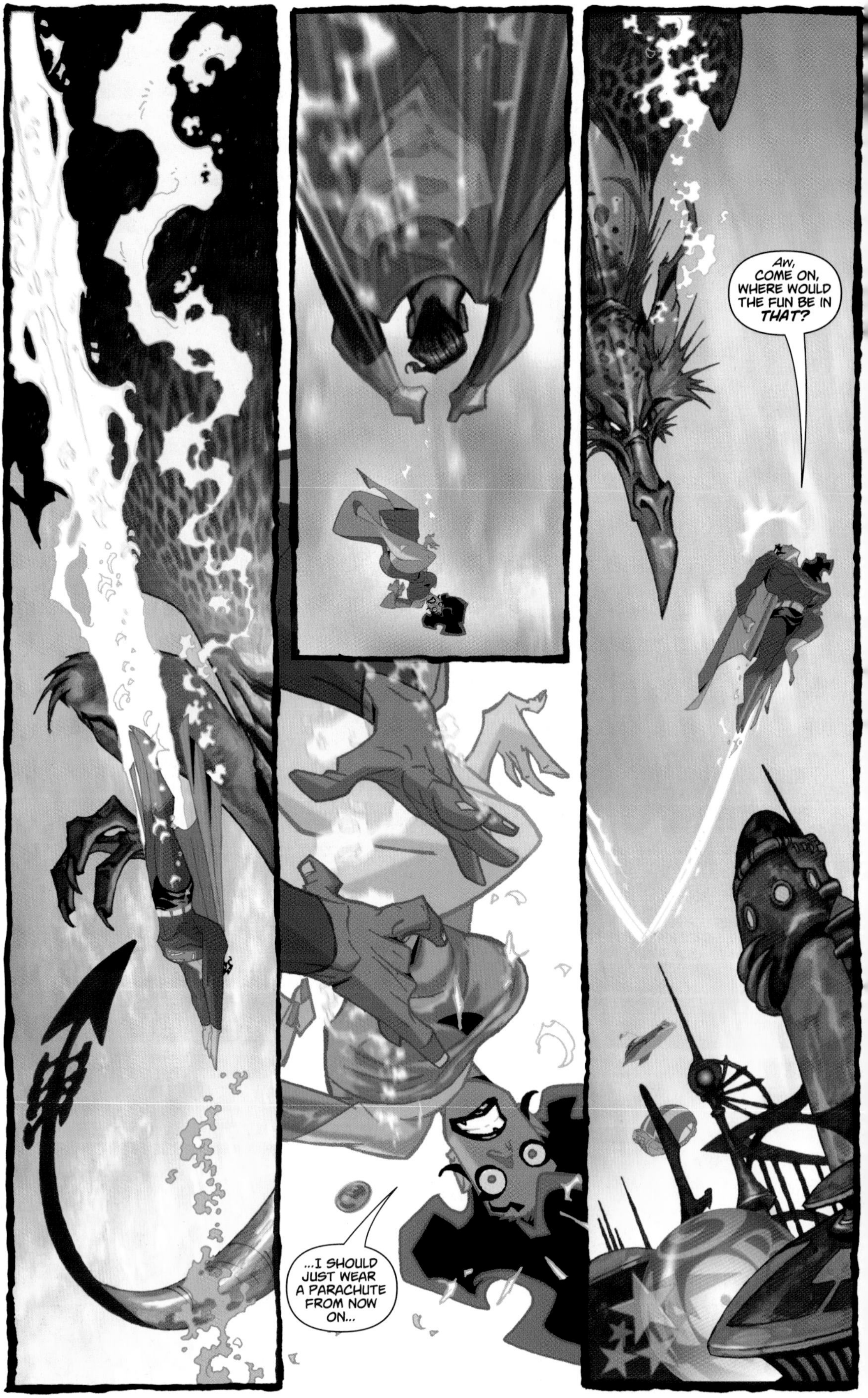
AW, COME ON, WHERE WOULD THE FUN BE IN THAT?
...I SHOULD JUST WEAR A PARACHUTE FROM NOW ON...

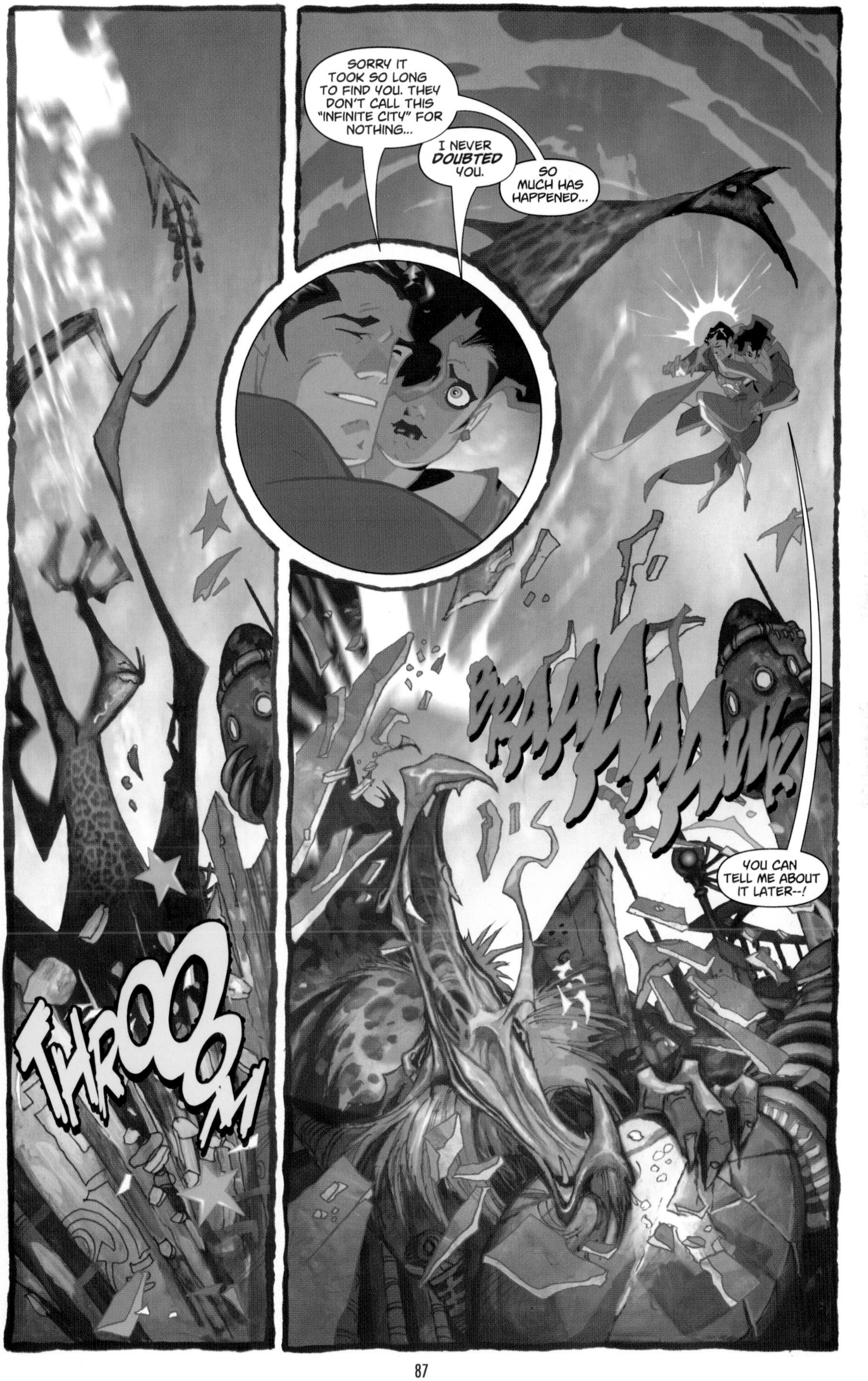

SORRY IT TOOK SO LONG TO FIND YOU. THEY DON'T CALL THIS "INFINITE CITY" FOR NOTHING...
I NEVER DOUBTED YOU.
SO MUCH HAS HAPPENED...
BRAAAAAAWK!
YOU CAN TELL ME ABOUT IT LATER--!
THROOOM

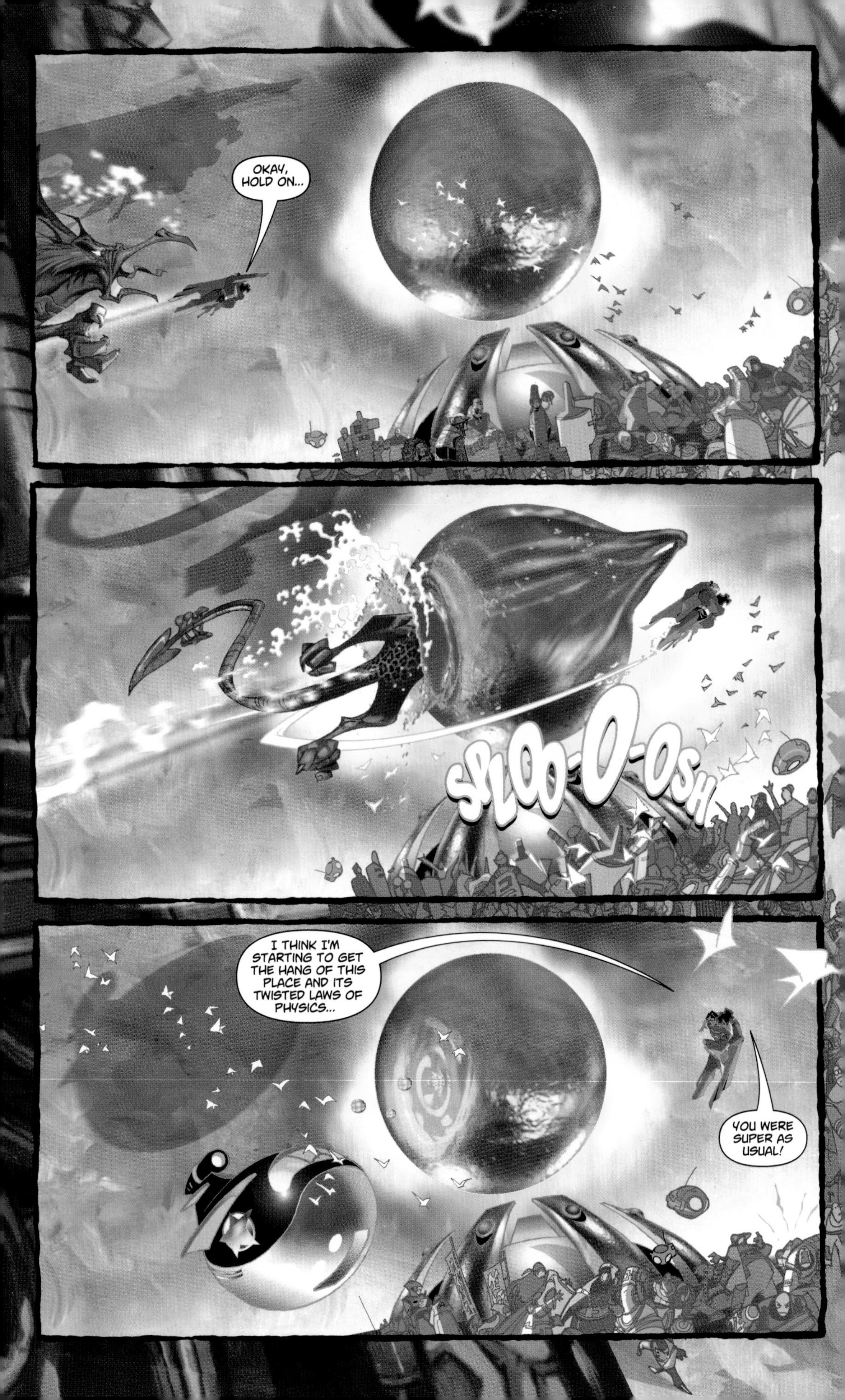
OKAY, HOLD ON...
SPLOO-O-OSH
I THINK I'M STARTING TO GET THE HANG OF THIS PLACE AND ITS TWISTED LAWS OF PHYSICS...
YOU WERE SUPER AS USUAL!

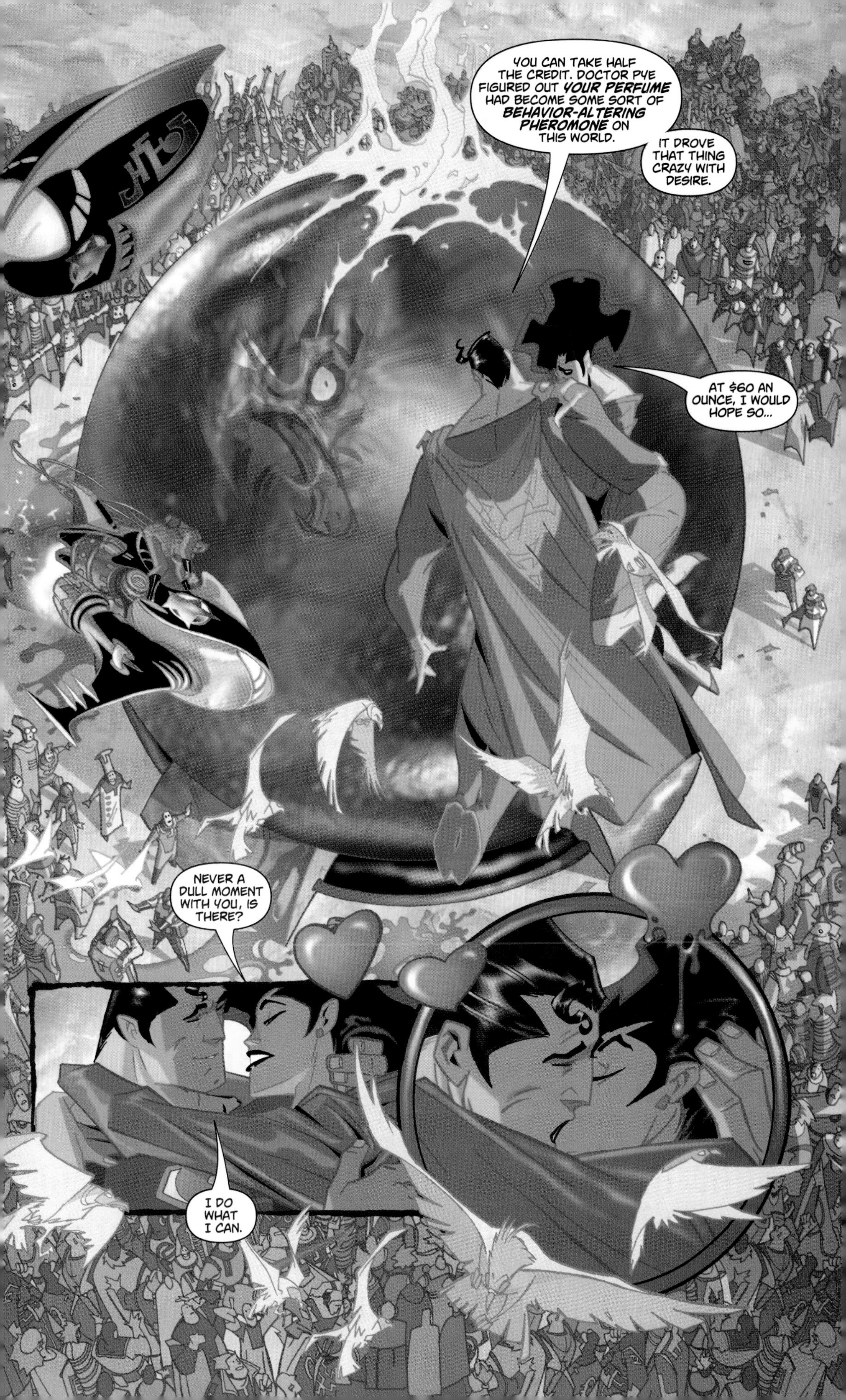
YOU CAN TAKE HALF THE CREDIT. DOCTOR PYE FIGURED OUT **YOUR PERFUME** HAD BECOME SOME SORT OF **BEHAVIOR-ALTERING PHEROMONE** ON THIS WORLD.
IT DROVE THAT THING CRAZY WITH DESIRE.
AT $60 AN OUNCE, I WOULD HOPE SO...
NEVER A DULL MOMENT WITH YOU, IS THERE?
I DO WHAT I CAN.

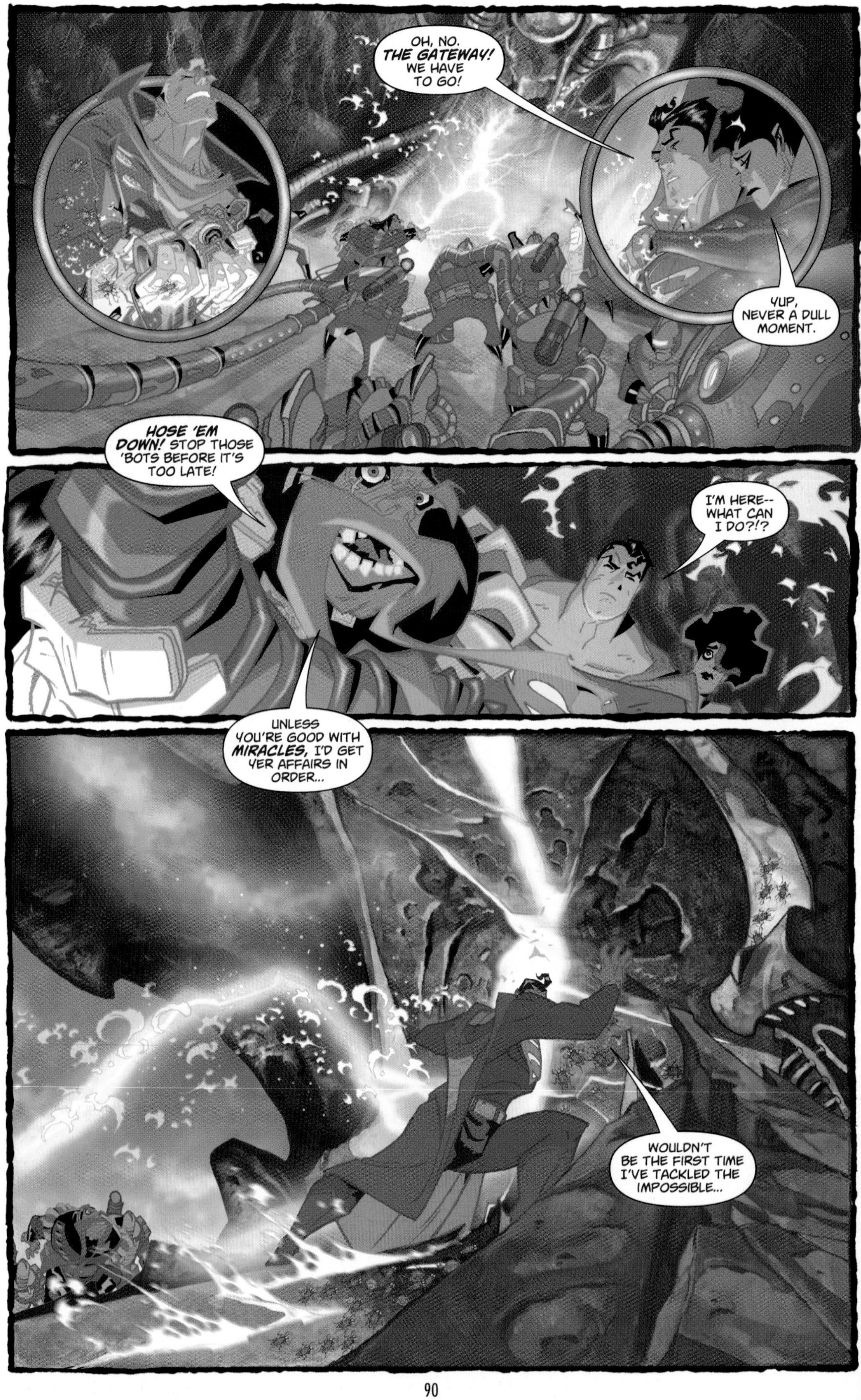
OH, NO. THE GATEWAY! WE HAVE TO GO!
YUP, NEVER A DULL MOMENT.
HOSE 'EM DOWN! STOP THOSE 'BOTS BEFORE IT'S TOO LATE!
I'M HERE-- WHAT CAN I DO?!?
UNLESS YOU'RE GOOD WITH MIRACLES, I'D GET YER AFFAIRS IN ORDER...
WOULDN'T BE THE FIRST TIME I'VE TACKLED THE IMPOSSIBLE...

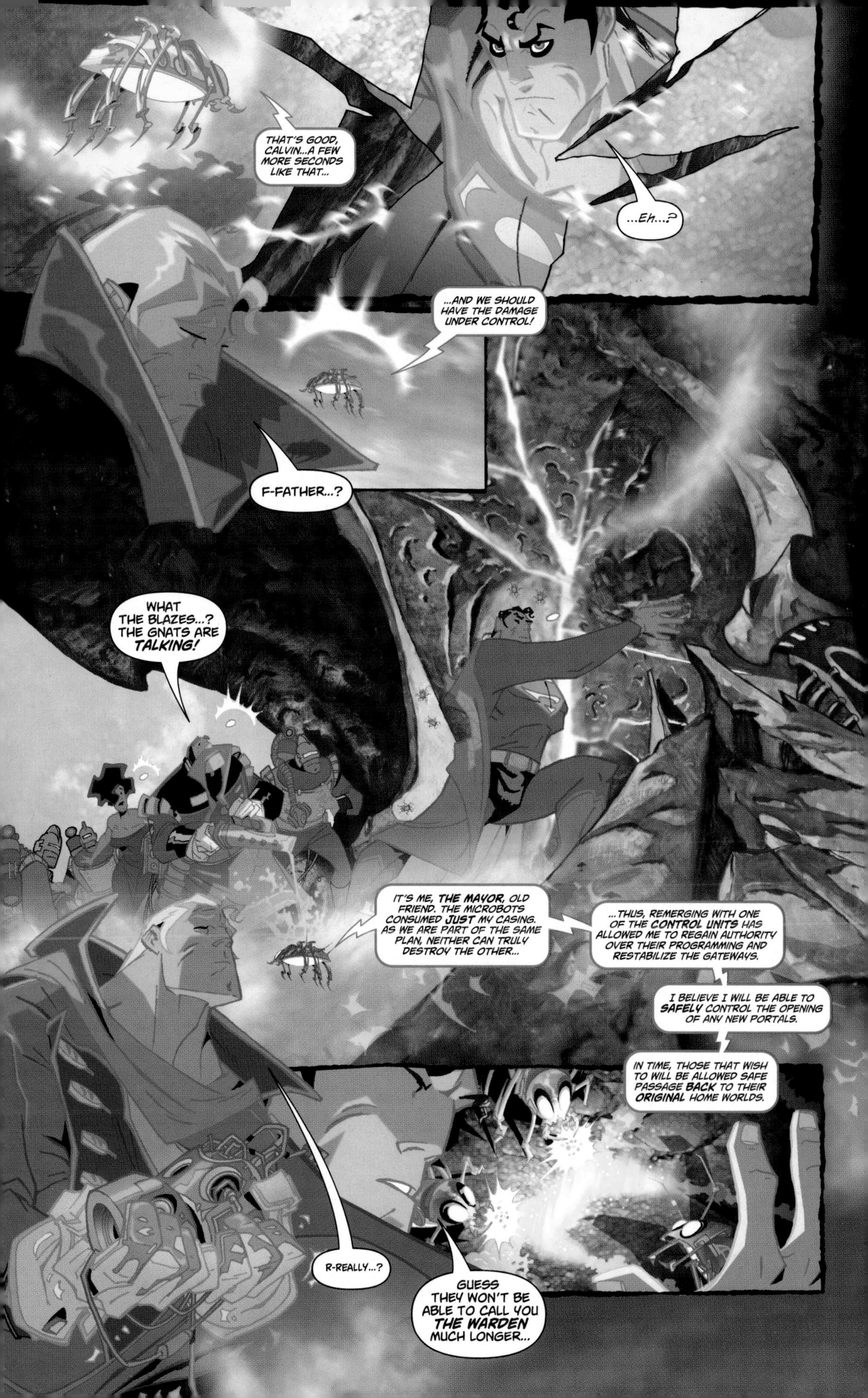

THAT'S GOOD, CALVIN...A FEW MORE SECONDS LIKE THAT...
...Eh...?
...AND WE SHOULD HAVE THE DAMAGE UNDER CONTROL!
F-FATHER...?
WHAT THE BLAZES...? THE GNATS ARE TALKING!
IT'S ME, THE MAYOR, OLD FRIEND. THE MICROBOTS CONSUMED JUST MY CASING. AS WE ARE PART OF THE SAME PLAN, NEITHER CAN TRULY DESTROY THE OTHER...
...THUS, REMERGING WITH ONE OF THE CONTROL UNITS HAS ALLOWED ME TO REGAIN AUTHORITY OVER THEIR PROGRAMMING AND RESTABILIZE THE GATEWAYS.
I BELIEVE I WILL BE ABLE TO SAFELY CONTROL THE OPENING OF ANY NEW PORTALS.
IN TIME, THOSE THAT WISH TO WILL BE ALLOWED SAFE PASSAGE BACK TO THEIR ORIGINAL HOME WORLDS.
R-REALLY...?
GUESS THEY WON'T BE ABLE TO CALL YOU THE WARDEN MUCH LONGER...

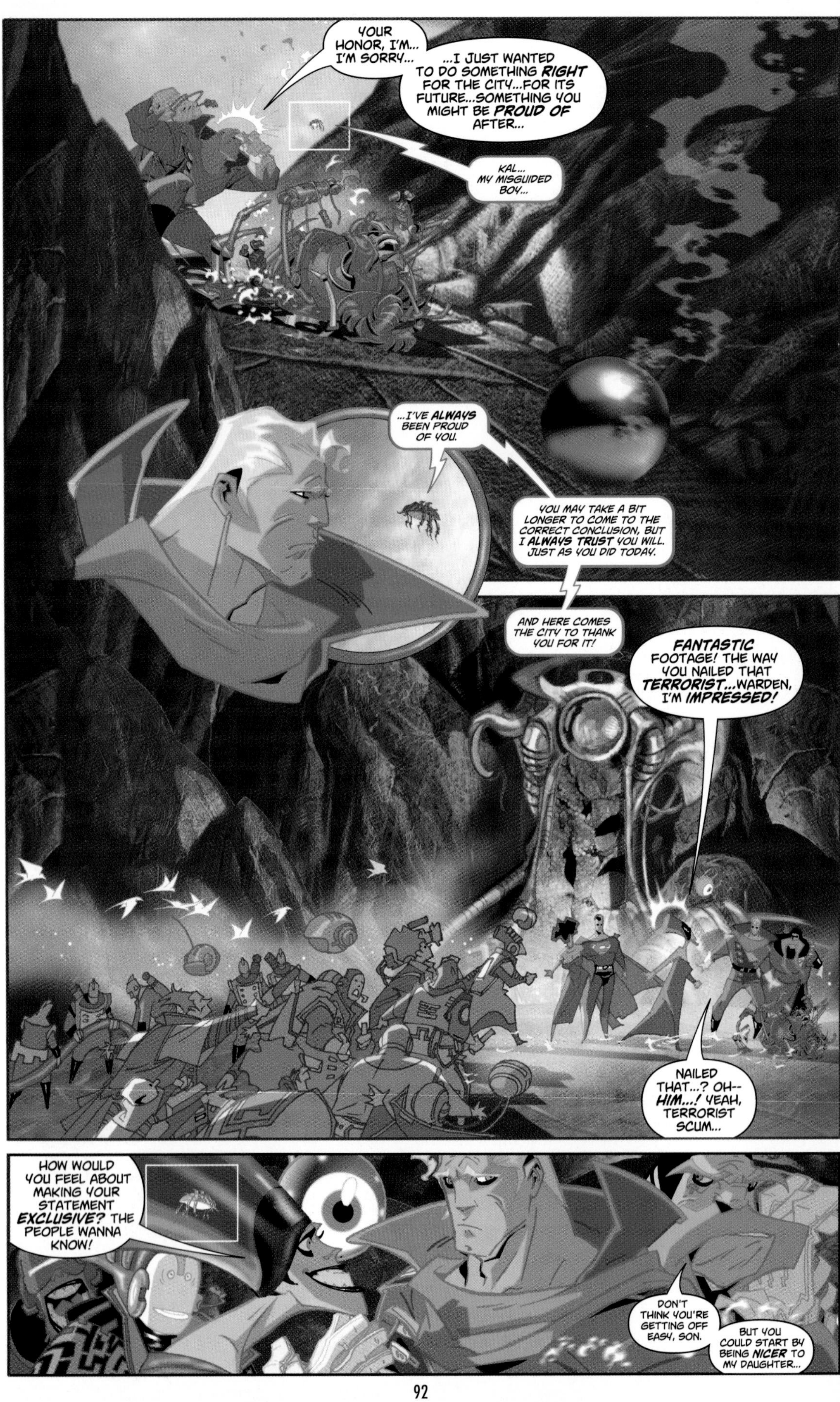
YOUR HONOR, I'M... I'M SORRY...
...I JUST WANTED TO DO SOMETHING RIGHT FOR THE CITY...FOR ITS FUTURE...SOMETHING YOU MIGHT BE PROUD OF AFTER...
KAL... MY MISGUIDED BOY...
...I'VE ALWAYS BEEN PROUD OF YOU.
YOU MAY TAKE A BIT LONGER TO COME TO THE CORRECT CONCLUSION, BUT I ALWAYS TRUST YOU WILL. JUST AS YOU DID TODAY.
AND HERE COMES THE CITY TO THANK YOU FOR IT!
FANTASTIC FOOTAGE! THE WAY YOU NAILED THAT TERRORIST...WARDEN, I'M IMPRESSED!
NAILED THAT...? OH-- HIM...! YEAH, TERRORIST SCUM...
HOW WOULD YOU FEEL ABOUT MAKING YOUR STATEMENT EXCLUSIVE? THE PEOPLE WANNA KNOW!
DON'T THINK YOU'RE GETTING OFF EASY, SON.
BUT YOU COULD START BY BEING NICER TO MY DAUGHTER...

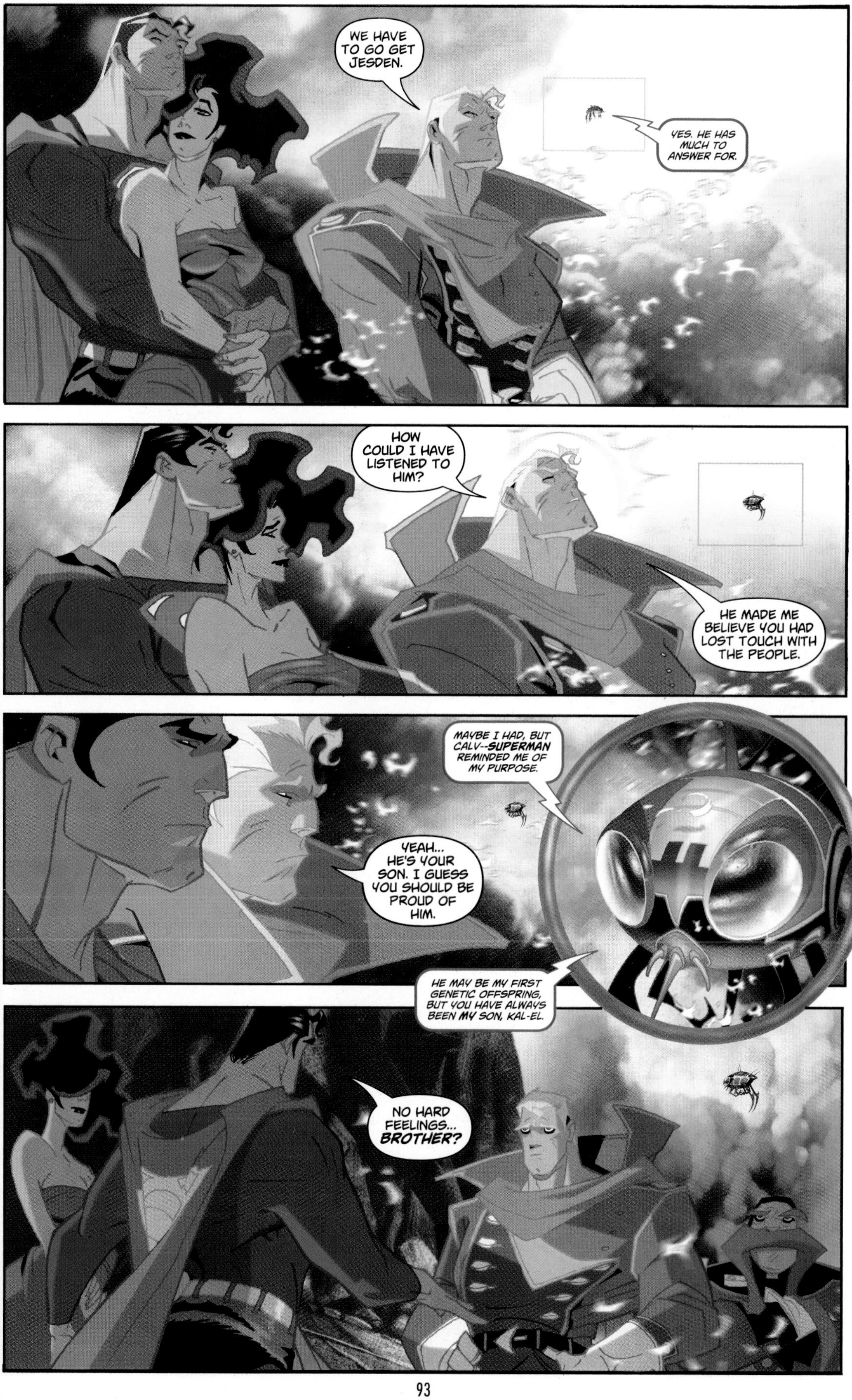
WE HAVE TO GO GET JESDEN.
YES. HE HAS MUCH TO ANSWER FOR.
HOW COULD I HAVE LISTENED TO HIM?
HE MADE ME BELIEVE YOU HAD LOST TOUCH WITH THE PEOPLE.
MAYBE I HAD, BUT CALV--SUPERMAN REMINDED ME OF MY PURPOSE.
YEAH... HE'S YOUR SON. I GUESS YOU SHOULD BE PROUD OF HIM.
HE MAY BE MY FIRST GENETIC OFFSPRING, BUT YOU HAVE ALWAYS BEEN MY SON, KAL-EL.
NO HARD FEELINGS... BROTHER?

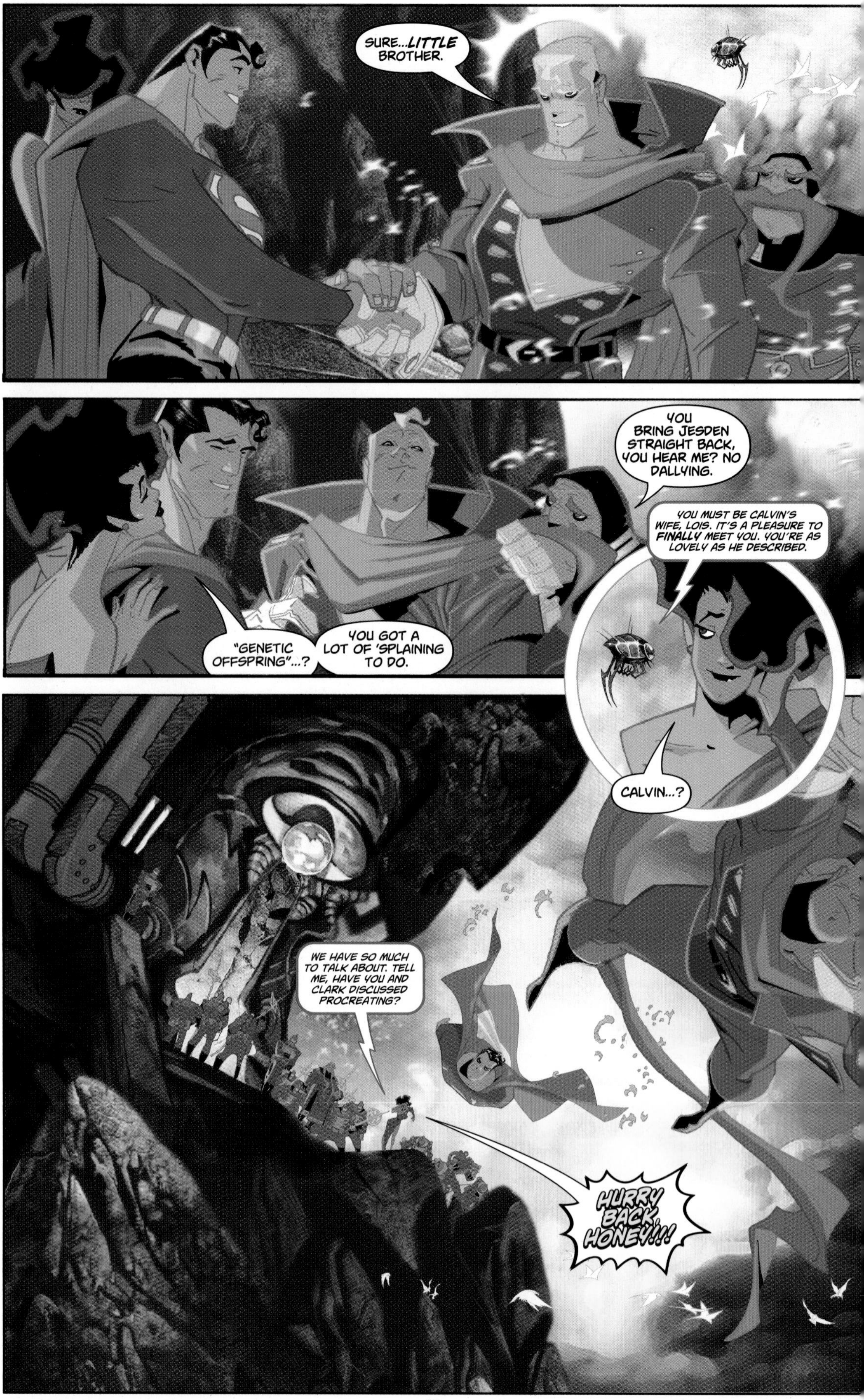
SURE...LITTLE BROTHER.
YOU BRING JESDEN STRAIGHT BACK, YOU HEAR ME? NO DALLYING.
YOU MUST BE CALVIN'S WIFE, LOIS. IT'S A PLEASURE TO FINALLY MEET YOU. YOU'RE AS LOVELY AS HE DESCRIBED.
"GENETIC OFFSPRING"...?
YOU GOT A LOT OF 'SPLAINING TO DO.
CALVIN...?
WE HAVE SO MUCH TO TALK ABOUT. TELL ME, HAVE YOU AND CLARK DISCUSSED PROCREATING?
HURRY BACK, HONEY!!!

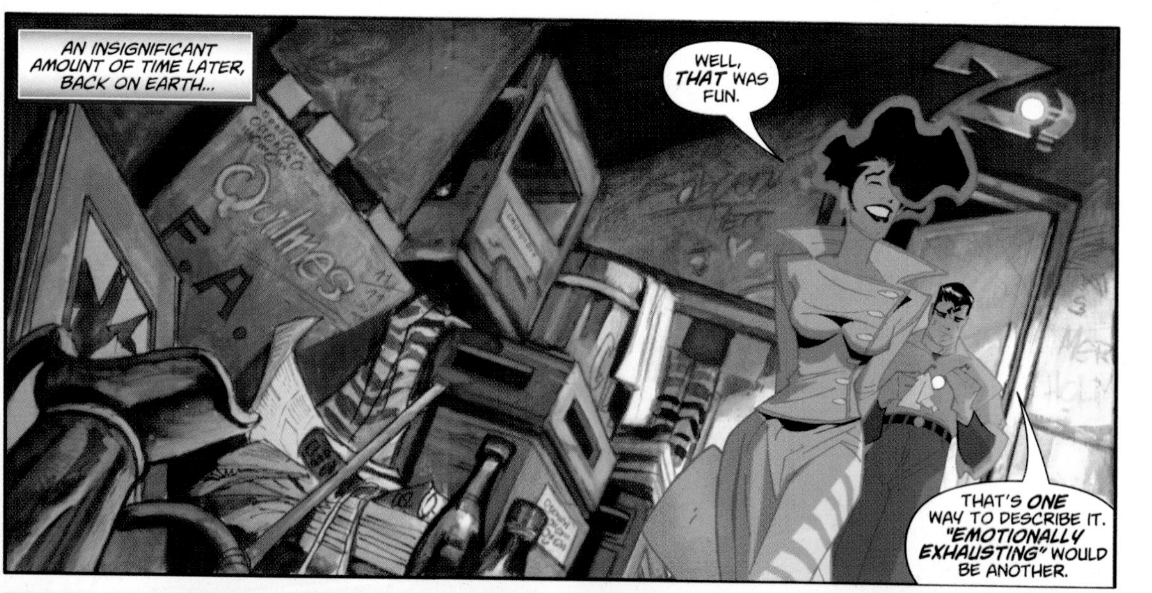
AN INSIGNIFICANT AMOUNT OF TIME LATER, BACK ON EARTH...
WELL, THAT WAS FUN.
THAT'S ONE WAY TO DESCRIBE IT. "EMOTIONALLY EXHAUSTING" WOULD BE ANOTHER.

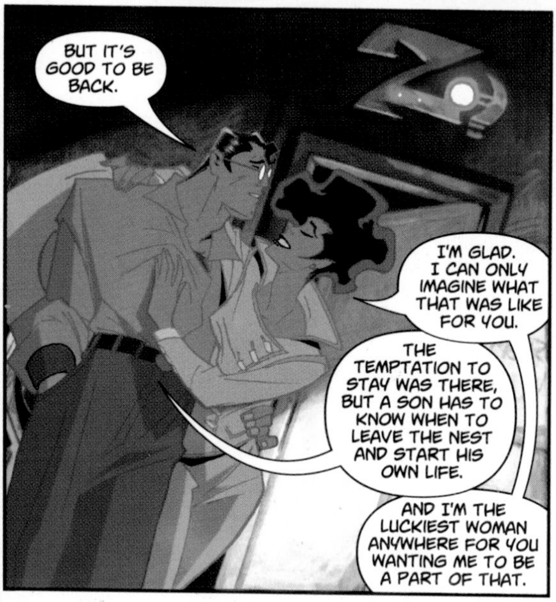
BUT IT'S GOOD TO BE BACK.
I'M GLAD. I CAN ONLY IMAGINE WHAT THAT WAS LIKE FOR YOU.
THE TEMPTATION TO STAY WAS THERE, BUT A SON HAS TO KNOW WHEN TO LEAVE THE NEST AND START HIS OWN LIFE.
AND I'M THE LUCKIEST WOMAN ANYWHERE FOR YOU WANTING ME TO BE A PART OF THAT.

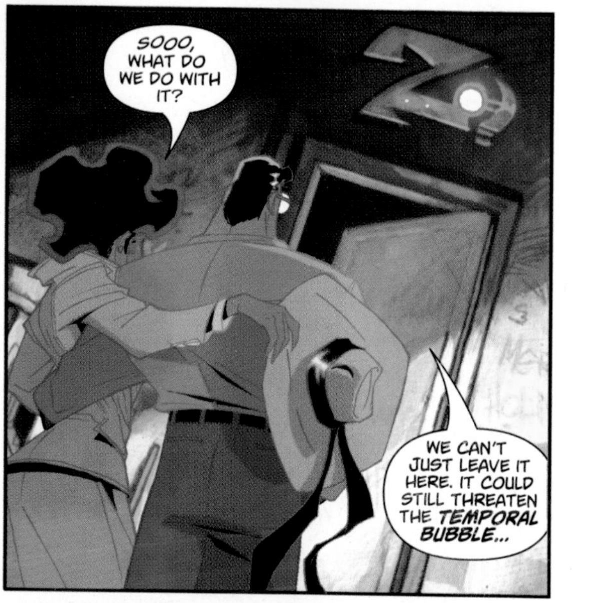
SOOO, WHAT DO WE DO WITH IT?
WE CAN'T JUST LEAVE IT HERE. IT COULD STILL THREATEN THE TEMPORAL BUBBLE...

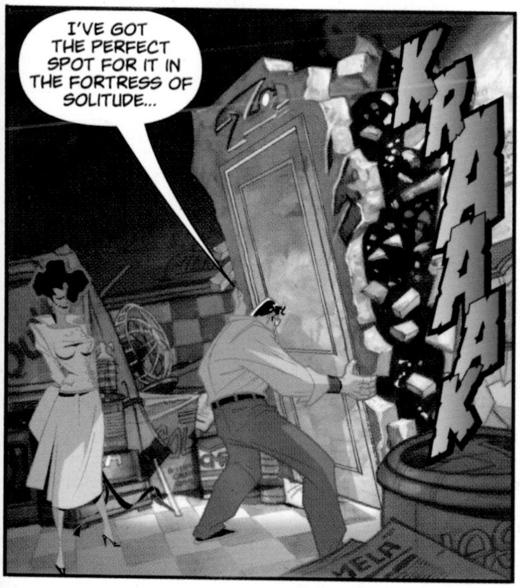
I'VE GOT THE PERFECT SPOT FOR IT IN THE FORTRESS OF SOLITUDE...
KRAAAAK

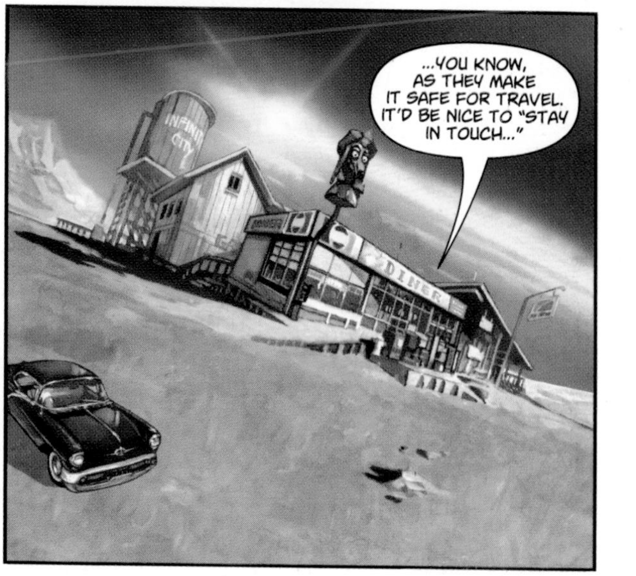
...YOU KNOW, AS THEY MAKE IT SAFE FOR TRAVEL. IT'D BE NICE TO "STAY IN TOUCH..."
DINER

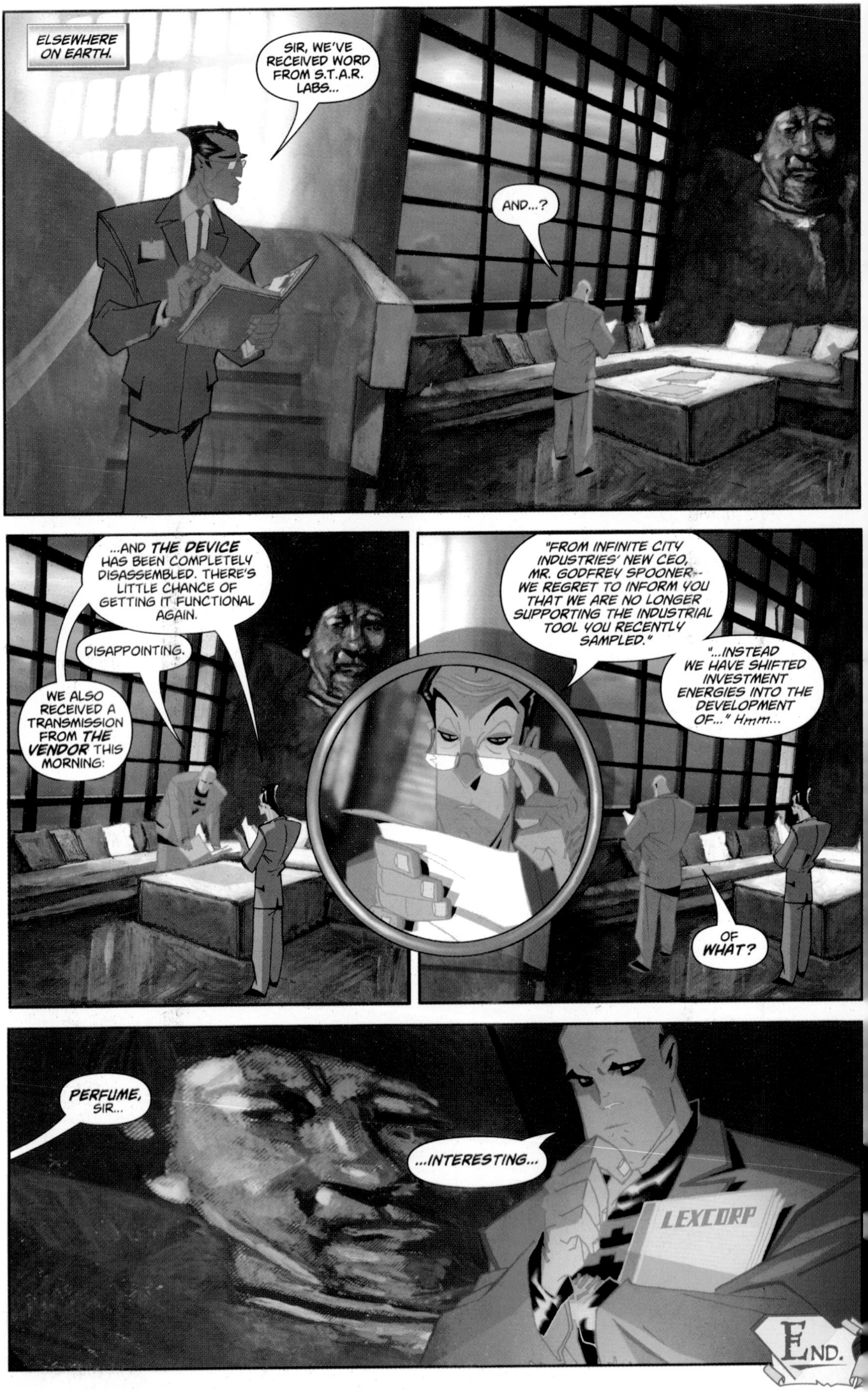
ELSEWHERE ON EARTH.
SIR, WE'VE RECEIVED WORD FROM S.T.A.R. LABS...
AND...?
...AND THE DEVICE HAS BEEN COMPLETELY DISASSEMBLED. THERE'S LITTLE CHANCE OF GETTING IT FUNCTIONAL AGAIN.
DISAPPOINTING.
WE ALSO RECEIVED A TRANSMISSION FROM THE VENDOR THIS MORNING:
"FROM INFINITE CITY INDUSTRIES' NEW CEO, MR. GODFREY SPOONER-- WE REGRET TO INFORM YOU THAT WE ARE NO LONGER SUPPORTING THE INDUSTRIAL TOOL YOU RECENTLY SAMPLED."
"...INSTEAD WE HAVE SHIFTED INVESTMENT ENERGIES INTO THE DEVELOPMENT OF..." Hmm...
OF WHAT?
PERFUME, SIR...
...INTERESTING...
LEXCORP
END.